P42 - descr. of Fort

CHITRÁL

THE STORY OF A MINOR SIEGE

CHITRÁL

THE STORY OF A MINOR SIEGE

BY

SIR GEORGE S. ROBERTSON, K.C.S.I.

WITH EIGHT ILLUSTRATIONS

A MAP AND FOUR PLANS

This edition published by

R.J. LEACH & Co.

38 Inglemere Road

Forest Hill

London SE23 2BE

R.J. LEACH & Co.   © 1991

First Edition	Nov	1898
Second Edition	Jan	1899
Third Edition	May	1899
Fourth Edition		1905
This Edition		1991

ISBN 1.873050.054

Printed and bound by A. Rowe
Chippenham, Wiltshire

AUTHOR'S NOTE

THE Author's acknowledgments and thanks are due to all those who have so kindly lent him pictures to illustrate this book, and particularly to the Hon. Mrs Gatacre for permission to use the photographs taken for General Gatacre during the march to the relief of Chitral, and to Colonel Atwell Porter of the 28th Regiment Bengal Infantry for those he obtained while stationed at Kila Drosh.

AUTHOR'S NOTE

CONTENTS

CONTENTS

ILLUSTRATIONS

MAPS & PLANS

CHITRÁL:
THE STORY OF A MINOR SIEGE

CHAPTER I

THE COUNTRY AND THE PEOPLE

THE dominant note of Chitrál is bigness combined with desolation ; vast silent mountains cloaked in eternal snow, wild glacier-born torrents, cruel precipices, and pastureless hillsides where the ibex and the markhor find a precarious subsistence. It takes time for the mind to recover from the depression which the stillness and melancholy of the giant landscape at first compel. All colour is purged away by the sun-glare ; and no birds sing. Life is represented by great eagles and vultures, circling slowly or poised aloft, and by the straight business-like flight of the hawk. The dull, ceaseless roar of the distant river changes, whenever you listen fixedly, to a sound as of supernatural voices shrieking in agony, but too remote for human sympathy.

Enclosed in such a mighty frame the space for human life and action seems almost microscopic, so small is the spot it occupies, so completely is it lost in its surroundings. It consists of tiny fan-shaped oases of cultivation on soil deposited by mountain streams, just before they noisily hurl themselves into a main river. These torrents are the tutelary deities as well as the creators of the village holdings, for they provide life and nourishment, through little canals, to the fields, which would otherwise vanish under the rainless sky. Such fertile patches,

A

completely dwarfed by the limitless expanse of rock, glacier, and crumbling hillside, are beautiful to the eye of the traveller wearied with the monotonous grey tones of the vast slopes of shale or shingle where his hazardous path has long undulated, or curved, when it was not climbing or descending bluff, spur, or cliff by toilsome zig-zags. To anyone thus tired, both in body and in mind, there is no pleasanter sight than the homely fields, divided by walls or low banks, the pretty orchards carpeted with soft grass, the gregarious cabins, or the occasional isolated fort, which resembles nothing so much as an overturned footstool with its legs in the air. After the fierce light and dust of the hillside there is something restful in the friendly willows, the hollowed-out plane trees, which offer the wayfarer shelter not only in their shadow but in their very substance, and the precise soldier-like poplars which stand about in stiff rows or singly as if on sentry-go. Such is this huge, crumpled-up, mightily-furrowed country in the hot summer weather.

Spring, in the villages, bursts forth like magic : one week is cold, the earth frozen ; the next finds the almond trees decked with gay blossoms, the willows in strings of green beads, the orchards scattering wide their superfluous glories. Autumn is perfect—still more beautiful—for the variegated leaves are lavish of their splendours, and the planes stand out as if stamped in copper. Winter is frigid and harsh, but dry and nearly windless, so sheltered are the great deep valleys with their hanging masses of snow ready, at any moment, to topple over and roll down irresistibly in thunder and smoke. But there are compensations for the prevailing dreariness ; red rhubarb leaves, dried for fodder, look pretty stacked in the branches of some convenient tree ; and with ice, frozen cataracts, fantastic snow-wreaths,

and snow-laden branches, beautiful objects meet one
everywhere.

The total area of this interesting region is small.
Fashioned from the ridges and spurs, which run downwards from the Hindu-Kush, it lies between Káfiristán
and the Amir of Kábul's other territories on the one
hand, and the Gilgit frontier district, Hunza and Puniál,
on the other. It is limited, and bounded on the south
by the high range which forms part of the northern
watershed of the Indus. Mountain-locked and moun-
tain-divided, its total area is a little more than that
of Wales, and its population certainly does not exceed
100,000. Level ground is rare, and where it exists
the soil is often swampy, or crusted with saltpetre.
A great mass of mountains, traversed by three important passes, runs from the Hindu-Kush to the
southern boundary range, and divides the little state
into two portions. It was the southernmost of these
three passes which was the grand obstacle to the
march of the Gilgit column to the relief of Chitrál.

The difficulties of travel in this mountain land are
great. All baggage and stores must be carried on
the backs of coolies or ponies. Food is so scarce that
a fat man has never yet been seen in the country ;
even the upper classes look underfed, and the most
effective of bribes is a full meal. The hill tracks,
which form the main lines of communication, are
seldom easy ; they are often difficult, sometimes
dangerous. Being narrow, and frequently high above
the river, whither the ground drops away in a steep
or precipitous fall, good nerves are necessary to ride
along them in comfort. The bridges are untrustworthy ; they are usually constructed on a rough
cantilever principle. One or two are strong, and have
lasted for years, but most are unenduring as the winter

snow. During the thaw the rising waters, at first far below, gradually climb upwards, throw their spray in derision over the puny structure, and finally, tired of the sport, carry it bodily away. The best of the bridges are easily destroyed by fire, so that any old woman with a pan full of charcoal and a bundle of dry straw might delay for hours, or even days, a column of British troops at certain crossings. Even when the rivers are moderately placid and shallow the fords are always bad, because of the boulders and stones in their bed; they are frequently devious also, and, consequently, always require a guide. It is dangerous to miss the proper line, for then one is liable to be carried into deep heavy water, or to find oneself in a quicksand. Yet it must be said that long, tiring marches, unsafe bridges, dangerous fords, shocking roads, and precarious supplies, do not make travelling in Chitrál as uncomfortable as might be expected.

One day, eight years ago, I was riding along one of those in-and-out, up-and-down rocky paths, which diversify the long, stiff climbs and the slow, dangerous descents of the Drásan division of Chitrál. Down below, several hundred feet, fumed the turbulent river; while beyond it rose, tier upon tier, great mountain ranges, the highest topped by perennial snow; there was also a lovely glacier. Leading our little cavalcade was a confidential servant of the Prince-Governor of the district mounted on a big, well-bred bay pony with every leg screwed from galloping over stony ground. The rider was perched so high on doubled-up blankets and cloths, to protect him from the hardness of the wooden demi-piqued saddle, and so short were the stirrups, that his knees reached nearly to the animal's withers. He chattered brightly to a companion on foot, who shuffled along holding a stirrup, when the road was wide enough; but at difficult places he grasped the tail, either to help himself up some severe incline or to steady the pony down a sharp descent. Both men were armed with curved swords in black leather scabbards, and carried old Snider carbines loaded, and, in the case of the runner, at full-cock. Between the shoulders of each hung a black shining bullock's-hide shield, embellished with four metal bosses.

Immediately in front of my horse trotted a happy-faced individual with flowers stuck all round his rolled-up brown cap, while his long, sad-coloured robe was dragged up through his belt to free his feet, and carefully pinned back on both sides in order that its gay chintz lining might not be hidden. From time to time he would glance back at me with the smile of one who never knew a sordid care, while now and again he trilled a high-pitched melodious song. Behind us strung out a dozen country ponies, some with one, others with two riders apiece. A few of the horsemen were arrayed in one or in two silk coats of astounding patterns, reaching to the soft leather riding-boots; on their wrists they supported hooded hawks. The remainder wore simpler clothes, some were even in tatters, but all alike were well armed and light-hearted; a pleasanter little party it would be hard to meet. At one point on the road one of my companions called out that the pathway we had just crossed was called the road of the double murder. This, of course, made me ask why it was so oddly named, and I settled myself in the saddle for the inevitable story, which ran like this:

"Once upon a time a young man lived with his mother in the hamlet you see among the sycamore trees below the spur yonder. He was unmarried, and in answer to his mother's incessant urging—you know

women never leave off chattering—always replied that
he did not want a wife. However, at last he fell
in love with a pretty girl, whom he married and
brought home to the great joy of his mother. But
the two women could never agree. They were always
quarrelling, and the unfortunate man led a miserable
life. He did all he could to make them friends, but
the hatred they had for one another grew worse and
worse. At last, in a fit of mad anger, both women
actually left their home, and ran away together, up
that very road we just crossed. The man followed
in dismay, and caught them up near a large stone
with a flat top which stands just off the path ; so he
placed the women upon it and cut their throats."

"What ? " was my shouted inquiry, as I abruptly
reined up the pony.

"He cut both their throats," rippled on the narrative, " and then a strange thing occurred. The two
pools of blood refused to mingle. The women hated
one another so that even their blood could not mix."

After a slight pause another of the Chitrális solilo-
quised, " Yes, it is a curious thing, but a woman never
can agree with her son's wife."

A third added—" Oh, my brother ! that is true ;
but in her heart a woman always loves her son-in-law,
although he invariably detests her."

Then followed more anecdotes pleasantly told, by
a kindly, soft-mannered people, of cruelty and bloodshed. Such and such a prince tied his eldest son
heels and neck and then cut his throat, so that the
family succession should fall to a younger son. The
then Mehtar * did dreadful deeds, it seemed, while his
immediate predecessor, " a handsome youth of fine
figure and frank countenance," indulged in so much

* Title of the ruler of Chitrál.

passionless slaughter that he earned the nickname of the "cannibal." Or for a change, tales of shameless perfidy would be described, or stories of the sudden end of horse and rider from falling through a bridge, or off a road over and over down to the river, and sometimes of people, whole companies at a time, being overwhelmed by avalanches or mangled by falling rocks. Most narratives, even fairy tales, had a crimson atmosphere. Sensuality of the grossest kind and murder, abominable cruelty, treachery or violent death, are never long absent from the thoughts of a people than whom none in the world are more delightful companions, or of simpler, gentler appearance. So happy seems everyone—the women are mostly secluded —so lovely are the little children, so much natural politeness is met with everywhere, that if it were not for the occasional glimpses of the famished slaves living on fruit or dying from starvation when past their first youth, a hurried traveller might almost imagine himself in a smiling dreamland!

In the evening at the end of a march a stranger is never allowed to feel dull. There is a band somewhere near, for certain, with dancing boys to twirl, attitudinise, shuffle, or prance to its music ; or a sitar-player will sing of love, begging someone or other "speak low for *her* heart is so tender," and declaring that his beloved one is so ideal and rare that she cannot bear the weight of even one diamond! The singer himself is possibly a refugee prince from Badakhshán or elsewhere who has fallen on evil days, and this adds to the general Arabian Nights character of the entertainment.

Sometimes a play will be acted, the theatre being soft orchard grass, with the boughs overhead glowing from the bright camp fire, which not only supplies illumination,

but enhances the surrounding gloom sufficiently for the
purposes of dressing-room seclusion. A favourite plot
is the adventures of a prince and his party beset by
Káfirs when on the march. The scene opens by the
Chitráli travellers swaggering gallantly into the firelight
with drawn swords. They prepare for the night by
taking off their accoutrements and loosening their
garments. A servant, with a small load still on his
back, sits down by the fire and goes through the motions
of cooking. Broad comedy is shown by the energy with
which this attendant is kicked by his master to make
him hurry. That always tickles the audience, and the
greater the laughter the more the poor actor suffers,
until his tremblings, at first feigned, end by being natural
enough. Suddenly a band of Káfirs, armed with tiny
bows and arrows, leap into the circle. They are black
and nearly naked, not because Káfirs are darker than
the average Chitráli, but because they are "devils" and
cannot be made too ugly. The Chitrális bolt and the
Káfirs express their joy by grotesque dancings; but
their triumph is short-lived, for the brave prince has
only been dissembling, and speedily returns with an
enormous sword, to put the Káfirs to death. Then it
begins all over again, and repeats itself until the most
distinguished stranger present declares he has had
enough. Afterwards the actors who played as Káfirs
have an interview with the priest to make sure no
stain is left upon their characters because of the part
they have sustained. The Lutkho men have a greatly-
improved *ballet d'action* (of course, for male performers
only) in which there is the same idea of a Káfir attack.
They, too, have to receive ecclesiastical pardon at the
end of the piece.

Sometimes instead of a play two boys sit down by
the fire to sing, beginning with one high-pitched, long-

sustained note, and then continuing with the shakes and quavers so admired in the East. After a moment or so, a musician with a kind of flageolet generally creeps up behind and tries to accompany them, but never seems to succeed. He keeps changing the key and lagging behind. However, neither the vocalists nor the audience pay him the slightest attention. The two boys press together and comport themselves like shy little maidens, whom they frequently resemble also in being pretty and feminine-looking.

Perhaps the pleasantest evenings of all are passed in listening to stories of fairies and of prodigies. A sympathetic attitude and an interested manner are frequently rewarded by tales of fairies, with their feet turned backwards, carried along on the wind, of hag-ridden horses, or of the terrible mischief worked by supernatural agency in those barns where tribute grain is concealed from the Mehtar. The speaker is usually telling of events which have come under his own observation or that of some of his friends and rela-tions. This gives a note of sincerity to the narrative. As in India your native groom actually sees the fright-ful ghost spring from a tree, and afterwards tells you the story, with starting eyeballs and a damp brow, so the Chitráli, in equally good faith, relates his fables, usually with this preamble :—" Was or was not ! Has been or has not been ! Do I tell you a lie ? The dark lies to the light, the day lies to the darkness ! It may have been or it may not have been. Either way, it is past. A man was in a cave, a mischievous man with a big head. The Mehtar was seated on a high place ; the Wazír sat in a corner."

And so the pleasant days and evenings pass.

There are few more treacherous people in the world than Chitrális, and they have a wonderful capacity for cold-blooded cruelty, yet none are kinder to little children or have stronger affection for blood and foster relations when cupidity or jealousy do not intervene. All have pleasant and ingratiating manners, an engaging light-heartedness, free from all trace of boisterous behaviour, a great fondness for music, dancing and singing, a passion for simple-minded ostentation, and an instinctive yearning for softness and luxury, which is the mainspring of their intense cupidity and avarice. No race is more untruthful or has a greater power of keeping a collective secret. Their vanity is easily injured, they are revengeful and venal, but they are charmingly picturesque and admirable companions. Perhaps the most convenient trait they possess, as far as we are concerned, is a complete absence of religious fanaticism.

CHAPTER II

GILGIT IN '95

ON January 1st, 1895—shortly after my arrival in Gilgit, to succeed Colonel Bruce, who had been acting as British Agent in my place for the greater part of a year—there was seemingly a prospect of continued peace all along the Kashmír frontier. In proof of this, superficially at least, many of the neighbouring chiefs and notables had come into Gilgit with large followings, to play polo, watch pony-races, and join in the general festivities of our Christmas "week."

The Gilgit district has a strange and enduring charm. Once visited, the desire to return is almost inevitable. In spite of isolation, of the difficulty of getting other than the plainest necessaries, of the inconvenience of four uncomfortably hot summer months, when the valley smells of dirty water, and the rice-swamps breed myriads of stinging insects ; in spite, also, of lofty passes, only certainly open from June to September, Gilgit has a fascination for all who have once lived there. Isolation leads to enduring friendships and generous sympathies ; plain food, if not invariably associated with high-thinking, certainly induces simplicity of thought and clearness of mind. Summer heats can be avoided by a little climbing, while the acrid bites of mosquito or sandfly can be escaped at the same time. Then the scenery is lovely and changeable as the face of a child. Eternal snows dazzle in the sunlight, or stand forth in virginal purity against the blue of a kindly night. The beauty of this upland country compels admiration at all times and seasons—the budding glories of spring, the riotous colouring of autumn, or even the tamer displays at the earth's drowsy time in midsummer or winter. Severe cold is practically unknown in the Gilgit valley itself, for, although it is 5000 feet above the sea-level, still, lying east and west, its temperature is mild.

The headquarters of this out-of-the-way borderland consist of a fort, picturesque, but useless, which contains within its walls an arsenal and barracks for the troops of the Maharajah of Kashmír. It is planted down on the high river-bank. On other sides it is environed by fields and orchards, dotted here and there with small drab-coloured hovels, groups of which, in different places, are dignified with the name of hamlet or village. At the southern edge of this expanse of cultivated ground, intervening between it and the barren-looking, stony slopes, which rise some thousands of feet, to form the southern boundary of the narrow valley, stands a gabled house, the official home of the British Agent, snugly nestled amidst fruit trees and willows, which, even at the end of November, are sparsely decorated with the tatters of their autumn foliage. Less than a hundred yards to the rear of this pretty dwelling, and a little higher up the slope, is a range of double rooms, serving indifferently as offices, or as lodgings for bachelors. Three miles to the east, on a bleak and high stony fan, long rough buildings can be indistinctly seen. These used to be occupied by the soldiers of the British Agent's escort of Sikhs. Close by, in similar barracks, altered for the purpose, were the quarters of the military officers, arranged round a central building, which served as a mess-house.

The European inhabitants of Gilgit, in 1895, were officials, without exception, and there was but one lady resident.

In those days Gilgit, for practical purposes, was, in winter, cut off from the rest of the world. The only convenient road to India, that through Kashmír, led over two passes, 14,000 and 11,300 feet high respectively, which were so deeply blocked with snow, that we sometimes received no mail-bags for thirty or forty days at a stretch. A track, indeed, did run up the Indus valley, whereby strong men on foot might reach Srinagar, after a tramp of 400 miles ; but down the Indus valley, and between Peshawer and Chitrál (220 miles to the west) the country was inhabited by cut-throat tribes, filled with a fanatical distrust of Europeans. Northward there was no outlet. There, lofty, snow-covered passes led on to those desolate rolling plateaux, more than 12,000 feet high, known as the Pamírs—"the roof of the world." A telegraph line, which was supposed to connect us with civilisation, was the winter plaything of avalanches and snow-slides. Its fractured or buried portions were valiantly hunted out by young men of the Indian Telegraph Service, who were constantly on the move all that winter, risking their lives, and suffering endless hardships in a hopeless endeavour to keep the wire intact for more than three consecutive days.

On the table before me as I write, there is a photographic group, taken by Lieut. F. J. Moberly,* the defender of Mastuj, who, consequently, does not appear in it himself. It is a picture of one of our Christmas gatherings. Eight officers are portrayed. Not many

* Mr Moberly, D.S.O., of the 37th Bengal Infantry.

weeks later, two of them, Baird and General Báj Singh, were killed, and two, Campbell and myself, severely wounded. One, Edwardes, was a prisoner in the hands of fanatical Patháns, expecting death at any moment. Another, Whitchurch, by an act of beautiful unselfishness and scorn of death, had earned the Victoria Cross ; and yet one more, Stewart, by his courage and invincible persistence, had gained the applause, as he had always possessed the affection, of his comrades.

CHAPTER III

FRONTIER POLITICS

IN spite of the seeming peacefulness of the political outlook, there were, however, not wanting one or two specks on the horizon to give cause for anxiety to the civil authorities—myself and my assistants. At Chitrál everything was thought to be satisfactory, until Lieutenant B. E. M. Gurdon* went there in December 1894, when he at once discovered the existence of a strong anti-English party. As Gurdon, though young, was remarkable for temperate and thoughtful judgments, his report on this point was disquieting. Bazaar rumours from Peshawer also continued to insist on the certainty of a frontier war as one of the results of a certain Boundary Delimitation Commission, then at work in the Kunár valley, under the command of an experienced Indian civilian, Mr Udny, C.S.I. The Commission was trying to arrange with the Amír's representative, the Afghán Commander-in-Chief, the somewhat complicated frontier lines agreed to, at Kábul in 1893, by Sir Mortimer Durand on behalf of the Government of India, and H.H. Abdur Rahmán, the astute Amír of the Afghán nation.

To the superficial observer nothing could seem more statesmanlike than to lay down distinct boundaries demarcating respectively the spheres of influence of the

* An officer of the Political Department of the Government of India serving under me at Gilgit.

Amír of Afghanistán and of the Government of India, and so to prevent all fear of collision between those two powers. A weak point, however, in the plan was the practical ignoring of all the intervening tribes, who, as they owed allegiance neither to the Afghán chief nor to the Government of India, not unnaturally objected to what they imagined was the parcelling out of their country without their consent. But a still greater danger was the opportunity it gave for a singularly acute Oriental diplomatist to play upon the bigoted sentiment of ignorant and easily-prejudiced tribesmen, and to misrepresent the honest intentions of the Government of India. Such a man could easily persuade those freedom-loving mountaineers that the real object of the ever-advancing military empire of India was to annex, sooner or later, all the country up to the boundary lines fixed by the joint commissions. Insinuations and suggestions of this kind would not be considered unfair moves in the game of diplomacy in most countries, eastern or western. The effect, all along the North-West Frontier of India, has been that ever since 1893, the tribes have become restless and distrustful, nervously anxious about every movement on our part, and always ready to hearken to the ravings of any rabid priest of Islám. Much blood and treasure have already been expended, at different times, on account of that well-intentioned agreement, which, though made in the utmost good faith and simplicity on our side, was from its very nature foredoomed to failure, temporarily, at anyrate.

Yet another discordant element in the political atmosphere was Umra Khán, the restless and ambitious ruler of Jandol and Dír, a spoilt child of our general border policy.

The love of buffer-states is deeply rooted in the

heart of British Foreign Offices, London or Indian ; but Indian Frontier Authorities have an inveterate tendency to improve on that cherished system, by erecting subordinate buffer-states against the larger varieties. One of these secondary buffer-states was that governed by Umra Khán. It was, no doubt, designed to counterpoise in some degree the growing influence of the Amír of Kábul. There is, of course, an obvious objection to such measures, in the impression they may possibly convey to our Oriental allies, that we are practising duplicity, and, therefore, cannot be trusted. They know little of "balance of power," or similar principles of political action, and when they find us proclaiming our friendship for the Amír, for instance, at the same time that we seem to be less openly inciting a minor chief to rival him, there is some fear that we may come to be looked upon as uncandid.

Umra Khán was at first encouraged, and then gradually dropped, as his heart began to swell, inconveniently, with a sense of his importance. Finally, he became estranged, because he conceived that his Pathán honour was wounded by a decision of the Durand mission, already referred to, that the little Khánate of Asmár, formerly seized by him, and whence he had been driven by the Afghán ruler, was to remain with the latter, although it had always been held that the Amír of Kábul must never be permitted by the Government of India to hold territory on the left bank of the Kunár river. Umra Khán was now therefore in a state of extreme irritation, and refused to collaborate with Udny's mission ; he was indeed more incensed against the British, by whom he considered he had been deserted, than against the Amír of Kábul, who had quietly secured the debatable land. The Government of India had already not only saved Umra Khán from

B

destruction at the hands of Abdul Rahmán, but it had helped him greatly in another way, by discountenancing the persistent attempts of the Mehtars of Chitrál to form a tribal league on behalf of the former ruler of Dír, whom Umra Khán had driven from his hereditary chiefship. But Umra Khán is one of that well-known class which is invariably less placable towards helpers, who eventually fail them in some wild dream of ambition, than to those who have always been consistent enemies.

Thinking over these and other probable converging influences, I convinced myself that a frontier outbreak of some kind was inevitable. There was no conclusive proof on the subject, still, it was in the air. Events proved me right in the generalisation, but wrong in particulars, for all my reflections had led me to believe that the danger would first fall on Udny's party in the Kunár valley.

Before Gurdon left Gilgit to take up the work of Assistant British Agent at Mastuj, Udny had telegraphed from Peshawer asking me that a political officer might be sent to meet him in the Kunár valley. To that I replied that the thing was impossible, unless a written permit and safeguard were first obtained for the journey through that part of the valley occupied by Umra Khán. Subsequently, the Government of India also telegraphed to say that it was desirable for a British officer to be sent to meet Udny, if this could possibly be arranged. It was at length decided that Gurdon should, at any rate, remain at Chitrál, after presenting his credentials to the Mehtar, and keep in correspondence with Udny, instead of returning at once to his headquarters at Mastuj where his escort of Sikhs was stationed.

But, feeling certain that my forebodings of trouble would be realised, I, with the senior of my special military assistants, Captain Colin Campbell of the

Central India Horse, went to Gupis, in Yásín, soon after my arrival in the district, to inspect that place, and to say some final words to Gurdon before he started. Amongst other things, I told him that if there was any outbreak in the Kunár valley, or danger to Udny, while he was at Chitrál, he must at once summon his escort from Mastuj, and take certain other steps, particularly in the way of quickly sending news of events to Gilgit. Captain Townshend, the senior British officer at Gupis, was ordered to repair a very bad piece of ice-covered road, over a neighbouring ravine, and to be ready to hurry forward a reinforcement to Mastuj, at any moment. We then returned to Gilgit, and Gurdon departed on his fateful journey.

A careful inspection of Gupis, and the Kashmír troops holding it, had been satisfactory, except in one important particular. Campbell discovered that the garrison was but ill-instructed in musketry. It seemed that during the year the soldiers had been continuously employed in building the fort, of course, at the expense of their military training; and that although Townshend, a diligent officer, had repeatedly applied for targets, he had never been able to get them. Serious, indeed, as was this defect, it was obviously irreparable at that frozen season. Campbell, who had only lately come up from India, was anxious on the subject, and he communicated some of his uneasiness to me; but Captain Baird,* who filled a post which may be best described as that of military secretary to the British Agent, was more optimistic. He thought the Kashmír riflemen were less bad than we believed, and that, though insufficiently trained, they might still give a good account of themselves, if need arose.

* Captain J. McD. Baird of the 24th Punjáb Infantry.

CHAPTER IV

OUR DEALINGS WITH CHITRÁL

GURDON arrived safely at Chitrál, where he was received with effusion by the ruler, Mehtar Nizám-ul-Mulk, and at once set to work to discover on the spot the true state of affairs. About this prince, Nizám-ul-Mulk, we shall have much to say later, but it is enough to remark here, that he was, for adequate reasons, disliked by his subjects, and merely retained his regal authority because he was the ally of the Government of India.

It is necessary, at this point, to relate shortly the history of our dealings with Chitrál, and to show how it happened that, on January 1st, 1895, British troops were stationed in that country, and British officers were trying to influence, however ineffectually, the councils of its chief.

The early history of Chitrál is interesting to the student only; to others it is merely a crimson-stained record, a monotonous tale of murder and perfidy—the slaying of brother by brother, of son by father. No gleams of generosity or magnanimity illuminate the lurid pages, but naked treachery, wholesale betrayals, and remorselessness, are only varied by the complicated and mean intrigues, which cement them into a connected story. It is but fair to add that public opinion in Chitrál, and many other Eastern countries, gives the same meed of applause to these villainies, when successful, that the West awards to high-minded statesmanship.

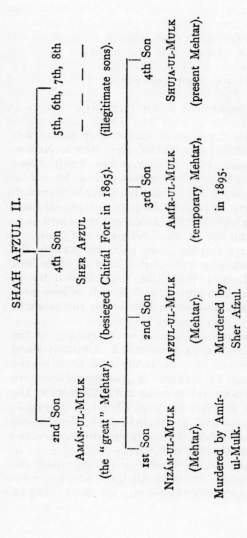

SHAH AFZUL II.

2nd Son
AMÁN-UL-MULK
(the "great" Mehter).

1st Son
NIZÁM-UL-MULK
(Mehtar).
Murdered by Amír-ul-Mulk.

2nd Son
AFZUL-UL-MULK
(Mehtar).
Murdered by Sher Afzul.

3rd Son
AMÍR-UL-MULK
(temporary Mehtar),
in 1895.

4th Son
SHUJA-UL-MULK
(present Mehtar).

4th Son
SHER AFZUL
(besieged Chitral Fort in 1895).

5th, 6th, 7th, 8th
— — —
(illegitimate sons).

There were more than sixty other children born to Amán-ul-Mulk, of whom three sons of doubtful legitimacy were murdered by Afzul-ul-Mulk.

The above are the personages chiefly referred to in the short historical sketch.

Amongst Orientals, ends justify deeds even more than with us, and the cruellest brute is the national hero.

In 1857, a remarkable man climbed to the throne of Chitrál, by steps slippery with the blood he had shed. His name was Amán-ul-Mulk, "the Great Mehtar." He was a man of sturdy frame, commanding features, and adroit tongue. Far in the future, he saw clearly the objects of his ambition. Scarcely less distinctly, the intervening difficulties, with the paths over or the burrows beneath them, were before him also. With this strong mental vision, Nature gave him a relentless heart, and inexhaustible vitality. She made him a scourge to a people who deserved no mild ruler. When he died in 1892, from being merely a younger son of the Mehtar of Lower Chitrál, he had gained possession of the whole of the hill country, bordering the south of the Hindu-Kush from the limits of Gilgit to Káfiristán, the Kunár valley as far as the Asmár frontier, and he also held real, if somewhat undefined, authority in Dárel, Tángír, and Eastern Káfiristán. With nothing approaching to a standing army, or the resources to support it, he was obliged to fight most of his battles vicariously, while his turbulent nobles and relatives were disciplined by secret assassins, or set to kill one another by false promises of lands or rulership. Cupidity always smothered their reason, as it quenched all natural affection, and after thirty years' experience of Amán-ul-Mulk's sinister ways, they were still his easy victims. But the terrible old man knew well the baser springs of human action—hunger, greed, lust, and the insatiable vanity of man, however cunningly it may be hidden—with their innumerable developments.

Three years before Amán-ul-Mulk came to the throne, Kashmír had made overtures to the reigning Mehtar of Chitrál for pressing reasons. In those days, all the mountain-land between Káfiristán and Gilgit was divided between two chiefs, descended from a common ancestor. The eastern portion, named the Khushwaktia district, was ruled by a prince, who was a most trouble-some neighbour to Kashmír ; the western part, the Katúr country, or Chitrál proper, was reigned over by Amán-ul-Mulk's father, whose subsequent death is somewhat remarkable in Chitráli annals, because it came about naturally. These two princes looked upon one another with jealous rivalry and undying hatred, in spite of, or perhaps because of, the fact that they were closely connected by blood and by inter-marriages. Conse-quently, as the Kashmír authorities were greatly troubled by the Eastern Mehtar, he of the West would naturally be inclined to listen to overtures of friendship from them. A coalition was accordingly arranged, and in 1855, the Katúr forces seized Mastuj, at that time the headquarters of the Khushwaktia chief, but they were driven out again in the following year.

In 1857, the place was again captured by the Chitrális. To give some idea of what the enmity to Kashmír of the Eastern chief meant, it must be told that he not only overran Gilgit, but, with the exception of two short intervals when the fortune of war com-pelled him to retreat, he maintained himself in that unhappy valley for twelve years, from 1848. His fiend-like temper vented itself in reasonless slaughter of the people, while his calmer moments were occupied in the equally disastrous sale of the inhabitants into slavery. The depopulation of the district, and the broken spirit of the Gilgitis at the present day, are mainly due to this Mehtar's cruelties. In 1860, his merciless grasp was relaxed by death, and the valley was recovered by Kashmír easily enough, while the dead man's sons fought over their remaining patrimony till all the border was in confusion, and reeked with blood.

The next memorable event occurred in 1870, when Heyward, the distinguished traveller, was murdered in Yásín by Mír Wali, who had succeeded to the Mehtarship of Khushwaktia. Poor Heyward was warned of the designs of his false friend, Mír Wali, and dared not go to sleep, for his few servants were useless to protect him, or to defend themselves. So, all night, he sat by a camp-table, armed and watchful. At the break of dawn, he became exhausted, for he had undergone much previous fatigue, and his head fell forward on the table. That was the opportunity long waited for by his cowardly enemies. A running noose was thrown over his shoulders, and he was seized and bound. It is said that he begged for one last look at the rising sun, and that the request was granted. But this is probably untrue. He was taken up the stream a short distance, and there cut down with swords, besides being subjected to other cruelties before he died. Everyone present flung a stone upon the dead body, that all might be equally implicated; but the actual executioners were three men well known to me. It was loathsome to have relations subsequently with such wretches, but it would have been unjust to hold them responsible for the murder, since they only carried out orders which it would have been death to disobey.

At this lapse of time, it is possible to give a calm opinion on this matter. Mír Wali, who eventually suffered for the crime, was probably instigated to it, not, as he falsely declared, because Heyward had tried to force villagers to do his transport work, but because Amán-ul-Mulk of Chitrál, and perhaps the Kashmír authorities also, dreaded the idea of English travellers visiting this borderland. Heyward's rifle was given to the Chitrál Mehtar, and many years afterwards was presented to me by Nizám-ul-Mulk.

After much intrigue, and long negotiation between Kashmír and the Chitrális, Mír Wali was ousted and slain by his own brother (nicknamed the Wrestler), who was accoutred for the task by Amán-ul-Mulk. The last-named was well rewarded by Kashmír, and the Wrestler, a dirty little man with a fierce spirit, reigned in Khushwaktia. But, as is usual with successful Oriental soldiers, surrounded as they are by flatterers, and by admiring wives, he gradually became intoxicated with his own glory, and fell an easy prey to Amán-ul-Mulk, who now wanted his country, and a further subsidy from Kashmír. Instigated by his treacherous relative and father-in-law, he marched an army, in 1880, against Gilgit, at the time that Colonel John Biddulph was our Political Agent there. No sooner was he well started on this surprising adventure, than Amán-ul-Mulk's forces invaded and captured the Khushwaktia country; the poor befooled Wrestler had to fly for his life over the hills, while Amán-ul-Mulk's Kashmír subsidy was doubled, and his territorial influence greatly increased.

Penniless, and almost without friends, the Wrestler had a brave heart. He kept the frontier ablaze, till Amán-ul-Mulk bribed the outcast's brother and nephew, with a promise of the Khushwaktia country, to murder him. This they did; whereupon Amán-ul-Mulk drew back from his word, and failing to persuade the son to kill his father, had to crush their combined resentment by force of arms.

In 1885-86, Colonel Lockhart (now Sir William Lockhart, G.C.B.) led a mission to examine the Hindu-Kush passes. He visited Amán-ul-Mulk, then in the zenith of his power, and entered into direct negotiations with him on behalf of the Government of India—relations which were not without profit to the Mehtar of Chitrál, both in the way of gifts of rifles and of money. In 1888 and 1889, Colonel A. Durand made similar journeys with an identical object. He was equally successful.

Before closing this chapter it is desirable to state briefly the political position of Chitrál towards Afghánistán. There is a strong probability that in former days Chitrál was in a subordinate position to the little state of Badakhshán, which lies to the north of the Hindu-Kush, and is no longer independent, but in the hands of the Amír of Kábul. Amán-ul-Mulk, in the year 1874, felt dubious about the Afgháns, his near neighbours on the north. He, therefore, experimentally suggested to the then Amír that Chitrál should become nominally subject to Kábul, and that a betrothal should take place between the Afghán heir-apparent and Amán-ul-Mulk's daughter. The marriage arrangement was accepted, but was never completed. For the rest, the Mehtar quickly retracted his tentative offers, and when, in 1876, the Afgháns threatened his country, he sought the protection of Kashmír. Thereupon, with the approval of the Government of India, an agreement was made between the two States, which served to protect Chitrál, although Kashmír obtained no advantage, except the honour of being recognised as the Suzerain of the Mehtar. The outcome of all was that the Amír of Kábul was definitely informed by the Government of India, that no claim by him to the overlordship of Chitrál could be admitted.

CHAPTER V

AN ORIENTAL INTERLUDE

ON the 30th August 1892, Amán-ul-Mulk died suddenly in open durbar, after a reign of some thirty-two years. His death was due to a failure of the heart, but the Hindustani native doctor stationed at Chitrál had only a short time previous administered an emetic; consequently, many people, including some of the dead Mehtar's sons, believed, or professed to believe, that the old king had been poisoned. He died, universally detested, but in the odour of sanctity, for he had, on three different occasions, sent men to Mecca, to perform the pilgrimage in his name. Besides, as years crept on, he, following the custom of so many Oriental rulers, began to turn his diplomacy heavenwards. In addition to listening to the exhortations of priests, he kept his fasts rigidly, and gave much in alms. Occasional murders had become a habit with him, but of late years he always wept bitterly for the unkindly fate of his victims, which was, perhaps, as much as could be expected from such a man. On the whole, Amán-ul-Mulk was faithful to his engagements with the Government of India, although he was sorely tempted to side against us during the long interval, in December 1891, between the capture of Fort Nilt and the forcing of the heights which commanded it. Again, he was greatly vexed by my long stay in Káfiristán, and his irritation became almost uncontrollable when the Government of India forbade him to attack openly, or intrigue secretly against, his son-in-law, Umra Khán of Jandol, who, in 1892, was approaching the high-water mark of his fame. Nevertheless, he crushed down his rage, and smiled (with eyes of fury) on the British. If it had been possible for his subjects to hate him more than they did—with the paralysed hatred of the mouse for the cat—it would have been for his Indian proclivities. For, after deliberately choosing between the infidels and his co-religionist neighbours, Amán-ul-Mulk perceived that his authority rested altogether on the prestige and strength he derived from his subsidies of breech-loading rifles and Indian rupees.

This old man left dozens of children, but in August 1892 only two were looked upon as important. Between them, seemingly, the succession lay, for they were legitimate, a matter of the first consequence in Chitrál, and the only other possible candidates were two little princes by a despised queen, who lived with their mother at Shoghot, and Sher Afzul, Amán-ul-Mulk's half-brother, a fugitive soldier of fortune at the court of the Amír of Kábul. The rivals were full brothers, but oddly contrasted. Nizám-ul-Mulk, the elder, was handsome and debonair, the admired of women, whom, in return, he abhorred, a keen sportsman and polo player, an utter coward, and a man whose soul was drowned in abject Oriental vice.

Afzul-ul-Mulk, the younger brother, had more of his father's character, fearless, implacable, and was as secretive as he was persistent in his schemes. A somewhat vacant gaze, and an open mouth, made him look like a fool, which he certainly was not. He was married to a Badakhshání princess, famous for the loveliness of her white throat. Scandal said she loved the gallant-

looking Nizám, who probably would have turned green
at the suggestion, for he abominated all women; but
Afzul heard, and suffered the more, because pride forbade him to show his wound.   He put his wife's
cousin to a cruel death for merely smiling at her,
and, no doubt, cheered himself with the thought of
how he would hack Nizám to pieces, if God would
only deliver him into his hands.

As may be imagined, the prime political question
in Chitrál was, who would succeed; and in Gilgit,
also, the chances of each brother were anxiously
calculated. Nizám was a miser, but as a result he
must have treasure to bribe with.   Afzul gave everything away to his adherents, and, therefore, had no
reserves. Nizám, from pure fecklessness, had hardly
one noble in his train; but then, on the other hand,
Afzul, in his frantic anxiety to ingratiate himself with
British officers, and show them the extent of his
civilisation, had forced the greatest personages in his
district, by insult and threats, to help to make roads
for his august visitors, who, in return, politely declared
that his work compared favourably with that of the
Government engineers in India.

One important circumstance, portentous, but invisible, was not thought of.   This was the inexhaustible
hatred of all classes in Chitrál, for differing reasons,
to Amán-ul-Mulk, and the certainty that this strong
passion, unable to expend itself on its real object,
would dam back its torrent till it could sweep away
and destroy his offspring; visiting the sins of the
father upon the children in the true spirit of Asiatic
vengeance. Amán-ul-Mulk himself had never definitely
said which son he desired to succeed him; but it was
generally thought that he favoured Nizám. As a
matter of fact, he feared both his sons, as they

feared him, and one another. When all three were together at the headquarters of the country, at Chitrál fort, it was a strange scene. Each of the three was surrounded day and night by armed groups, while at critical moments, priests of Islám might be seen fluttering from one to the other, swearing them on the Koran to abstain from bloodshed. The father occasionally received a son in durbar, drawn sword on knee, and with a sermon suggested by thoughts of parricide and cold steel.

Nevertheless—and here comes in the Gilbert-and-Sullivan side of the court—tears were rarely seen, even amongst the abject peasantry and the slaves. For the rest, all was gaiety and bright raiment, picturesque polo games, hunting parties, polite discourse, with prayers at orthodox times, and the music of tabor and pipe, giving a dancing measure to unspeakable but beautiful boys. A false atmosphere of quiet enjoyment covered everything, and a near relative, on his knees before the king, might be relating a story with jestful lips, while his cold fingers trembled, and his scared eyes never left the face of the grim old man.

The question of the succession was quickly answered. Afzul was close at hand, while Nizám was shooting in Yásín. The former pounced upon Chitrál, seizing the fort with its arsenal and treasure. That settled it. Having now the power to bribe added to his strong native store of vital energy, he was able at once to wind round his head the enormous turban of Mehtarship. Every personage at such a ceremony has to help with one or more of the folds of this gigantic head-dress, for the action is held to signify his acquiescence in the royal investiture.

Afzul at once sent off expresses to Gilgit, asking

to be recognised as Mehtar. His letters were full of
friendship and affection for the Government of India,
and he begged that a British officer might be sent to
him at Chitrál as a visible sign to all men of his
subordinate alliance with that great power. In the
meantime, Nizám had become, by turn, piteous, angry,
frightened, and warlike ; but never of one mind for
long. Half-heartedly he collected troops. When he
discovered that the British Agent at Gilgit was determined to stand and watch the game in a neutral
attitude, and would not even make suggestions to
Afzul for a division of the country with his brother,
he became scared. Afzul, on his part, magnified the
force Nizám had at his disposal, and made overtures
all round for help. He withdrew the Chitráli garrisons
from Narsut fort, which was thereupon promptly occupied by Umra Khán, and started for Yásín with all
the men he could muster. But Nizám had no stomach
for the encounter ; his troops read their leader clearly,
and rapidly melted away, while he himself fled to
Gilgit, there to be hospitably received.

The triumphant Afzul hurried back to Chitrál, and
in the excitement of his easy victory, let loose the
savage instincts which are always hard to hold in a
Katúr. He had already slain three of his half-brothers
in cold blood, treacherously as well as cruelly. Now
he began to torture women suspected of knowing where
treasure was hidden, and threw the reins on the neck
of his dæmonic temper. Kalash Káfirs were summoned
to dance before the new king to the disgust of orthodox notables, who were still more scandalised at the
extravagant largess squandered on others than themselves. Finally, the fatuous Mehtar remarked that his
past killings were insignificant compared with what he
intended to do. If there had been any doubt before,

that doomed him. Everyone trembled, and a collective terror soon changed into despairing fury.

Amongst the possible, though unlikely, candidates for the Mehtarship, Sher Afzul's name was mentioned. He had done good soldier service to the Amír of Kábul, who was said to trust, as well as like, the exiled Chitrál prince, and to treat him with much honour at the Afghán court. All Chitráli hearts and eyes now turned to this refugee, who, by something more than a coincidence, was at that moment crossing the Dorah Pass from Badakhshán into the Lutkho Valley, with less than a hundred followers.

Eastern peoples have a well-known faculty for keeping a secret. Even amongst their fellows, Chitrális are remarkable for this power. So, in spite of the fact that the whole country was against Afzul, and a dreadful enemy was within ten miles of him one night when he went to bed at Chitrál, yet he never dreamt of danger, although numerous conspirators were actually inside his fort walls. At midnight an alarm was raised, and Persian war cries filled the air. "The Afgháns are on us" was whispered by pale lips, as men, wearing tall Kábul-made caps, were seen to swarm over the corner towers. Afzul sprang up. His women tried to induce him to dress in their clothes and so escape in the darkness, but he was a brave if a bad man, and scorned such a disguise. He shouted for a fire to be lit, so that the real extent of the danger might be discovered, and by its light he was at once shot down and hacked to pieces. Joyful shouts, starting from the fort, were taken up all round in the darkness, that Afzul, the dæmon, was slain, and Sher Afzul, the saviour, was Mehtar.

CHAPTER VI

MY FIRST MISSION

So the poor "dæmon" was slain. I say "poor," for a man-torturer is only less to be pitied than his victims. We were now, indeed, at the parting of the roads. Sher Afzul had roughly installed himself as Mehtar. Nizám was a fugitive at Gilgit. What was our policy to be? A further complication was added by the fact that we had a news-writer, and a Hindustani doctor at Chitrál, in a position full of risk.

Now, it must be confessed, that the Indian Government does not thoroughly confide in the Amír of Kábul, who heartily distrusts them in return. Putting aside all sophistry, it was certain that Sher Afzul would not have attempted his adventure, without the tacit consent of the Amír, and was, in short, the Afghán nominee. Abdur Rahmán obviously sought to obtain indirectly through this prince what the Indian Government had disallowed—the suzerainty of Kábul over Chitrál.

It is just possible that an elaborate diplomatic compromise was the best way out of a difficulty, which might become extreme. In those days, however, no certainly open road of communication lay between Gilgit and the Government of India, so the British Agent had to decide on the spot what should be done. The holder of that office at the time was a clever and conscientious man, who arrived at important decisions with no light heart, but diligently, and with anxious thought. Nizám claimed his right to try for his father's throne, and argued forcibly that he was not a prisoner, but a guest, as free to go as he had been to come. Colonel Durand believed that to be unanswerable, and that Nizám could not be forcibly prevented from starting for Yásín. Troops had already been marched over the Yásín border, and remained within that district as a guarantee for the safety of our Indian officials at Chitrál, a moderate and reasonable precaution. Nizám advanced fearfully, but he had with him some Hunza men, the chief of whom had long been an exile in Chitrál, and was well known for clear-headedness and force of character.

Absurd rumours of the intention of the Gilgit authorities frightened Sher Afzul, and more particularly the Chitrál nobles, who, in those days, looked upon British troops as irresistible. A comical mistake is said to have intensified their terror. Some grain—a feed for a horse—and a few melons were sent out from Gilgit to the native servant of a British officer. By misadventure, this small load went astray, and got handed on from village to village, until it eventually reached Chitrál, where it created consternation. It was held to be the warning of a friend in Gilgit, that the advancing troops were as numerous as grains of corn, and that all who opposed them would be cut into pieces like melons.

Nizám reached Mastuj, and moved over to Drásan, where Sher Afzul's son commanded. A loose skirmish, cleverly won by the Hunza leader, combined with the adroit behaviour of a young prince, a supposed opponent of Nizám, who spread dismay in the other camp by ingenious lies told with the fervour of conviction, made the Sher Afzulites retreat up the Lutkho valley. Thereupon, the princes and nobles of Chitrál lost their heads in panic. Weeping, but with unwavering persistence, they compelled their new Mehtar to leave the country by the Kunár valley, and return to Kábul. Nizám, however, was with difficulty induced to move on to Chitrál, and when there his senses became numbed with fear, his face wearing the look of a hunted animal. He despatched messenger after messenger to Gilgit, imploring that some officer might be sent to advise and help him. There was no promise he was not prepared to make. He frantically offered his country with both hands, if he only might be allowed to live under the protection of the Government of India.

Now, as previously mentioned, Afzul, during his short, bloody reign, had asked for a British official to be sent to him, to tighten, as he said, the existing bonds which held Chitrál and India together. He was anxious for formal recognition as Mehtar. Unaware of the state of terror in Chitrál the Government of India acceded to his request; he was recognised as Mehtar, and I was deputed to visit him. Subsequent events simply stopped the clock temporarily. When Nizám, trembling over his triumph, was asking wildly for someone to hold him on the throne, I was again ordered to Chitrál.

Fully alive to all the difficulties ahead, I prepared for this mission in January 1893. It was sufficiently adventurous. We had before us a march of over 220 miles, some parts of which were as bad as is conceivable. Beyond Mastuj, we knew the people were bitterly hostile to their king, and disliked us honestly. The whole country was in a turmoil. Authority had, in many places, disappeared altogether. In short, our only safety lay in the fact that everything was disorganised, and there were no leaders of the people.

The great religious heads of the numerous Maulais, a heretic sect of Shiah Muhammedans, the chiefs of the noble class, and the headmen generally, were sullen and resentful. By that time they had discovered how feeble was the force that owned Nizám as its leader, and their hearts went out in contrition to Sher Afzul, for the pusillanimous part they had played. They also perceived their present powerlessness. What we in the West call "the people" could not rid themselves of the servitude of many generations. Custom, even the cruellest, is hard to eradicate, and though, on the whole, the villagers wished us well, they would sooner have shot us down at the order of the Adamzádas (the nobles) than have dared to break the chain of centuries which bound them to their petty tyrants.

My escort was of the 15th Sikhs, 50 men all told, but commanded by an admirable officer, named Gordon,* a soldier by instinct, as well as by training. Captain F. E. Younghusband, the well-known traveller, went as my assistant, and Lieutenant the Hon. C. G. Bruce of the 5th Gurkhas, famous all over the frontier for muscularity and his power of influencing Orientals, helped with the camping arrangements, and proved his utility in innumerable ways.

I had been having some rough fighting in the Indus valley at Chilás, so the mission marched forty miles ahead, while I stopped at Gilgit to rest, arrange details with Durand, and provide for all discernible contingencies; then Bruce and I rode out to Gákuch, where we caught up our party. Before we started, one of Nizám's Wazírs arrived, and, on learning the smallness of my escort, besought me to increase it to

* Lieut. J. L. R. Gordon, not to be confounded with Lieut. B. E. M. Gurdon of the Political Service.

two hundred men. On discussing the matter, he was, however, obliged to admit that it would be impossible for me to feed such a number.

As a minor complication, Yásín had now risen against Nizám, and had proclaimed a Khushwakti prince, Muhammed Wali Khán, the son of Heyward's murderer. The rebellious party needed someone to lead it, so this daring, enterprising youth was chosen. He had some right by heredity, and more from his energetic character; but, probably, the majority of the Yásínis honestly desired British rule in those days. They knew what the Khushwakti and Katúr tyranny was, and they imagined that our sovereignty meant peace and happiness for all; but a critical examination of their thoughts and wishes left an impression on the mind, that each man desired to have no one in authority over him, but that he himself was to have the power to harass, bully, and control as a master, all those of an inferior social position. Happily however, for Yásín, it has none of the noble class. There the most influential men are the religious teachers, who are of that strange sect already referred to as the Maulais. They are really the "assassins," the followers of the lineal descendant of the "Old Man of the Mountains."

All along the Gilgit frontier, the most tractable men, in my experience, if you can only get personal contact with them, are the ecclesiastics, especially those of this somewhat persecuted faith. They hate one another, and their jealousy is as intense as their dislike. Muhammed Wali Khán was influenced by one of these men, who was equally ambitious and bribeable; thus our way was smoothed. Indeed, my chief difficulty was to keep at arm's-length the people who wanted to put the Government of India in the place of the prince they themselves had lately selected.

Until we neared the Shandúr, we had only the customary difficulties of ponies skating over frozen roads, or being lowered down steep places or sudden drops by the leverage afforded by their tails and bridles. It daily grew colder. The last march to the pass was over deep snow, with a temperature which could not be measured, for the mercury sulked at the bottom of a thermometer which did not register the severest cold. At that point we said goodbye to Muhammed Wali Khán, who had ridden with me all the way through Yásín. He was a capital companion, but had a temper like flame. Nevertheless, we became very good friends, and parted regretfully, I with a feeling that if disaster were in store for us ahead, we had behind us a well-disposed country to retreat through.

Some of our marches had been most pleasant. The young prince—he was only seventeen, and looked younger—appeared more like the pantomime fairyland variety than an everyday wear-and-tear specimen. He was short, slight, and graceful, a bold rider, and unconsciously threw himself into graceful poses, while his gestures, when he was roused, were highly dramatic. His face was girlish, with its bright eyes, white teeth, and fair colour; long ringlets fell over his gay silk coat. He was elaborately armed, and the caparison of his horse was covered with metal studs. Amongst his attendants was one boy, certainly not more than twelve years of age, who ran immediately in front of his master when the pace was not too good, and caught us up at other times in a surprising way. This boy had long fair curls, on his back hung a shield of large size, and he carried, painfully, a man's sword. "Prince, who is that?" I asked, on first seeing the mannikin. "Why, that is my servant, a soldier," was the surprised answer. After this, a detachment of young lady warriors, from Her Majesty's Theatre, Drury Lane, would hardly have astonished me.

Mastuj was reached without mishap. The night before we crossed the Shandúr, one of the Sikhs was brought into camp frozen stiff; but Bruce and his Gurkha orderly, who, like his officer, had learned mountaineering not only on the Himalayas, but also on the Alps, flung themselves upon him, so to speak, and tore off the strips of blankets in which his feet were wrapped. Then they spanked, rubbed, and wrung the numbed limbs with an energy that seemed ghoulish. At last, agonised yells proclaimed that the blood was again circulating. Whereupon the grateful patient was allowed to approach the fire, and given a hot grog, preparatory to being swathed in blankets and left to sleep in the cheery warmth. So cold was the night, that a sturdy Yarkand galloway belonging to me could not be kept alive in spite of thick clothing, although we lit fires all round him and administered hot rum and water. Curiously enough, my grey Arab pony, lately brought up from Bombay, withstood the low temperatures easily.

On the pass itself we had good luck. There was no wind, so an altitude of 12,000 feet gave us but little trouble. We got over without a single frost bite. It was a curious sight to watch the tall Sikhs tramping through the snow. Although plainsmen, they were very resolute, and their inborn fire told with them just as much as with my Arab stallion.

Sikhs cannot use Balaclava caps, for dread of their sacred hair being injured, but they were muffled up to the eyes, and their big turbans came down over the ears. Each man had a pair of blue spectacles to protect him from snow-blindness. Long sheep-skin coats reached nearly to the heels, while their feet,

well anointed with mutton fat, were swathed in
blanket bandages.   Thick woollen gloves protected
the hands from burning gun barrels.   Gordon marched
at the head of his men in single file, and their line of
march curved and undulated over the broken tortuous
track in the frozen snow, like some big, wounded serpent.

On the Chitrál side of the pass my anxieties increased.   There we came into contact with the nobles
and the religious heads of the people.   They were
frankly chagrined at our coming, and could hardly
force the smile of Oriental politeness to their down-
drawn mouths.   However, we were not to be defeated.
We gave them tea and cigarettes, not to speak of more
substantial presents.   They were petted and talked to
confidentially.   In the end, they almost invariably
brightened up, and became happy for the time being.

I had with me as a "native attaché" a singularly
clever diplomatist named Abdul Hakím.   At such work
as this he was irresistible, while his ubiquity and
ingenuity in keeping me supplied with a correct knowledge of local feeling and villager politics were surprising.   Then Gordon kept an unwinking eye on his Sikhs,
ready to punish on the instant any attempt to bully or
ill-use the porters, whom Bruce paid with his own
hand.

It is hard to find in the world better soldiers than
good Sikhs, but their discipline must be rigid ; for a
peculiar religion accentuates the extraordinary natural
vanity of these military sectarians.   Slackness in manag-
ing them is always liable to be followed by grave trouble.
Otherwise they are simple-minded, except in money
matters, where they are always crafty and miserly.   One
of them remarked to an officer, with single-hearted com-
placency, just after we had emerged from a village,
" I suppose these folk, after seeing us Sikhs, always

ask, 'Whence come these splendid, handsome young men?'" They are also amusingly thick-headed.

The country people were delighted with us. Never had they received such sums for porterage, and the money was actually put into each man's hand by Bruce himself, to make sure that everyone got his due. So overcome were certain of these men at finding themselves the owners of four or five veritable rupees, that they had to sit down and speculate what to do with it. The most common decision was that the silver must be worked into ornaments for their wives.

At length we turned into the Chitrál valley, four or five miles from the fort. Just before, Nizám-ul-Mulk and the native Indian officials stationed at Chitrál—the news-writer, a Bengal cavalry officer, and the Punjábi doctor—had met us with a numerous retinue. Across the river, to our right, the rocks were covered with Chitrális. There it is customary for a salute to be fired, in honour of distinguished visitors, from huge matchlocks which cannot be put to the shoulder, and compel the operator to waltz about after each round to lessen the recoil, or from ordinary *jezails* and Snider carbines. On the present occasion this ceremony was pretermitted for unanswerable reasons. The Mehtar and the Bengal cavalry man considered that the saluting companies could not be trusted to abstain from loading their pieces with ball, and shooting us. We rode onwards with the haggard, frightened Mehtar, many of my Káfir friends forming part of the mob of horsemen and runners. Near the bridge is an open sandy stretch, free from stones. There the Wapenshaw pole had been put up, and the gallantest of Chitráli cavaliers raced past, one by one, in attempts to hit the egg-shaped silver ornament suspended near the top, by firing at it as they stood in their stirrups, galloping hard. This was too much for the Mehtar's nerves, so, with a sickly smile of apology for the restiveness of a horse as quiet as a cow, he pulled back behind my Arab, to concede me the honour of first meeting any bullet which might be fired in our direction.

Everything was wrong in Chitrál, in very truth. The Mehtar, palpitating with fear, could only think how to strengthen the defences of the fort. Sher Afzul, when he fled, had distributed, or the Chitrális had plundered, all the treasure, as well as the rifles and ammunition. Dozens of men were now swaggering about, armed to the teeth, most of them with their Sniders loaded. They carried their chins in the air, and scowled defiance in a manner which amazed any-one who had visited Chitrál in the old Mehtar's time. But Nizám had neither the moral ascendancy nor the military strength to disarm these dangerous folk.

We were lodged all together, in a house of two storeys; the living part being above, while the lower portion was used as a storing-place for grain and fire-wood. In front, to the east, there was a forecourt, with a range of stables against the end wall, and, at the sides, sheds and rough dwelling-rooms, which could be utilised for the Sikhs. Behind was a large oblong orchard, intersected by water channels, sloping gradually up to the edge of a ploughed field, which was fringed on the west by a small grove of plane trees. Farther still, the ground rose more and more steeply, until it merged into a moderately difficult hillside. At 700 yards our flat roof was completely commanded. The house and its enclosures, on the north, one of the long sides, edges a high cut-away bank, down which slanted a narrow track to the verge of the noisy Chitrál stream. Across the torrent were two or three small water-mills,

looking like military block-houses, except that they were
not loopholed. On the south side, far too close to our
walls, were the large Musjid (Muhammedan temple)
and the enclosed burying-place of the Mehtars of
Chitrál. Across a lane, and beyond some narrow
open ground to the east, were high garden walls and
buildings, then used as a hospital and as quarters for
the Punjábi doctor and his staff.

Our house was by no means a good one to defend,
but there was no other. In the event of hostilities, to
get down to the water would be a great difficulty,
for the mills on the opposite side could not safely be
held by tiny detachments of our small escort, particularly at night ; while in the hands of an enemy
they would constitute little forts, which would entirely
prevent our reaching the only drinking water. Then,
again, the power of controlling the Musjid, and the
walls and buildings near at hand, on the south and
east, from our roof, was of small advantage, for, as
already stated, that spot could itself be rendered untenable by rifle fire from the hills to the west.

To be prepared for all eventualities, we busied
ourselves in collecting stores of food. We also elaborated plans of defence, which included schemes for
loopholing, for getting flanking fire along certain walls,
and for making barricades ; a little tank was also
made in the garden, which would give us a day or
two's supply of water before it ran out. Distances
in every direction were carefully measured, to get
correct ranges for rifle fire. All was done secretly.
We were ready to act at a moment's notice ; but we
desired that the Chitrális should not know that we
distrusted them.

At two, or at most three, days' journey, for mountaineers, lived a famous fanatic, who devoted the tributes

of his congregation and admirers to the support of a large number of young disciples, who came from all sides, even from Káfiristán, to sit at his feet, and imbibe red-hot doctrine. Dír, where this man Shah Baba, or Sheo Baba, lived, was a kind of primitive academy for Musalmán theology. The holy man was known far and wide for his piety and learning, as well as for his blameless life. His influence was enormous. A word from him, at any time, would have started several hundreds of religious enthusiasts against us. Happily, he was somewhat dubious of Umra Khán, the recent conqueror of Dír, and was, on the whole, rather well-disposed towards Nizám. But such lukewarm sentiments were always at the mercy of his priestly fervour, for he was sincere, and would make no terms with infidels. On one occasion, two years before, he sent out a party to try and kill me, for the glory of God, and he had given up the use of a sulphur cure in Chitrál, which always eased his rheumatism, simply because those hot springs had been visited by British officers. Nevertheless, according to his lights, he was really a saint, although a less estimable person would have been a pleasanter neighbour.

More than once, it looked as if the electric atmosphere of Chitrál was on the point of detonating spontaneously. At other times, an onslaught of fanatics seemed inevitable. There were plenty of alarms of all kinds. Once, the end seemed to have certainly come, and a letter was laboriously composed in French, to be sent by a heavily-bribed secret messenger to Peshawer. Its meaning was obvious, if its idioms were of surprising novelty. Happily, it was not required.

A matter which at this time angered the Chitrális very much, was the occupation of the Nursut fort by Umra Khán of Jandol. He had moved his men there when Afzul summoned away its garrison for his advance against Nizám, and now he declined to give it up. It cannot be certainly affirmed what promises, if any, were made to Umra Khán by Afzul, as a bribe for his countenance or neutrality. But, independently of any such compact, Umra Khán conceived himself entitled to the Nursut district, in virtue of his position as conqueror of Dír. In former days, before Amán-ul-Mulk occupied the valley, the people of Nursut paid tribute, when they could not avoid it, to Asmár and Dír, as well as to Chitrál, while the Káfirs blackmailed them. Asmár and Dír had both been humbled by the Chitrális, and the Bashgul Káfirs had, for an equivalent, accepted Amán-ul-Mulk's nominal suzerainty; therefore, the Chitrális looked with angry contempt upon Nizám-ul-Mulk, who, they declared, could neither keep Yásín, nor force the usurping Khán of Jandol to leave the Kunár valley. "This," said they, "comes of the British Alliance." When to these troubles were added the general unrest and irritation of the whole people, caused by their annoyance at Sher Afzul's failure, combined with the seeming success of one of the hated family of Amán-ul-Mulk, the dreary outlook of the general situation can be understood. But everything turned upon the Sher Afzul problem. The Chitrális were convinced that he would come again, so even those who might not care for him personally felt it necessary to dissemble their feelings, for fear of his future vengeance.

Nothing could prevent Nizám stupefying himself with intoxicants, nor could any influence rouse him to be intelligent in durbar, or even to understand the questions discussed there, in the face of the whole nation, as it were. Vaguely, he perceived that unless Yásín were recovered, and Umra Khán were compelled to leave Nursut, his prestige must be lost, and the people would grow more and more clamorous. Beyond this he could not go, and it took some trouble to induce him to hold durbars at all—a necessary condition of Mehtarship in Chitrál.

Taken altogether, the influences favouring the success of my mission, which had now to stiffen Nizám, and keep him on the throne, seemed to be far outnumbered by hostile converging circumstances, which threatened at any moment to topple over and crush the Mehtar, and us with him. Nevertheless, luck favoured us, and gave us some measure of success. Formerly I did not look at the result altogether in this light, but thought my own cleverness had something to do with it. Later events and further musings have, however, shown the true relative dimensions of the different agencies which were at work.

What helped me much was the kindliness and geniality of all my officers, in their relations with the Chitrális, and the good behaviour of the Sikhs, who were ever ready to amuse the people by running races, by athletic performances, or by playing hockey with them, and were equally ready to be amused in return.

Another favouring influence was the adroitness of the before-mentioned Abdul Hakím, and the all-pervading nature of the special intelligence service he organised. There is fair reason to believe that we saved the Mehtar on one occasion from an attempt upon his life, which was to be made as he rode to prayers in the evening. Most of all, we were indebted to the cupidity of the notables generally, and particularly of the influential Maulai ecclesiastics (the orthodox Sunni priests anathematised us), and to the strange absence of fanaticism, except amongst a small proportion of the Chitrális.

As no religious antipathy prevented the people from coming to see us, or from accepting our hospitality, it was easy to win their hearts, for the time being, by kindness, fair words, and presents. It was simply wonderful how quickly they came round, and how cordial they grew. Like their marvellous spring, which first vivifies the almond tree, and almost the next day gives place to summer, the winter of their distrust seemed to disappear with an equal magic ; other difficulties smoothed themselves out, more or less.

Umra Khán's grip could not be unfastened from Nursut. I tried hard to get a personal interview with him to try the effect of persuasive arguments ; but it was not to be. But there were compensations, for Nizám could now assume the most warlike ardour, certain that he would not have to fight. He might even gain some popularity at our expense, as a patriotic Mehtar, held back with difficulty by his English allies. There was no doubt of his sincere desire to displace Umra Khán, but he obviously wished the necessary force to be supplied and directed by us, in continuation of the policy of all Chitráli statesmen, who had consistently tried to embroil us with the Jandol ruler. Lastly, Yásín had been restored to Nizám, with certain limitations to compel better government, and little Muhammed Wali Khán, in his turn, had retired to brighten Gilgit with his picturesque *entourage*.

A little incident helped us greatly. At the various ceremonial visits I paid to Nizám, at the fort, we used to ride in procession, with a guard of Sikhs in full dress—scarlet tunics, and the national thin, steel quoit encircling the large variegated turbans. Our soldiers were capital shots, so the conversation one day was made to turn on marksmanship, and the Mehtar was asked if my men might display their skill before him.

Anything in the form of a show pleases Chitrális, and all present were delighted at the suggestion. I was a little nervous, for just then the political outlook was thunderous, and although I knew that Sikhs are always at their best when playing to a gallery, I was desperately anxious for them to make a deep impression by their good shooting. A small fragment of rock some 900 yards distant was selected as the mark. The rifles rang out as one, and light-footed Chitrális raced away to examine the target. After a short period of suspense, they came running back in round-eyed astonishment, to declare that every bullet had hit the rock. It was quite true; and the awestruck assembly stared at the complacent Sikhs with a mighty respect.

This little story lost nothing in the telling. Rumour magnified the distance, and diminished the size of the mark, and men went about saying, " If anything happens to these soldiers, without doubt their brothers at Gilgit will come and destroy the whole countryside."

Month by month our prospects brightened. Bruce and I made an experimental journey up the Lutkho valley, to find everything quiet there, and, finally, in May, we two marched back to Gilgit without escort, and through a country as quiet as an Indian district.

Our future policy in Chitrál had been anxiously considered by the Government of India, and much correspondence had passed on that subject; moreover, I had indited a long report, the gist of which was that the British Agent at Gilgit, if his hands were strengthened, could certainly control Chitrál, provided always, that the Government of India was able to keep Umra Khán from troubling, and, more important still, could trust the Amír of Kábul to keep Sher Afzul under effective surveillance. These, indeed, were the essentials of any arrangement : first, that Sher Afzul must be kept out of the country; and next, that Umra Khán must be restrained by the Peshawer authorities.

Indian frontier management has been gradually developed from day to day, and, for the most part, fortuitously. Local events have been dealt with as they arose, usually without reference to fixed central principles, but by accepting the opinion of some local official with decided views and detailed knowledge of the particular case. Consequently, our policy has never aimed at being logical or consistent, but has always been of the hand-to-mouth variety. Another characteristic feature has been the complicated nature of the various intermediate jurisdictions between the Executive Political Officer, in charge of the borderland itself, and H.E. the Viceroy, as head of the Government of India; for example, officially, the British Agent at Gilgit had nothing to do with Umra Khán, although that chief was so important a factor in the Chitrál problem, nor was there any way for me to know the real nature of the hold which the Peshawer political officers had over the Khán. It was, however, supposed that he was greatly influenced by them.

We were now committed to Nizám, and, poor creature as he was, he could not be abandoned, either in honour, nor without distinct loss of prestige. It might not have been absolutely necessary to recognise and support him at first, but once my mission was at Chitrál, I found that its only hope of safety, and the avoidance of a big frontier war, to avenge, or to deliver it, was to throw in my lot with Nizám, and openly to use every means in our power to persuade the people to accept his rule. We had, in this compelled action, been extraordinarily successful, and there was fair reason to hope that a little more time, and a little more work on the same lines, might set the Mehtar securely

D

on the throne, with hardly more than the ordinary risks of assassination, provided only, that he would behave reasonably, and govern in agreement with his promises and protestations. The fact that he now seemed to have no rival in the field was of great moment.

Ultimately, the Government of India left it for me to decide whether, upon my return to Gilgit, I should leave an officer behind at Chitrál, or whether I should take back everyone with me. After much reflection, I decided that it was safe to leave an officer in Chitrál, provisionally, and that, unless I did so, all our past work must be thrown away. It must be remembered that in 1893 the satisfactory agreement between ourselves and the Russians, which was so happily come to in 1894, did not exist, and, therefore, I felt strongly that until an Anglo-Russian Boundary Commission had delimitated the Pamírs, and terminated all jealous friction between the two great civilising powers in Asia, it was imperative for us to maintain some obvious hold of any part of the borderland of the Hindu-Kush which might intervene between the territories we actually occupied and those of the Amír of Kábul. Otherwise, it would be always possible for a small party of Russians to swagger across the Hindu-Kush, as had been done once already, and madden the "hard-funkers" in India into some such cry as "Russians in Kashmír!"

The real risk of the so-called Russian menace to India is not the danger of any invasion, but the wild alarm of the English Russophobes, who never consider that they may communicate their own fears to the general native population of India, and so stimulate that capacity, inherent in Orientals, for vague pessimistic speculation, as well as their instinct for trimming, and for setting their houses in order against the advent of another possible conqueror. The loyalty of the timid Indian peoples is more highly strained by our own outspoken fears of Russia than in any other conceivable way.

So I left Younghusband and Gordon with the whole of the escort of Sikhs ; and, with Bruce only as my companion, marched back to Gilgit, as already mentioned.

Subsequently, the Government of India settled that it was inexpedient to have an Assistant British Agent at Chitrál, other than temporarily, so, a few months later, they ordered back both the officers and the whole of the escort to Mastuj, where they occupied the fort. It was moreover, intended that, as soon as practicable, they should be moved out of the country altogether.

In the autumn of 1893 I left India for England, returning to Gilgit at the end of the following year, when the only officer then across the Shandúr Pass was Lieutenant H. K. Harley, who was at Mastuj with his detachment of the 14th Sikhs, which had relieved Gordon's company some months before to enable them to go back to India, while Lieutenant B. E. M. Gurdon, of the Political Department, was preparing to start from Gilgit for Chitrál, which he reached in December, as mentioned in Chapter III.

CHAPTER VII

THE UPHEAVAL

ON the 6th January 1895 an exhausted messenger galloped into Gilgit from Yásín to repeat a rumour that Nizám had been accidentally shot by his half-brother while out hawking. The man brought a letter from the senior British officer at Gupis to say the news was believed by all the magnates there; and that fugitives were already flocking in for protection. Of its truth I never doubted for an instant, except the part which referred to the accidental nature of the killing. People who knew Chitrál best would be the last to accept any explanation of that sort.

It was impossible to minimise the gravity of such a catastrophe. There could be little doubt that some subterranean conspiracy had exploded, and, as there was no word from Gurdon, who had only seven or eight Sikhs with him in Chitrál, we grew restless with anxiety about his safety ; and, to a less degree, about Harley's also, but the latter had nearly a hundred stalwart soldiers with him at Mastuj, in a sufficiently good fort. He was, moreover, much nearer to Gilgit, and in a fairly safe district. As he had not written, and yet must have heard the evil tidings, the inference was that all roads were blocked.

Reinforcements were hurried off to Gupis, five marches distant, and hard-riding *estafettes* raced thither with instructions for local men to be despatched to

Mastuj, both by the ordinary way and over the hills also, in case the roads might be stopped, to discover what was happening.

As no news came on the 7th, it was a day of gloom, which culminated in the evening at the Agency mess dinner, when conversation died, and a sense of calamity weighed us down. For everybody was fond of Gurdon, who was the kindliest of quiet good fellows, and we knew the danger to be expected from excited Orientals, who, for a while, have the upper hand. Sorrow endured for the night, but the next day, the 8th, a letter came in from Gurdon himself, telling of all that taken place, assuring us of his safety, and quite unconsciously revealing the wonderful *sang froid* with which he had faced and mastered a grave danger. If the previous evening had been miserable, that night was gay, and we amused ourselves with an imaginary picture of Gurdon's characteristically kind smiles and placid voice, when confronting a critical position.

The facts were these:—Nizám-ul-Mulk had been murdered on the 1st January by his half-brother, Amír-ul-Mulk, generally believed to be a semi-idiot. Broz, a village ten miles below Chitrál, was the scene of the crime. Nizám, fond of hawking, had ridden up a certain odd-shaped mound to watch his falcons work. About mid-day, when on the point of descending, his turban came unfastened. While an attendant held his horse, the Mehtar put up both hands to re-arrange it. The supposed idiot was riding close behind with an attendant on foot, who had a loaded Snider carbine hidden under his long robe. This wretch, at a sign from his master, who perceived the helplessness of Nizám, pulled out the rifle and shot him in the back He fell from his horse, screaming for help, and vainly trying to pull out a revolver. Attendants ran to cut down the assassin, when the real culprit rode calmly forward, and shouted out that Nizám had been killed by his orders. Whereupon guns were let off in the air for a salute, and he was acknowledged Mehtar as soon as the life ebbed out of the miserable Nizám, who expired with a solitary trembling servant to tend him. Such methods of determining the succession are by no means uncommon in Chitrál history. We learned later that, had he not been murdered on the hill, the fated Nizám was to have been despatched while he sat at meat with a noble who was, at the very moment, waiting to conduct him to his mid-day repast, and to his doom.

Probably everyone except Nizám suspected that some catastrophe was pending, for one of his half-brothers, eminently sane, as the result shows, had for some time past stationed a man at the river bank, a short way below and opposite to Broz, to warn him when danger was near the Mehtar. This brother was sitting at home, playing with his little son, when he heard the report of a matchlock, the signal agreed upon between him and his servant. Springing up, he seized the young boy, and without waiting even to pull on coat or riding-boots, jumped on a horse, and galloped out of the valley, thereby saving his life, for he was a devoted adherent of Nizám and would have received no mercy from the idiot.

In Chitrál in those days most men of importance preferred to sleep in the daytime, and to pass the night with a loaded rifle across their knees, while a faithful servant sat on the roof over the central smoke-hole of the apartment, to prevent enemies shooting down through it. Murder was so common, and too many magnates knew they deserved the vengeance of those they had wronged in their homes or of their possessions.

During the end of my mission to Chitrál, in 1893, the weather was hot, and we used to sleep in the garden at the back of the house, with a sentinel on the roof. I was roused one night by the somewhat near explosion of a gun, which made me sit up in bed. Nothing more was to be heard. "'Tis some murder or other," I remarked to myself before lying down again to sleep. In the morning we learned that a noble, an old friend of mine, had been shot dead, as he slept, by some person said to be unknown. A prince, or prominent personage, in Chitrál, must generally be a man with exciting reflections, when he lets himself go, as the phrase runs.

The fratricide, who had so violently seized the Mehtarship, was only wrong from a Western standpoint. In Chitrál, his deed was everywhere applauded. "See," observed several of the people to me subsequently, "we thought Amír-ul-Mulk an idiot, and lo! he has killed Nizám." Such remarks were made with smiles of self-depreciation that the speaker had not formerly given the young murderer his proper meed of admiration.

The new Mehtar, astounded at his own resolution in doing the deed, confused with success, and troubled by some very natural doubts as to how he should dispose of the British officer, rode off to Chitrál with jubilant attendants. Ill news travels quickly. Gurdon was shooting up a big ravine, behind and to the west of my old mission house, which had been used ever since as quarters for European visitors, when anxious messengers sought him out to tell their story. The solitary young Englishman was too clear-sighted not to recognise his danger; nevertheless, he hurried back to search for, and carefully read over, certain instructions I had left behind in 1893, explaining how Younghusband or Gurdon was to act in the event of Nizám being assassinated. In consistence with this beginning, Gurdon never allowed the excited Chitrális to perceive that his pulse was quickened. Very likely it was not hastened one beat. At interviews with the pale and trembling Amír-ul-Mulk, who, besides stopping his messengers, had all the roads guarded, only to grow frightened at his own temerity, the lonely British officer remained calm and unruffled. On those occasions, he so placed his eight Sikhs that he and they could not be killed without cost, and then smiled forbearingly upon the demonstrations of armed men, with rifles at full cock, that crowded his apartment.

To Amír-ul-Mulk's demands, that he be officially recognised as Mehtar at once, Gurdon replied that such matters were beyond his powers, and must be referred to me at Gilgit. He also insisted on summoning fifty Sikhs from Mastuj.

In the end, unemotional determination and unwavering persistence overcame the passionate Chitrális. The thoroughgoing amongst them protested loudly that the " Frank " must be killed forthwith, for in that way only could the situation be cleared of nonsense. But a new complication at this point revealed itself. A short retrospect is necessary to explain the case clearly.

When Sher Afzul fled from Chitrál to Kábul in 1893, Amír-ul-Mulk, who had left his mother at Shoghot, to join his adventurous uncle, quitted the country also, and went to his brother-in-law, Umra Khán, at Jandol. After much negotiation with Nizám, he finally agreed to return, and did so the following year. He at once demanded a governorship, which was as promptly refused. To explain his reluctance to come back, Amír-ul-Mulk averred that he had been forcibly restrained by Umra Khán. He also told a romantic story about his adventures, which ended with his digging a hole through the wall of his fort prison, and thereby escaping.

By Nizám he was looked upon as an idiot, because of a vacant gaze, a bad mouth, and a thick manner of speaking. Although naturally dull, and slow of thought, Amír-ul-Mulk had cunning, and played his rôle cleverly enough. Subsequently, I discovered that he possessed a good deal of histrionic talent of a certain kind. He was, all the time, a prominent member of a far-reaching conspiracy. Umra Khán was by no means the greatest personage in it. Amír-ul-Mulk's part was to cheat Nizám into a feeling of security by acting as a fool or a madman. He rather overdid it, as a matter of fact, and used to appear on the crowded polo ground without turban or shoes. There he disported himself in most unprincely fashion. Nizám was ashamed of his brother, and regarded him with equal dislike and loathing. Nevertheless, he was not blind to the truth that even a half-demented son of a Mehtar of Chitrál might serve for the disaffected to rally round. So he kept Amír-ul-Mulk under his own eye. No doubt, he refrained from having his brother killed, because he believed him a lunatic, and therefore half-sacred. All the conspirators were aware of this. Finally, the supposed madman became so silly and drivelling that Nizám's caution was disarmed. He felt that no one, however rabid, could dream of supplanting him by such an imbecile. Soon afterwards Gurdon reached Chitrál.

Nizám had seen the wonders of the British Alliance which had kept him on the throne, in spite of the dislike of his subjects. Naturally enough, he began to exaggerate its power of ensuring his personal safety. Therefore, when Gurdon appeared, with eight Sikhs guarding his baggage, the frugal Nizám decided that he might safely dismiss to their homes the bodyguard, whose support he felt as a vexatious expense, and that he could trust solely to the moral influence of the British officer. Thereupon, one of the carefully-prepared mines was exploded, with the result we know.

So remarkably astute and secret are the Chitrális, that our agents on the very spot had been blind to a conspiracy which numbered the great majority of the upper classes and was known, or suspected, by a large number of other people. Its object was, first of all, to remove Nizám, who was to be succeeded by Amír-ul-Mulk, temporarily, but was shortly to resign the throne to Sher Afzul, in return for being adopted as the son of the Kábul candidate. Amír-ul-Mulk had agreed with Umra Khán to call the latter in to help as soon as Nizám was slain. Umra Khán, on his part, had particular personal views. To him the scheme opened wide, selfish aims. He was really playing fast and loose all round, relying upon his destiny to get him the Chitrál fort, and the rifles known to be in the country, and perhaps upon the fulfilment of a famous dream, wherein he was promised the whole of the western half of Chitrál. But he himself was being fooled to the top of his bent by the Afghán Commander-in-Chief, Udny's fellow-commissioner in the Kunár valley.

All these people were thoroughly insincere, and traitors to one another, but all were agreed on the one necessity of killing Nizám. In this they had the cordial sympathy of all Chitrális. That Mehtar, true to his blood, had followed in the crimson footsteps of his predecessors. Secret murders multiplied themselves. Fear added to a naturally cruel disposition, and Nizám reached a lowest depth of infamy when he caused a half-brother to be killed, and then, in terror, handed over the ministers of his will to the vengeance of other members of his family. Seven men expiated Nizám's crime on the polo ground of Koghazi. He sold whole families into slavery. There was a man who robbed me of certain articles in 1889, but whom I dared not report to the Mehtar, for fear of the terrible punishment he would receive. Meeting this individual in January 1895, we talked about his former rascalities. He declared miserably that now he would gladly be killed, for he was the only one of his family left; all the others had been sold out of the country by Nizám. It was quite true, and the village where the man lived was almost empty of inhabitants.

But, besides all his other vices and cruelties, which angered the people generally, Nizám displayed one other which infuriated the orthodox Sunni priests of Islám, the sect he belonged to himself; this was drunkenness. It was bad enough of him to get intoxicated with eastern drugs, and sit in open durbar breathing heavily, and with lack-lustre eyes, but to besot himself with infidel's wine, so especially forbidden by the prophet, was unforgiveable. Nizám was thorough in his sins, if in nothing else, and his drunken habits were a public scandal.

At his death, it is probable that not a dozen men in the whole of Chitrál sincerely regretted him.

Immediately after killing his brother, Amír-ul-Mulk wrote to Umra Khán to relate what had happened, and to summon him to his help, feeling sure that the Government of India would seek to avenge Nizám. Gurdon's diplomatic imperturbability, however, made him doubt if that was so certain as he had thought, and he began to discuss with his counsellors the possibility of conciliating the British authorities. His ambition also took fire, and led him to speculate on his chance of keeping the Mehtarship. Anything might happen to prevent Sher Afzul coming, and the innate sentiments of all Chitrális for Jandolis are not unlike those of cats for dogs. As Amír-ul-Mulk was looked upon by everyone as merely a puppet king, acting as a place-warmer for Sher Afzul, who not only might be prevented from leaving Kábul, but whose real feelings towards his nephew were open to doubt, all the chief men of Chitrál thought it prudent to stand aside and watch the stream of events, until the moment seemed more opportune for them to step in, with some certainty of obtaining their desires. Consequently, Amír-ul-Mulk's sole advisers and ministers were two or three reckless young nobles, not much older than himself.

The savage young Mehtar indulged his instincts by putting to death several of those he hated. He exterminated one Adamzáda family, the sons being cut to pieces, one by one, in front of their anguished father, who, it is said, nearly died of horror before his own turn came. At the same time, his youthful ministers discovered the delights of power. They transferred estates and holdings, and comported themselves as the actual rulers of the unhappy country. It occurred to them, also, that, Sher Afzul might not get away from Kábul, and that it was easier to invite Umra Khán into the country than to get rid of him afterwards. So, from varying reasons, doubts about Sher Afzul, suspicions of Umra Khán, and elation at the novel exercise of unfettered authority, they indited a second letter to Umra Khán, telling him he was not wanted.

They decided to try and ingratiate themselves with the Government of India, to ask pardon humbly for what they had done, and to strengthen, as much as they could, the rule of Amír-ul-Mulk, at any rate, until events developed. Gurdon was, therefore, permitted to send out letters, and to increase his escort by getting down fifty Sikhs from Mastuj. Every attempt was made to obtain his good-will, and the atmosphere seemed to be clearing rapidly. Of course, all the facts were not known till later. Those obvious to everyone were the anxiety of Amír-ul-Mulk to rehabilitate himself in our eyes and the lapse from truculence of his followers.

Gurdon at once saw his chance, and put a stop to more bloodshed, by convincing Amír-ul-Mulk and his supporters that such courses would irrevocably alienate the Government of India.

CHAPTER VIII

MY SECOND MISSION

BUT the Government of India was in no haste to recognise a youth, who was probably a mere puppet, liable to be kicked off the throne at any moment by Sher Afzul's partisans, a man guilty of the murder of their own nominee, Nizám-ul-Mulk, and one whose capacity for governing, or even for behaving sanely, was by no means evident. They subsequently ordered me to examine the position of affairs at Chitrál, when, and not till then, they would come to definite decisions. It was insisted that I was to commit them to nothing, nor was anyone to be recognised as Mehtar of Chitrál, until they were in a position to consider the matter from every standpoint.

When Gurdon called down half of Harley's Sikhs from Mastuj, a reinforcement was started for the latter place from Gupis, Lieutenant H. A. K. Gough of the 2nd Gurkhas marching on the 12th January with 150 of the Kashmír Rifles, and Captain C. V. F. Townshend of the Central India Horse, on the 14th, in command of another detachment of 100 men of the same regiment. For I determined to take as large an escort to Chitrál as I could feed, since the risks of the journey were considerable, and there was still the possibility of an outbreak.

At this time, Amír-ul-Mulk's subjects seemed to acquiesce in his rule, with the exception of the Yásín province where the people again rose and vowed they would have no more kings. The Chitrál Governor's house was plundered, and he was hunted into Gupis fort, followed by the hostile shouts of the country folk, who crowded round the place, cursing him. They swore they were now subjects of the British only, and were ready to carry loads, or do any servile work for them.

On the 15th January 1895, I left for Chitrál, with my senior soldier-assistant Campbell as a responsible military adviser.

Notwithstanding the improved outlook, those left behind at Gilgit were in desperate case. No one who has not studied young British officers can understand their tragic emotions at not being allowed to go where there is even a remote chance of a fight. Just before we started, my office witnessed conferences too sincere for laughter, yet almost too absurd for gravity. Everyone wanted to see me on pressing business which could only be conducted personally. This quickly resolved itself into earnest, even pathetic, prayers to be allowed to go to Chitrál. All kinds of arguments were used—some ingenious, others comical, even nonsensical—but all alike the outspring of that dauntless spirit of enterprise which makes the British officer a delightful memory, an ideal of irresistible pluck and energy to every civilian who has had close dealings with him in time of action. He is not coldly to be dissected or analysed. It is his unique personality and vital force which make him, taken as a whole, the most romantic figure of our modern time. Poor Baird, a man of no common mould, who combined great ability with surprising courage and the suavest manners, fairly burst into tears when told he must stay behind to act as Staff Officer to Colonel Kelly, in case that officer had to march to Chitrál for our relief. He pleaded that, as my particular assistant for secretarial work, his place was logically with me. In the end, it was settled that he might have Beynon * in, from the Hunza line, teach him the details of the office work and then go to Gupis, upon the understanding that, in the event of trouble, he should be at once summoned to Chitrál. Captain G. H. Bretherton, the head of the Commissariat and Transport Service, a lean individual with iron nerves and joints of steel, who loves an uphill task or a craggy argument for its own sake, brought all his hard-headedness and perseverance to show that, whoever else accompanied me, he was indispensable. But he, also, had to stay behind, for the contingency that Kelly might want him.

Colonel J. G. Kelly, now introduced for the first time, a man destined to be so famous hereafter, occupied a somewhat strange position in the Gilgit district. After my return from the Chitrál mission of 1893, a regiment of British India troops was sent from the Punjáb to Gilgit, to act as backbone, and general stiffener to the soldiery there. Previously, the garrison employed to guard that distant frontier consisted entirely of Kashmír troops, and at the time of which I write it numbered three regiments of the Maharajah's infantry (mostly Gurkhas and Dogras), a mule battery of mountain artillery, and some sappers and miners. There was also the British Agent's escort, formerly a small company of Afridís, who did splendid service in the Hunza-Nagar expedition, and lately a strong detachment of Sikhs, two hundred in number, commanded by British officers. With a view to economy, and because there was so much road-making to be done, the British India regiment selected for duty, at Gilgit, was what is known as a Pioneer regiment, an

* Lieutenant W. G. L. Beynon of the 3rd Gurkhas.

organisation peculiar, I think, to India in the Imperial forces. In the ranks are a few skilled artisans, even cabinetmakers are to be found there, while the mass consists of men willing to work at road-making, or similar rough engineering projects, for which they get remuneration in addition to their ordinary pay as soldiers. These special corps are mainly recruited from a low-caste people, in former days wandering thieves and robbers, who have been settled, and given land in the Punjáb, while the flower of their manhood is enlisted in these "class" regiments. By faith they are Sikhs, in stature middle-sized, and of sturdy build. Somewhat coarse in feature and dark in complexion, they form a striking contrast to the stately Sikhs, of the 14th, 15th, and 45th Infantry, for instance, who, in spite of the avowed levelling nature of their creed, shrink from contact with their low-born co-religionists in almost Brahminical horror.

Known colloquially as Mazbi Sikhs, these Pioneers are good fighters, and admirable soldiers. In addition to their ordinary equipment, each man carries a pick or a shovel on his back. Colonel Kelly was at the head of one of these Mazbi regiments, the 32nd Pioneers.

Theoretically, Kashmír troops are managed by native officers, hence, the Gilgit General was Báj Singh, a brave Dogra; and each regiment and battery has its own Oriental leader. All British officers are supposed to be merely "attached" to the Kashmír regiments to instruct and advise, but never directly to control. In this way, the chance of wounding delicate susceptibilities is obviated. Such is the arrangement in peace time; but when there is war, everything is changed, and the whole of the garrison, Kashmír and British, comes under the orders of the

E

senior British officer on the spot. Consequently, Kelly was simply in charge of his regiment of Punjáb Infantry, employed in making roads down the Indus valley, while there was peace, but, as soon as hostilities occurred, he would be commander of the whole district, and all military responsibility would rest on him alone.

CHAPTER IX

BY THE WAY

WE rode to Gupis in a couple of days, and halted for twenty-four hours, to interview the local headmen, and see what could be done about the Katúr Governor, whose occupation, as already mentioned, had been rudely snatched away from him by the revolted country people. He was a small, eager man, and far from being discouraged or depressed by his recent misfortunes, was as buoyant as ever. In perfect seriousness, probably with some idea that the Mehtarship was to be put up to auction amongst the legitimate princelings, he suggested that he should be made Ruler of Chitrál, in the place of Amír-ul-Mulk, and began to make astounding promises. On being told that his claims were not to be thought of, neither could he go with me to Chitrál, he grew mightily angry. Certainly his position in Yásín was not pleasant. I summoned all the district headmen before me, and required them, as a first test of the loyalty they professed, not to molest their late Governor, who was to remain in his old house, under their protection. They obeyed these orders scrupulously, although several people longed to shoot the little tyrant, who, Katúr-like, had been carrying off girls from their homes.

At Gupis, and throughout the Yásín province, the people were enthusiastically for us. When questioned about the toilsomeness of the Shandúr in January, they protested that they would tear the whole pass away with their fingers, sooner than the Colonel Sáhib (the British Agent) should suffer fatigue. And thus, with Eastern hyperbole, and also with practical help in the way of carrying baggage, they emphasised their hope that they would not again be handed over to any tyrant to be harried and outraged. My fiery little friend, Muhammed Wali Khán, with his picturesque following, had disappeared. While I was in England, he, for some reason or other, grew suspicious, and left Gilgit silently, by night, to wander wrathfully in Dárel and Tángír.

We left Gupis on the 19th January, and after a shockingly bad bit of road, where the snow had been trodden into long slides, we reached the almost deserted village of Pingál in eight and a half hours. Townshend's detachment on ahead was to wait for us at the cold, wind-swept Ghizr, two marches farther. We made a fairly large party, whose most striking members were four young rajahs, who accompanied me as Musáhibs (aides-de-camp). One of them, Sifat Bahádur, whose name will frequently recur, was an unusually handsome young man, fair-skinned, and powerfully built. He was a soldier, and a leader of men by heredity. In 1892 he saved me on one occasion in the Indus valley, by a really splendid charge, which changed, in masterful fashion, a doubtful-looking fight. Naturally, I placed great confidence in him, knowing that if there were any rough-and-tumble fighting in store for us, he would be invaluable. These young Musáhibs were jealous of their privileges and of one another. In strict rotation, one rode in front of my horse each march, with pride and a keen sense of responsibility stamped on his features and displaying itself in every gesture.

The cold in Yásín during the month of January is great, but exhilarating. Nobody, without actual experience, could believe the marvels country ponies can perform over an ice-covered track, on a steep hillside. A slide of several feet is a common incident, yet they never leave the pathway, even when a corner has to be rounded. If they fall, it is on their noses, never sideways. After bad stumbles, they may bleed at the mouth, but even that is rare. When one's nerves get used to it, the best plan is to sit perfectly still, or as quiet as one can, and not to dismount, for, unless wearing special boots, it is most difficult to walk over these ice sheets. Of course, when there is time, and the ground close by is not frozen too hard, it is a capital plan to throw earth upon the glassy surface, and this precaution must always be taken if the loads are heavy. Soldiers on the march have to use picks, when the journey, though tedious, is safe enough.

On the 21st we caught up Townshend and his men at Ghizr, and, with them for an escort, started for Langar, at the foot of the Shandúr. Gough, with whom was Whitchurch,* had already crossed the pass on the 19th, at the cost of a few cases of frost-bite, but none of any severity.

Every care was taken of the Sepoys, who were provided with Balaclava caps and snow-goggles, and had their feet cased in strips of blanket, sent up by the careful Baird. Gloved, with thick wrappings on the feet, and woollen mufflers round their faces, the men looked comfortable in yellow sheepskins worn over their greatcoats, and trudged along sturdily.

The cold was now too great for our thermometers to register. After Ghizr, the soft snow caused more falls than the naked ice lower down the valley, but in that fine dry climate a well - fed man accepts such incidents with equanimity. Just beyond the village

* Surgeon-Captain H. F. Whitchurch of the Indian Medical Service.

of Teru there is a sharp descent to the river. Riding first, my horse buried himself and me in the snow, each of us struggling out of the drift independently. Campbell was riding next, and, in a voice striving in vain to keep down its merriment, he expressed a polite hope that I was not hurt. In the early morning a man is apt to be irritable, and a snow bath, added to a comical mishap, is only cheering to onlookers. So I was answering with a surly growl when Campbell's pony slid its hind legs gracefully between its fore feet, and then went over backwards, a bit of the red lining of its rider's cavalry cloak asserting itself gaily in the swirling commotion. No bones were broken. I then discovered how much fun there is in an overwhelming cropper in soft snow, soothed myself with anxious inquiries of exaggerated civility, and we were quits.

At Langar the three of us crowded into one small tent, seven feet square. We had a little fold-up Canadian stove, which, with its chimney, quickly got red-hot under the ministrations of a lucky Sepoy who had been told off to keep it fed with chips of wood. Within a yard or so of the glowing iron water froze solid. It was almost impossible to keep warm, even beneath a mountain of blankets and furs. Revolvers felt sticky, while iron tent-pegs could not be touched by the bare hand. Such was the care of the military officers, however, that not a single Sepoy, although all were practically in the open, was frost-bitten. The only shelter for the men was a long wedge - shaped erection of willow branches fixed in the ground, and interlaced at their free ends. Happily, there was no wind, and Baird's admirable letters about clothing had been carefully read.

Next day, the 23rd, the Shandúr was crossed. During the winter, a dreaded wind at times sweeps this broad mountain plain. Fortunately, on this day, although it was blowing somewhat, the wind was at our backs, so we got to the melancholy village of Laspur with little trouble. We found great bonfires blazing at the top of the pass and on the farther side. Headmen and notables, with a numerous following, met us half-way over. While crossing one of the two frozen lakes which are on the Shandúr, this mob of people made the ice crack with a report like a pistol-shot. My horse slipping badly at the same instant, jerked me suddenly forward and gave Campbell, who was riding near, the momentary impression that I had been shot treacherously from behind. It is curious to reflect what serious troubles might perhaps be originated by a mistake of this kind, when the air is overcharged with the elements of suspicion.

On the 25th January, the dreary valley of Laspur was quitted, after a long march, and we reached the dismal Mastuj fort, which stands bleakly among saltpetre swamps, in a wind-swept solitude. In the days of bows and arrows, even in matchlock times, this was a formidable place. History tells of much desultory fighting, sieges, and bloodshed in connection with it. Placed at the meeting point of three main roads—to the Shandúr, to the Baroghil Pass, and to Chitrál—it is still of importance, although it is commanded from a hill slope in front, and the walls have fallen into decay.

There is a sorrowful garden at the south side, and the only attempt at decoration is a carved balcony front, which looks into the central courtyard. Adorning it, just under the eaves, is a cabinet photograph of Sir William Lockhart, inserted in the woodwork. The fine presence of that famous fighting general and soldier-statesman seems to have fascinated the imaginations of the Chitrális as much as his geniality and grave kindness of manner.

Gough and Whitchurch reached Mastuj, on the 23rd, with their detachment. Harley, a light-hearted, young Irishman of gregarious instincts, commanded the remnant of his company of the 14th Sikhs, the greater number having gone to Gurdon at Chitrál. Amidst the desolation of Mastuj he had lived alone for months, no doubt praying always for a fight. The young officers, and all the countryside, were in readiness to salute us new arrivals formally, and then cordially.

CHAPTER X

BAD NEWS AND A RACE TO CHITRÁL

AT half-past six the night before, we had been galvanised by news from Gurdon, that Umra Khán had crossed the Lowari Pass from Dír into Chitrál territory with between 3000 and 4000 men, and had sent peremptory letters to say that he had entered upon a holy war against the Káfirs of the Bashgul valley; that he had no hostile designs against Chitrál; but that if Amír-ul-Mulk did not join him, and give help, he must take the consequences.

This was a bolt from the blue. All our thoughts had been occupied with the progress of events at Chitrál. About Umra Khán, at that time, we knew comparatively little, except that, as far back as 1893, he had been warned by the Government of India that he must not commit further aggression on Chitrál. He was known to be in a state of irritation, and to be a disturbing spirit on the frontier; also, I had suspected that his dissatisfaction and restlessness might find vent by starting troubles in the debatable land of the Kunár valley, where Udny and the Afghán Commissioner were marking out the frontier, or, at any rate, discussing its limitations. But it was impossible, in our then state of ignorance, to guess what had possessed Umra Khán to invade Chitrál, which he, of course, knew to be under the suzerainty of Kashmír. The temerity of the enterprise, the sufferings his men must have undergone

73

travelling through the snow of the Lowari Pass, and the wildness of any conceivable scheme that he had formed, were equally subjects for reflection.

At the same time, the Chitrális were evidently scared. Only a limited number of them knew that Umra Khán had been invited into the country by Amír-ul-Mulk, that he had started on that not un-expected call, and had afterwards been told he was not wanted, and must not come. The dislike of Chitráli to Jandoli is bitter, and of long standing. Umra Khán's renown as a warrior and conqueror created a panic amongst the villagers and the poorer classes of the people.

Gurdon was once more in a position of grave risk, from which all his coolness and tact could not rescue him. A stampede from lower Chitrál was beginning. Amír-ul-Mulk was suspected of double-dealing. Gurdon could not retreat to Mastuj without help. His road lay through a country incredibly bad; he would get no supplies, and no transport. He must be overwhelmed by a mob of fugitives from the Patháns, whose flight would be hastened as well as justified, in their eyes, by Gurdon's retirement. Worst of all, he and his handful of Sikhs could be stopped and surrounded, hopelessly, in a dozen places, either by Umra Khán's men, or by disaffected Chitrális, who might grasp the occasion to gratify their hatred of the British. Finally, any such movement would be viewed by Amír-ul-Mulk as an open rupture with the Government of India and would make him desperate. There was only one thing to be done. It was to push on to Chitrál, by double marches, with as many men as possible, for only thus could Gurdon's safety be secured. I knew that he would not retire except upon my distinct orders, and unless he did so it was nearly certain that there would be some sort of opposition to Umra Khán, sufficient, at any rate, to delay his advance and probably give me time to reach Chitrál, where I intended to seize the fort, if necessary, and hold it.

Three telegrams from the Resident in Kashmír, delayed a few days, owing to the line being broken, are of some interest here. The first, dated January 7th, inquired, "Has Gurdon an escort with him in Chitrál?" The second, dated the 9th of January, hoped I had received a telegram from Udny, reporting a letter received by him from Gurdon, which stated, amongst other things, that the latter had asked Harley to send him fifty Sikhs from Mastuj to Chitrál, at once. This second telegram went on to say, "Please let me know if men have been sent to Gurdon's assistance, and whether there is any further news. Send help to Gurdon, if possible, as his position is very risky." The third telegram, dated the 10th January, said: "When reinforcements reach Mastuj, will it not be advisable to raise Gurdon's escort to one hundred men? Please do this without waiting for orders, if you think it necessary for Gurdon's protection." These messages showed that the Government of India knew of the Chitrál catastrophe before I did, and not only approved of Gurdon's summoning the Sikhs from Mastuj to Chitrál, but were anxious that the men should be sent to him, and also that they should be reinforced.

Some months afterwards, I was asked by a high official why I had not ordered Gurdon back to Mastuj. He added philosophically, "Even if he had been killed, it would only have been one officer, instead of four—Battye, Peebles, Ross, and Baird." As a similar line of argument would have left me to my fate in Chitrál, I did not think it necessary to answer this strange reasoning. Acting upon my decision to march to

Gurdon's help, we sent letters off hastily to say that Colonel Kelly might shortly have to be asked to move to Gilgit, and take command of the district. Baird was also ordered up to Ghizr with 200 men, and Moberly to Mastuj with another 100. It was found necessary to halt for one day while we hunted up transport, harangued headmen, and set all hands to patch up the dilapidated fort, especially the corner towers, for we could only leave behind fifty men as a garrison. Harley was sent off a long ride in the Chitrál direction, to discover the state of the roads, fords, and bridges.

During the day, news came that Umra Khán had burned the Chitrál Kalash village of Utzún, and was threatening Kila Drosh. No time, evidently, was to be lost. We ordered up Snider ammunition from Gupis, to be replaced from Gilgit, and I sent an indignant letter of protest to Umra Khán, and hurried on our preparations though with great difficulty, for transport animals and porters were hard to find. Townshend was sent off on Sunday, the 27th, with 100 men. As he required help on the road, it was hinted to Whitchurch, the doctor, that I should be glad if he would consent, for the nonce, to act as a combatant officer. He agreed, and marched all the way to Chitrál as Townshend's subaltern, doing the work admirably. A great ecclesiastic came in the morning to tell me, in confidence, that it was Amír-ul-Mulk who had invited Umra Khán into the country. This was the first trustworthy statement on that point. The nobles, he said, were angry about it, as they distrusted the Jandol chief.

If it had been hard to get transport for Townshend, it seemed impossible to move the second detachment, under Harley, who commanded 33 Sikhs and 100 Kashmír rifles. They did not leave till half-past eleven, and it was nearly two o'clock when our private baggage—small as it was—left Mastuj, because the Sepoys' kits and the reserve ammunition had to be arranged for first. We had a twenty-mile march before us, to join Townshend at Buni. It was a calamitous journey. The ponies could hardly be induced to face the icy waters of the fords. The glassy paths were execrable.

Campbell and our party got into camp at a quarter to eight, but Harley was a mile or two behind, and lost his way upon the big plain, at one end of which is the village of Buni. It was then one wide stretch of ice, three or four miles in length. An Adamzáda acted as guide. He pretended to be hurt at something which was said, but, in reality, he was anxious to get under a warm roof; so he abandoned Harley, who did not get in till half-past five o'clock next morning, with several of his men frost-bitten. Our baggage was also belated, but we dared not wait, for word came that Umra Khán had defeated the Chitrális in front of Kila Drosh, killing and wounding about thirty men. As Kila Drosh was but twenty-five miles below Chitrál fort, this meant grave peril for Gurdon. A trusty messenger was sent forward with orders that, if the danger became imminent, Gurdon was to leave Chitrál, and try to reach us; but he was assured that we were making strenuous efforts to get to him in time.

We were passing through a country where an attack might be made upon us at any time, whilst the road could be completely destroyed in a dozen places within half-an-hour. Once in Chitrál, we should be comparatively safe, for there the fort would give us some protection, and food could be obtained. But if Umra Khán arrived there first, and Gurdon contrived to reach us, there was but one alternative, and that was to ford the river and return to Mastuj by way of Drásan, a perilous adventure, but less dangerous than trying to retrace our steps through the country we had just traversed, with enemies pressing behind, and an untrustworthy population in front.

Harley had to be detached to rest his men, and bring them on afterwards with the baggage, as quickly as he could. Townshend started at seven o'clock for Baranis, another bad twenty-mile march. There we arrived, all out, as the saying is, at half-past eight of a pitch-dark night. Just short of the village is a terrible cliff, with a narrow track hanging in festoons, or curving out from its face high above the river, which is heard roaring dully far below. Travellers have to go in single file, and cautiously. At one spot the path had broken away; therefore we had to crouch, each where he stood, till it was mended. The darkness was absolute, and the roadway so narrow that one could not pass a pony at all, nor a man without risk, for a stumble might be fatal. Some ineffectual repairs were attempted by the villagers, but in the end almost everybody had to be helped over the gap, by the light of a few flaring torches.

The delight of at length throwing one's self on the dirty straw of a hut full of smoke, and of tearing off with the fingers a portion of a roast fowl, tough as india-rubber, had in my case to be paid for. My feet being eased of riding boots, some night horror or other seized upon my big toe, as hungrily as I had seized upon the ancient bird, and half-crippled me for days afterwards. The days were as hot and stuffy as the nights were frozen.

On Wednesday, the 30th, our camp was at the village of Koghazi, twelve and a half miles farther on. The day was insufferably hot in the blazing sun, although the frozen snow under foot betrayed one constantly.

Baranis is the last village of the old Khushwaktia country, which formerly extended thus far down the left bank of the Mastuj river, while on the right bank it included Drásan. Therefore, on this day our road, for the first time, lay through Chitrál territory, to speak pedantically.

The track was extremely slippery and bad. As we were leaving Baranis village, Campbell had a droll experience. He was riding a diminutive, but lively black pony. A great horseman's cloak lined with red, golden cavalry forage cap, a long sword, and similar appurtenances adorned his smart, soldierly figure, but the *tout ensemble* was somewhat ludicrous, for the charger he bestrode was hardly bigger than a rat. At one spot, where the path was steep and very greasy, the little animal sat down on its tail, and shot forward several yards, from between its rider's knees. Campbell was left standing on his feet and gazing in surprised inquiry at his boots.

On this march we met some of the slain from the Kila Drosh fight, being carried on rough stretchers, to be buried amongst their own people. There were many touching sights: an old greybeard, supervising the removal of the dead body of his only son, and other tragic groups. Then we came upon five or six Patháns, who complained that they had been sent by Umra Khán to see Gurdon at Chitrál, but that Amír-ul-Mulk's people had made them prisoners. "Why," they asked in Eastern idiom, "are we to be interned at Drásan? This is tyranny." I promised to make inquiries, and if their statements proved true, to do my best to get them released.

The next day, Thursday the 31st January, a last thirteen and a half miles brought us to Chitrál. The road is abominable until the main valley is reached. It runs for a considerable distance over a gallery constructed by the villagers along the face of a cliff, the famous Baitári *puri*. The roadway is formed by simply packing earth over branches, which, in their turn, rest upon rough staples, driven into holes in the rock. Chitrális are clever at making these frail-looking galleries, especially when their lack of good tools is remembered. But such structures are always liable to break, and one inconsiderable hole may stop baggage ponies for hours. If an Eastern enemy were to catch one on such a place, he merely has to break down the hanging road, before and behind, and roll down stones from above, when nothing on earth could save one from a horrible and ignominious death.

But, if the way was rough our hearts were light, for the news from Chitrál had improved. Umra Khán was pressing the siege of Kila Drosh, but the old fort was said to be defending itself sturdily, while the fact of our coming seemed to have screwed up the Chitrális to the sticking-point. Gurdon rode out to meet us—a happy man, but no happier than we were to see him safe and well and find that he was none the worse for the terrible anxieties he must have endured, in spite of his great heart and placid nerves.

There were some of my friends, the Káfirs, skirmishing about characteristically, as dirty and as agile as ever. With wide grins and nods they ran round my horse, a few kissing my fingers in the Chitrál fashion, or pressing my hand on their foreheads after their own custom. Others, shyly and awkwardly, tried to salaam from a distance. The day was close and cloudy, and snow about to fall, so we pressed on to my old house on the high right bank of the Chitrál torrent. We officers occupied the living rooms on the upper floor, while the men were got under cover in and around the house and its enclosures.

CHAPTER XI

THE GATHERING OF THE STORM

SOME sixteen miles below Chitrál fort there is a strong rocky position, pierced by the river, at a place called Gáirat. Such positions are called by the people "darbands," literally, closed doors. Amír-ul-Mulk had stationed himself there, with several hundred men drawn from all parts of the country. It was an easily defensible place in the winter time, when the hills are covered with snow; then a few hundred stout-hearted, well-armed men could make it impregnable, if a certain turning road were faithfully guarded. This long turning road started up a valley, nearly opposite Kila Drosh, passed over a high ridge, and then ran down another long valley, which debouched immediately behind Gáirat, on the right bank of the Chitrál river. Consequently Umra Khán, even if he captured Kila Drosh, which was ten miles farther down the river, ought to be still completely blocked, and unable to move against Chitrál. Everything, therefore, depended upon the trustworthiness of those defending Gáirat.

Amír-ul-Mulk had excused himself from coming to receive us in person, on the plea of military duties, but his only (full) brother, a little boy named Shuja-ul-Mulk, afterwards known to Mr Tommy Atkins as "Sugar-and-milk," had travelled with us nearly all the way from Mastuj. He had made himself very popular, chiefly, perhaps, because of his princely gravity, which sat oddly, though picturesquely, on his boyish personality.

It was easy to perceive that Amír-ul-Mulk had deputed his brother to welcome us, and was remaining himself at Gáirat, not because he was valorous, but because he was timid and distrustful. In short, he was still wavering and doubting whether it would not be better after all for him to try and make it up with Umra Khán rather than trust to us. He misdoubted that he might have to expiate the murder of his brother, Nizám-ul-Mulk, if he came into Chitrál. Thus he vacillated. We, consequently, had to be ready for all eventualities. The day after our arrival rain fell heavily. As we were under cover, while Umra Khán's large force was presumably in the open, the bad weather was not without its compensations.

Campbell went down to the fort, 1100 yards away on the river bank, to see as much of it as he could. He afterwards made rough plans from memory of its defences. Gurdon tried hard to get supplies. There was food to be bought, but we found difficulty in getting villagers to carry it in. Nearly everybody was away on military duty, either at Gáirat or at Drosh.

On the 3rd February, Campbell, taking Townshend with him, rode down to Gáirat to inspect and report upon its power to resist attack. With them I also sent the native cavalry officer alluded to in the earlier chapters, Rab Nawáz Khán; but alas, I no longer had with me the astute Abdul Hakím, who, in 1893, had kept me posted up in everything that was going on, and even reported the opinions held by the queens in the harem, and the talk of aged crones squatting round a fire in the evening. The information brought back by Campbell was fairly satisfactory, but the political news was less so. It seemed, according to Rab Nawáz

Khán, that all the nobles with Amír-ul-Mulk were Sher
Afzulites at heart, and confidently expected the return
of that prince. But, stranger still was the report that
Umra Khán had no less than eighty Chitrális of the
same faction in his camp, and that he had won his
fight before Kila Drosh by the treachery of one of
Amír-ul-Mulk's half-brothers, who had drawn off his
men at a critical moment. It was also hinted that the
commander of Kila Drosh was not above suspicion.

Evidently there was some conspiracy abroad, which
I did not understand. The possibility of Sher Afzul
appearing in the field was not thought of, for Gurdon,
a fortnight before, had written to Udny on the subject,
and had received a reassuring answer. Udny answered
that he did not even think it necessary to speak of the
matter to the Afghán Commander-in-Chief, but would
send word to Chitrál if he heard of Sher Afzul's leaving
Kábul.

Further precautions were now necessary, so, under
the excuse of carefully guarding certain stores which
were in the fort, I sent there next morning a fine old
Kashmír major, a surly, trustworthy soldier, with a
hundred men, to hold the main gate; Campbell reconnoitred the neighbouring hills, and Harley measured
ranges all round. The princes in the fort, and the
Mehtar at Gáirat were given explanations about this
movement of troops. As no British officer accompanied
them, no objections were raised at the time, but on the
5th February rumours began to be spread amongst the
common people, that the English were acting in con-
cert with Umra Khán. It was declared to be strange
and suspicious that letters were permitted by Umra
Khán to pass between Udny and Chitrál. I therefore took occasion to say, emphatically, that the
Government of India had not the slightest intention

of annexing the country, and that the presence of my soldiers in the fort was of real help to the Chitrális, since it would save them all anxiety about its safety, as well as set free many fighting men to resist Umra Khán.

The same evening, without previous notice, Amír-ul-Mulk rode in from Gáirat to see me. It was our first meeting. He was a dull, stupid-looking youth, and neither spoke much himself, nor even listened to what was said. Every now and again he would smile in a heavy, absent-minded way while gazing into vacancy. With him came four or five notables, who conducted the conversation. Their prime object was to induce me to send part of my escort to Gáirat, to give confidence, they said, to its defenders. My determination was to do nothing of the kind; it was all very well for them to protest that Umra Khán could not otherwise be withstood. But I could not afford to separate my escort while rumours were industriously conveyed to me by the nobles themselves that the people generally were shocked at my having soldiers in the fort.

My visitors continued to urge their point, while I kept exhorting them to reinforce and strenuously defend Kila Drosh. The discussion was eventually adjourned till the following morning, to be then restarted on the same lines. After I had carefully explained anew the precise position of Kashmír, and the Government of India, in relation to Chitrál, and had convinced everybody present that there was no danger of their country being annexed, our interview closed. Amír-ul-Mulk rode back to Gáirat, carrying away with him his young brother, whom, he evidently feared, we might perhaps put in his place.

A stream of reports was poured in, that all the

Chitrális were depressed because I would not send troops to operate actively against Umra Khán, but Amír-ul-Mulk's spokesmen doubted the good faith of these, and I correctly guessed, as it turned out, that most of these rumours were set on foot by them, with the object of influencing me in secret ways when they had failed by open methods. The net result was, that I sent fifty more men down to the fort.

The next event was the surrender of Kila Drosh to Umra Khán, with all its rifles and stores, by the calm, open treachery of its commander. It was simply handed over, without any pretence of fighting. Amongst the unblushing nobles there were indeed a few who murmured excuses about the water supply of the place having been cut off, and other extenuating details; but, in the end, they could not but admit the plain facts of the case. Thereupon I decided to move all my people into the fort.

No coolies could be obtained, consequently the soldiers had to carry all baggage and stores. There was not one argument, plausible or ridiculous, left unuttered to stop our making this move. Everybody was listened to politely, but the work went on all the time. The Mehtar's uncles and cousins tried every device to make me change my intention. A resident of Peshawer, a British subject, but the son-in-law of the dead Mehtar Amán-ul-Mulk, was put up to advise, as a friend and as one loyal to the British, that we ought to stop outside the fort. He was a member of a highly-respectable, almost sacred, sect of Patháns, and declared that my not doing so would irritate the headmen and alienate the people; that every one would consider it tantamount to annexation, and so on. The chagrin of the princes and nobles when we were safe inside could not be disguised.

Gurdon's industry in getting in supplies had been more successful than was expected. Other prudential measures were also taken, and every contingency which could be thought of was provided against. Campbell made a covered way down to the river, and rapidly put the summer-house corner of the garden into a good state of defence. The troops were regularly practised at alarm post drill, and everybody was on the alert, for bad faith and treachery thickened the atmosphere.

It was explained in an earlier chapter that the whole of Chitrál was formerly divided between the Katúr and the Khushwakt descendants of a common ancestor, and it was shown how the strong ambitious rule of the Mehtar Amán-ul-Mulk had brought all the country under his control. But, though compelled to acquiesce in Katúr domination, the Khushwakt magnates and nobles (there are none of the latter east of the Shandúr) had always hated it. They fiercely desired a prince of their own nationality, and their seeming submission was merely the result of fear. When Kila Drosh was surrendered to Umra Khán, there were many Khushwaktis on duty at Gáirat. They broke into rebellion, and hurrying back to Chitrál, declared to me, in a body, that they refused thenceforward to accept any rule other than that of the Government of India. In this they were probably actuated more by dislike of Amír-ul-Mulk than by any sentimental attachment to us. The Mehtar also came back hastily. After much negotiation, Katúrs and Khushwaktis were received in durbar together to see what could be done. The Katúr nobles, by their furious glances, showed clearly how they would have solved the difficulty, but the others held firm, and the only way out of the *impasse* was by making a temporary truce between the factions, wherein the Mehtar bound himself to be responsible for all the Katúr part of the community, while I similarly guaranteed the good behaviour of the Khushwaktis.

In the evening all started again for the Gáirat position, the Khushwaktis reluctantly enough, but in obedience to my wishes. On the whole, this incident had not been without its advantages, and it was clear to me that a certain proportion of the Gáirat garrison would, in existing circumstances, resolutely oppose Umra Khán if he advanced.

Amír-ul-Mulk, on his arrival, had asked that the south half of the fort might be reserved for him and his women folk ; and that the northern half only should be occupied by us. But, as the former commanded the latter, a strong dividing wall separating the two, he was desired not to press the point.

To my view, our prospects were now improved considerably. It only remained for us to ensure that Gáirat should be properly held. That was the chief anxiety, for it alone intervened between us and the triumphant Umra Khán, if the latter should be bold enough to attack us ; and there seemed no limits to his audacity.

As we held the fort, and the Khushwaktis, at any rate, were on our side, though it was certain that they would not long remain so, unless we actively supported them, I decided to send some of my escort to help in the defence of Gáirat, and give the Chitrális there that moral support which was still more important. Amír-ul-Mulk and I came to an arrangement, whereby he agreed to remain always with me while any detachment of my men remained at Gáirat. The importance of that place became more and more evident, for we were surrounded with wooden buildings, a musjid, and stables, besides guest and store rooms. It was not safe to leave these structures standing, yet it would have been inexpedient to demolish them without urgent cause ; and to clear them away properly would take three days. Consequently, on the 15th, Townshend was sent to Gáirat, with a detachment of Kashmír Rifles, to occupy a block house on the left bank of the river there. He was provided with signalling apparatus, including lanterns for night use.

I went to Gáirat on the 17th, with Amír-ul-Mulk, to let its defenders see us together and realise that we were co-operating for the defence of the country. Chitrális, though constantly on horseback, cannot ride even moderately long distances at a rapid pace. They love to walk their marches, with occasional furious scampers over the rarely - occurring level stretches, which are always short and narrow. On this occasion, General Báj Singh and myself rode the thirty-two miles somewhat quickly, with the result that all the Chitrális and their horses were knocked up for the next three or four days, the men with abrasions, the horses with sore backs.

Everything began to look more cheerful. No storm-clouds were to be seen, except that one at Kila Drosh, where, however, Umra Khán seemed impotent, for Gáirat was secure, its defenders being reported, by British officers, to be confident and of good cheer. Late at night, on the 18th, news came that Gurdon, with a small escort, reconnoitring a little too far down the right bank of the river, from Gáirat, had been fired upon by a party of Umra Khán's men. Here then was that first shot, often fateful, and always to be dreaded. Campbell was hurried off to take military command of the *darband*, and to acquaint me, by mounted messengers, of all events.

He almost at once sent back word, that Sher Afzul had actually come to Drosh. Amír-ul-Mulk, open-

mouthed, brought the same story. But I scoffed, and
pointed out the impossibility of its being true. I
declared it was a foolish trick of Umra Khán. Two
days later, this opinion seemed confirmed, for Campbell
wrote that Umra Khán was rumoured to be growing
anxious, also that many of his men had deserted to
their homes. Now, our sun was surely about to shine
splendidly, for on the 22nd Campbell believed "that
Umra Khán was throwing up the sponge," although
there were indeed some discredited whisperings, that
the men who had left Umra Khán were, perhaps, not
deserters at all, but Chitrális hurrying away to receive
Sher Afzul at Dír. Townshend, on the 22nd and 23rd,
confirmed Campbell's letters, that there were large
desertions from Umra Khán's camp. But, on the latter
day, Campbell sent me disquieting evidence of Sher
Afzul having ridden into Drosh the night before. Yet,
there still seemed room for doubt, for how could Sher
Afzul get away from Kábul without Udny hearing
of it?

Baird marched in with a hundred rifles on the 20th.
He had been gradually moved up to Mastuj, convoying
ammunition, and was then told to join us. After
spending a day looking critically over the military
arrangements of the fort, he left on the 22nd with a
hundred men for Aiún, in support of Campbell.

There had already been some passing of letters
between Umra Khán and myself, wherein he had
developed a new style of diplomacy, which consisted
in making his letters meaningless, or full of vague
complaints when they were not unintelligible. As an
excuse for their want of coherence, he explained that
his Persian secretary was a badly-educated man. On
my part, I promised to send him the final orders of the
Government of India, as soon as they reached me.

On the 24th February, important events happened. Despatches from India arrived, with instructions for me to discharge an ultimatum at Umra Khán, while Udny, in the Kunár valley, was to send him a similar document. I was also authorised, consistently with my own safety, to help the Chitrális, morally and materially, to turn Umra Khán out of the country. These instructions were sent, doubtless, because the Government of India perceived that the Chitrális might possibly whip round sharply, and perhaps war against me, unless I actively helped them. In times of unrest, half-civilised people are quickly distrustful of mere moral support. Those not energetically with them are apt to be counted as secret enemies. But I was unable to attempt more than had already been done, for it was out of the question to risk any of my small force below Gáirat. However, by joining in the defence of that place, we raised our credit for sincerity in the wavering minds of the populace.

As an additional support, the Puniál and Hunza-Nagar levies were sent for from Gilgit, and other military movements were arranged. It was thought that when the levies came upon the scene, in the improbable contingency of Umra Khán not having by that time gone back, their help would enable the Chitrális to compel him to retire, especially as we helped to garrison Gáirat and held Chitrál with our regular troops. It was certain that he could not support himself on the country indefinitely, particularly if he were harassed, without cessation, by tribesmen as well armed, as light-footed on hills, and as brave as his own Patháns.

I sent Umra Khán the ultimatum, explaining that he must at once leave Chitrál territory, and if he disregarded this requirement, that I was authorised to aid the Chitrális to enforce it. With this letter I sent another to Sher Afzul, for that he was now at Drosh seemed certain though inexplicable. His presence there might or might not be a serious danger. In any case it added to the general tangle of affairs. That a great majority of the people wanted him as their king was so evident, that, in a recent despatch, I had explained to the Government of India, that Amír-ul-Mulk was nothing more than a makeshift figurehead, to be cast aside and broken by the people at any time; and that there was little hope of a peaceful settlement in Chitrál, while such a *roi fainéant* held the nominal power. I expressed the opinion, that the only possible Mehtar was Sher Afzul.

Amír-ul-Mulk had all this time never been recognised, even as temporary Mehtar. He and his friends were invariably told that his claims would be laid before the Viceroy, and that the more they showed their capacity for government, by prudence, justice, and patriotism, as well as by gaining the goodwill of the people, the better undoubtedly would be his chances. By these means, they were induced to make some show of moderation. They restrained themselves, with a great effort, from murdering opponents at the time of the Khushwakt revolt, for the paramount necessity of keeping in the good graces of the British officers compelled them to forego their craving for vengeance.

Sher Afzul's advent made it probable that the backers of Amír-ul-Mulk amongst the nobles would be reduced to a group of the smallest size, even if he contrived to retain one sincere adherent, in addition to the always faithful foster-relatives. He became frightened. Timidity was the keynote of his character. To fear of Umra Khán, and half-distrust of me, was now added a terror of Sher Afzul, for he knew that he had not consistently acted the part of place-warmer to that prince as the original plot ordained. Lately personal ambition had overridden solemn vows.

The connection between Umra Khán and Sher Afzul could not accurately be measured. It was optimistically believed that they were not friendly, that each was suspicious of the other. Reflecting upon the probable strength of the various—and many of them conjectured —motives of action animating these two men, it seemed best to try to get Sher Afzul to come into Chitrál, and put his case before the Government of India in a reasonable spirit. Most people still thought that Umra Khán would gladly retreat, from what he must now perceive was a dead enterprise, if he could find some bridge of honour to pass across. Sher Afzul, it was known, would be rapturously acclaimed by the people, and Amír-ul-Mulk would be satisfied to resign his fitful power, if he were certain of a reconciliation with his uncle, when he might hope once more to be adopted as his son, and made heir-apparent, or at least to be given a governorship. The Chitrális were convinced that I inclined towards Sher Afzul, so it seemed as if only the details of some comprehensive arrangement had to be thought out.

Sher Afzul made the first move through secret emissaries, who tried to induce the people at Gáirat to go to him at Drosh. Hearing of this, I sent him a frank letter inviting him to Chitrál. It was promised that he would be treated with every respect, and his personal safety was guaranteed. The letter went on to say that although, of myself, I had no power to formally recognise him as Mehtar, yet it was nearly certain that the Government of India would raise no objections when they knew that all classes were anxious for him to rule over them, although they might make stipulations.

But, just before he received this letter, an unlucky incident befell, which was little short of a catastrophe. A few headmen, who wanted to show Sher Afzul how energetic they were in his service, by a clever intrigue, convinced the defenders of Gáirat that the British officers there had no objection to their leaving their posts to go and salaam to Sher Afzul, and then bring him to me at Chitrál. So they trooped away, and this invaluable military position was left to the care of a few Khushwaktis and Campbell's troops — a force insufficient for its defence.

Surely some kind change of fortune was due to us now. It seemed to come in the evening with two letters, one from Umra Khán, of which only the beginning, "To the brave and great Colonel of Chitrál," was decipherable; but the second, from Sher Afzul "To his kind friend the Colonel Sáhib Bahádur," was more encouraging. With complimentary hyperbole, it told how the writer had received my "orders"; that their purport and my friendliness were known to him, and that his great desire was to become the friend and servant of the Government of India. He would, if I wished, send me a trustworthy agent, and he was ready to carry out all the wishes of the Government of India, and to accept any terms that they might impose upon him. In conclusion, he apologised for the general appearance of his letter as unbefitting a person of my exalted rank. There was, however, no answer to my invitation for him to come to Chitrál, so I wrote again. As this failed to produce a reply, I grew anxious.

Next day a reconnaissance was made down the right bank for a few miles. Everything was quiet. We noticed, in the distance, a string of horsemen toiling over the rough track on the farther bank. They were too few to be an attacking force, so we were inclined to believe what we were told, that, without doubt, they were a deputation from Sher Afzul. When I rode back to Aiún that night, it was to find the people there overjoyed at the seemingly peaceful end of the crisis, and at all danger having passed away. Nevertheless, no military precautions were omitted at Gáirat, where Campbell commanded with cool vigilance.

On the 27th, riding back to Gáirat, we found everybody cheery and hopeful. A deputation had certainly arrived, though it was a surprise to find it composed merely of a single gorgeously-dressed Afghán, with one dirty, mean-looking attendant. The former presented a short, polite note from Sher Afzul to say that he now sent me his confidential agent, whose words I must consider as Sher Afzul's own. It ended, " Make known to him whatever you have in your mind, so that action may be taken accordingly."

We went into a tent together, where the envoy at once began to speak in blunt style, and with an arrogance of manner surprising in an Oriental. First of all, he remarked that he was an Afghán, a race that never told lies, and that Sher Afzul had escaped from Kábul secretly, and without the knowledge of the Amír. This was said with a leer, the man intending me to disbelieve him. Next he observed that there was but one place in Chitrál fit for a Mehtar's residence, which was the fort ; therefore, I must evacuate that place at once, and march back, with all my soldiers, to Mastuj. He was not unprepared to modify this condition to the extent that I, and sixteen Sepoys, might remain at Chitrál, outside the walls, but all the rest must leave forthwith. If these preliminaries were accepted, then Sher Afzul would be friends with the Government of India, provided that he were given a specified annual subsidy, and that no British officers remained in Chitrál territory. A native Indian news-writer and the Punjábi doctor might live in the country, but no Europeans. He wound up with the significant remark, that unless all these conditions were complied with, it would be impossible to restrain Umra Khán from advancing. Though designedly truculent and rough of speech, the man must have known western rules concerning the inviolability of envoys, for he would never have ventured to behave so rudely to any frontier chief; nevertheless, considering that by race and religion he was avowedly sceptical of western assertions about honour, he showed much courage in acting as he did.

I answered coldly that Sher Afzul's message was improper both in tone and in spirit, that neither Umra Khán nor any one else could impose a Mehtar upon Chitrál, and that Sher Afzul would not be allowed to seize the rulership in any such high-handed fashion, but must first ask the permission of the Government of India. Although the envoy afterwards moderated his manner, yet, in the course of further conversation, he merely iterated his first demands in politer phrases. Upon his departure, I gave him a letter of protest against Sher Afzul's messages.

We subsequently learned that the Chitrális who left Gáirat for Sher Afzul's camp at Drosh, as already described, begged that prince to send some of their number to arrange matters with me. They knew the individual he had chosen, and understood what was implied by his selection, for, though a faithful servant and a valorous fighter, to employ him as a delegate could have but one meaning—that there was not to be peace. But Sher Afzul declined to permit even one of them to accompany his agent, as witnesses might be inconvenient, although all these frontier men tacitly maintain that written words alone are evidence; on the ground simply that all men being manifestly liars, verbal statements are worthless. Sher Afzul, like Umra Khán, wrote words of friendship, which might be produced thereafter as proofs of his good intentions, if things went wrong, while he consistently acted upon a pre-arranged scheme. Eastern rulers of far higher importance than these two chiefs are no less addicted to strange diplomatic methods.

Why Sher Afzul did not negotiate in a milder way is uncertain. His success in getting the defenders of Gáirat into his camp perhaps puffed up his vanity at the cost of prudence. Both he and Umra Khán, after that event, looked upon the first stage of their plans as completed. We were believed to be help-less, and without a possible chance of reinforcement at Chitrál. All that remained to be done was to act cautiously, so as to capture the troops, by means of Oriental stratagems, at small cost. They felt that plentiful hostages would strengthen flabby excuses for deeds, perhaps indefensible, but past and irrevocable. Another view is that Sher Afzul, from the moment of his entering Umra Khán's camp, became simply a tool of that chief, and was not responsible for any-thing that followed. The third, and by no means ill-grounded opinion, bases Sher Afzul's action on a scheme devised, long before, in agreement with the supposed teachings of history. According to it, the frontier powers, from the greatest to the least, sought to find a cure for the alleged ambitious designs of the Government of India in some such catastrophe as that which overwhelmed the British at Kábul in 1842, and resulted, so the border people believe, in Afghánistán obtaining a long rest from invasion. They were convinced that in no other way could the sleepless military yearnings of the Government of

India be checked. Afgháns exult in the thought that they compelled us to evacuate their country, both in 1842 and 1880, by stubborn fighting.

With this one object before their eyes, aided by a common religion, all joined together in a temporary alliance of that loose kind peculiar to Orientals, who can never organise a simultaneous outbreak. The confederacy started from the high level of the Afghán Commander-in-Chief, who was so carefully "protecting" Udny in the Kunár valley, that it seems he was almost a prisoner in his own camp, and included even the smaller peoples of the Indus valley. All existing difficulties were to be hung up until the British were driven back, when there would be leisure once more for the chiefs to settle their own affairs after ancient methods. It is enough merely to mention these different theories without examining them minutely. Each, probably, contains some portion of the truth. The certainty is, that there was a widespread conspiracy, having, as its bed-rock, an invincible suspicion of the real intentions of the Government of India.

G

CHAPTER XII

RETREAT

ON the night of the 27th all of us officers stayed at Gáirat in an unpleasant frame of mind, for it was clear that we might be attacked at any time. Except our own men, we had but a few desponding Khushwaktis to help us. The party, which had been guarding the all-important side-road, was now known to be either starting to go or to have already gone to Sher Afzul ; but, on the other hand, it was certain that no enemy could reach us from that direction in less than twenty-four hours, by the most unfavourable calculations. That we must get back to Chitrál as fast as possible was obvious ; also that we must keep up appearances before those Chitrális who were still nominally loyal to us. But how to get the baggage carried was a perplexing question. The fort was far off, and during a long night-watch one has time to magnify distance and exaggerate difficulties ; besides, however confident we might feel of eventually reaching Chitrál safely, there was certainly the possibility, even likelihood, of rearguard fights on the way.

On the west—*i.e.* on our side of the Shandúr—we had, at this time, the following soldiers, namely :—

At Gáirat	. .	{ 80 of the 14th Sikhs, and
		{ 67 ,, ,, 4th Kashmír Rifles.
,, Aiún	. .	80 ,, ,, ,, ,,
,, Chitrál	. .	150 ,, ,, ,, ,,
,, Mastuj	. .	102 ,, ,, ,, ,,
En route to Mastuj		95 ,, ,, 14th Sikhs, and
		20 ,, ,, Bengal Sappers and Miners.

There were at Ghizr, as our next support, 106 of the
4th Kashmír Rifles and 100 of the 6th Kashmír Light
Infantry.

Early on the 28th Amír-ul-Mulk, half-distracted,
came to Aiún.   Thither Baird and I rode quickly,
after a messenger we had sent *ventre-a-terre* to hurry
the collection of porters.   The young prince was wavering badly, but without his help nothing could be done,
because, by the custom of centuries, the peasantry
invariably give obedience to the Mehtar of the moment,
even if they are certain that his power has already
slipped away.

We had an interview squatting on the roof of one
of the houses that flank the polo ground.   Pressing
us closely, from all sides, were agitated young Chitrális
who controlled, almost with pain, an impulse to chatter
excitedly and to gesticulate.   All eyes watched my face
with fierce intentness, while every neck was strained
for fear one word should be lost ; but Amír-ul-Mulk
himself sat with downcast gaze and with hands that
trembled.   A firm, confident manner on my part was
imperative.   The young prince caught fire for an
instant, when I loudly declared that, temporarily and
subject to official confirmation, I recognised him as
Mehtar of Chitrál.   But it was hard to keep him at
the glowing point.   The shouts of the people brought
a dull light into his face, but it died away almost at
once, and his features contracted again into an anxious
frown.

Nevertheless, he bawled out some orders which
others interpreted and amplified with so much energy
that coolies were soon on their way to Gáirat in small
groups, and with a fair show of zeal.   Amír-ul-Mulk
had to be kept close by my side all the day.   At
2 P.M. Campbell signalled with flags that transport

coolies were collecting, and that he hoped to start in half-an-hour. About four o'clock, Baird galloped away to help. He was to start off at once as much of the baggage as there was transport for, and bring in the rest by a second trip of the villagers. All ponies were at the same time requisitioned and sent to Gáirat, whether they belonged to princes, British officers, or to anybody else. Just as darkness fell, Campbell's rearguard came in safely. Another night of stringent precaution followed. A small force of Sher Afzul's men had been lying close to Gáirat for some time. When we left he marched in. His advanced party was in such haste that it walked into the midst of some Kashmír Sepoys, who disarmed the men and brought them to Aiún.

On Friday, the 1st March, daylight was the sole welcome fact. Amír-ul-Mulk still needed to be watched carefully. He knew that the road between Chitrál and Mastuj had been destroyed by Sher Afzul's men in several places, but, notwithstanding, he repeated a proposal made by him the day before, that he, the British officers, and all the troops should retreat quickly to Mastuj, there to await reinforcements. I had been warned by a Chitráli friend that this plan would be proposed in the hope that we might be trapped at the formidable Baitári cliffs, referred to on page 80. Amír-ul-Mulk was simply told in reply that his suggestion was thought impracticable.

All day long the rain fell without ceasing, and saturated baggage and clothing. Once again there was terrible delay about carriers. Some precious food stores having to be abandoned, they were given as a present to a party of Káfirs, sent by their tribe to ask me how to preserve their country from the out-stretched hand of the Amír of Kábul. At last, every-

one, wet through and miserable, got into Chitrál fort
without mishap. I had contracted dysentery at Gáirat;
but contentment at seeing the last man enter the big
gates made me for a time happy and well.

Baird wrote to Gurdon from Aiún, instructing him
to hold the bridge at Chitrál and the towers defending it, and also to send a detachment to command an
awkward piece of river-road, which has to be traversed
just before the broad open Chitrál plain is reached.
These orders were promptly carried out; consequently,
the safety of our retreating force was practically
assured, although there would have been a certain
loss of baggage if Sher Afzul had ventured an attack.
But that wily individual was over-confident of his
powers of trickery, and felt certain of obtaining all he
wanted in a few days, and without loss. The essence
of his plans was to avoid present hostilities, and to lull
me into false security by diplomatic means. Next,
after getting into close contact with us, under the plea
of negotiation, he trusted that his cleverness would show
him an adroit way to turn some chance occasion into an
opportunity for an irresistible surprise. We, suspecting
no evil, were to be enticed, under the plea of friendly
discussion, into a position where we could be surrounded
and closed in upon suddenly by an overwhelming crush
of men. After the fright his envoy had given us at
Gáirat, it was supposed that we should naturally be
inclined to treat. Our rapid march to Chitrál had
disconcerted Sher Afzul for the time. It was thought
to indicate that we required handling in a gentler way,
and that I was either too "hot-tempered" and insistent
upon fighting, or too timid; probably the latter.

From my standpoint, everything pivoted on Umra
Khán. Even yet there seemed some reason to doubt
the nature of his alliance with Sher Afzul. It is a pity

one cannot know exactly what is behind a big stone wall, without going round it to see. Dozens of reports were secretly conveyed to me, that Umra Khán only waited for a sign to seize Sher Afzul, declare himself on my side, and so regain his old position in the good favour of the Government of India ; and, on the other hand, that Sher Afzul was constrained in all his actions by his false friend, and would, if encouraged, desert to my camp ; and so on endlessly. The truth, perhaps, was that they wanted to inveigle me into a wretched underground correspondence with both, which would convict me of bad faith, and deprive me of the sympathy of my eccentric fellow-countrymen, who were, notoriously, more than half-mad on such points. But I was determined merely to sit tight, as the saying goes, and watch not unhopefully the manœuvres of my opponents. I was, moreover, firmly resolved to allow no possible enemy to come within arm's-length.

A letter written by Gurdon on this day, March 1st, to Moberly at Mastuj, was the last news of us for fifty days. It is convenient at this point to interrupt the narration of events at Chitrál, and relate what was occurring in other places, as a direct result of the mystery of silence in which we were shrouded.

CHAPTER XIII

DISASTER AT MASTUJ

ON the 26th February Baird wrote from Aiún to Moberly, who was now in command of Mastuj Fort, to send Lieutenant J. S. Fowler, R.E., then journeying from Gilgit to that place, on to Chitrál. Moberly was also told that, when Captain C. R. Ross, marching from Gilgit with his company of the 14th Sikhs, reached Mastuj and took over command, he, Moberly, was to remain there as political officer—that is to say, he was to be my mouthpiece in the district, and was to manage all the relations between British officers and the country folk. Lastly, Baird asked that sixty boxes of Snider ammunition, escorted by a trustworthy Kashmír officer and forty Sepoys, should be sent down to us as soon as coolies were obtainable. The cartridges were for the Gilgit district levies ordered to Chitrál, as already explained on page 90, who might be expected in about a fortnight. Moberly was to send word to me when the convoy could start. Lieutenant S. M. Edwardes,* a smart athletic officer, had also been summoned from Gilgit to Chitrál to help manage the levies on their arrival, but two days later (the 28th) Baird again wrote to Moberly, altering these plans, and bidding Edwardes stop at Mastuj till further orders.

Gurdon wrote on the 1st March to tell Moberly that certain mischievous people were trying to stop our mail-

* Of the 2nd Bombay Grenadiers.

bags, and consequently, if letters arrived irregularly for a few days, he need not be surprised.

On the morning of the 3rd March the political sky was lowering at Chitrál, as will be related in the proper place, and Baird sent off an urgent despatch to Moberly, the gist of which was this: If communications between Mastuj and Chitrál should be interrupted, the following steps must be taken to restore them. The levies, timed to arrive at Mastuj about the 12th March, were to be sent, unaccompanied by a British officer, to seize Drásan Fort, a position of great importance marked on the map; one day later Fowler was to follow them with two hundred of the Rághunáth regiment, Moberly going also, both for political work and to command the Kashmír soldiers; Ross and his Sikhs were to hold Mastuj. The road between Drásan and Mastuj could be kept open without much difficulty, and would enable us to use the track along the right bank of the Mastuj river for several marches, unless the enemy were in great strength.

Our occupying both Drásan and Mastuj would probably insure the good behaviour of the surrounding people, as well as make us independent of that terrible road running above the left bank. Unfortunately these letters were seized on the way, and Moberly had nothing to guide him except untrustworthy rumour and completed events. The instructions about the ammunition reached him on the last day of February; also vague gossip of what was going on in Chitrál, the oddest bit of which was that the Viceroy of India had given Sher Afzul a letter to me recommending him for the Mehtarship! Nevertheless, there was a stampede of certain people inimical to that prince from the village of Reshun to Mastuj. The convoy, under the command of an admirable young Gurkha subadár, started the next morning down the valley to Sanogher. A day later certain obviously untrustworthy reports that we had been defeated at Gáirat, already current amongst the people, were renewed, and the convoy was stopped, but, on further consideration, again permitted to march.

Ross, with his Sikhs, was said the same day, the 2nd March, to be at Laspur, from over the Shandúr Pass, so Moberly wrote begging him to make a forced march into Mastuj. Gurdon's letter, pointing out the possibility of letters being stopped, was brought into Mastuj on the morning of the 3rd, cunningly concealed in the lining of the messenger's breeches. Then a note came from Subadár Dhurm Singh, the Gurkha above mentioned, to say that the villagers were helpful, but that he was assured it was hopeless to try and go farther until the broken-down road had been mended.

The same day Ross, with Lieut. H. J. Jones, his subaltern, and Captain Bretherton, the commissariat officer, marched in from Laspur with one hundred of the 14th Sikhs, and Moberly ceased to have a commanding voice in military movements, and could merely offer advice in virtue of his position as political officer. Ross listened to all that had occurred, and after hearing Moberly, and all the evidence producible, finally decided that Dhurm Singh and his party were to halt at the village of Buni and not return. As soon as Edwardes and Fowler, known to be near at hand, arrived, they were to hurry on to Buni also, when the total force guarding the ammunition would amount to sixty rifles. It was then to advance with great caution, repairing the roads as it went; if it were obstructed or attacked, he, Ross, would set out and help it after summoning every available man from Ghizr. Poor Ross, an officer gallant almost to the verge of eccentricity, had delivered a momentous judgment. It was his own death sentence,

and that of many others besides. How often we sigh
for lost "ifs"! In this case, if Ross had but listened to
the advice of Bretherton, a man of experience, or would
not have made up his mind irrevocably, a double
massacre might have been avoided.

It is a little difficult to understand the precise view
Ross took. The next day, March 4th, he sent a letter
to England, which eventually appeared in the London
Times of 17th April 1895. He wrote: "We are to
stay here for further orders, but I fancy I shall have
to give my own orders in a day or two. The Chitrális
have turned against us, and Robertson's communications with us are cut. I fancy he will be blockaded
in Chitrál. In that case I shall be senior officer for
160 miles, and will have to organise a column to re-
open the communications. The column won't be a
big one, 350 men at the most—transport, what we
catch—food, what that transport can carry. The road
runs along the Yarkhún (or Mastuj) river, first on the
right bank, then by a bridge to the left, and then
again to the right by another bridge they have broken.
On the other side of the road the hills rise up steep
—generally precipitous—in fact, it is a continuous
defile. A pretty job it will be, will it not? . . . We
are here in a crazy old fort, with, however, lots of
supplies. . . ." Thus he seemed to recognise the
gravity of the situation and evidently understood its
salient feature, that the Chitrális had declared against
us; but no man appreciates the various factors which
influence responsible action until that knowledge has
been forced upon him. Slight instinctive antipathies,
little personal peculiarities of temper or disposition,
even a passing qualm of ill-health, may, in an inex-
perienced man, unaccustomed to reflect upon and weigh
the opinions of others, produce incalculable effects.

The day Ross wrote his published letter, two items of information were brought to Mastuj. A well-known noble was accused of stirring up the people of the district, and Subadár Dhurm Singh, from Buni, sent in word that he was about to be attacked. Ross thereupon resolved to start at dusk and march all through the night to Buni. He also agreed to Moberly's request, that he would try and seize the troublesome Adamzáda on the way.

On March 5th Edwardes and Fowler also set off down the valley, as arranged, and Bretherton recrossed the Shandúr Pass for Ghizr. Jones returned at eleven o'clock the same night with a few men and the prisoner so much wanted. The man had been cleverly caught by Ross in a village five miles short of Buni, and sent back to Mastuj; Ross then continued his march. All manner of false intelligence was brought into Mastuj during the next twenty-four hours, no doubt designedly. Its chief points were that Sher Afzul, having been given a local governorship, was very friendly with me; and that I was sending happy letters to Mastuj, by a special messenger, to announce the end of all disagreements. Ross came back at 2 A.M. on the 6th, pleased with the results of his journey. He said that the right bank road was much better than that on the opposite side, and that everything seemed satisfactory at Buni, whence Edwardes and the augmented guard of the convoy were to start for Chitrál that very day. Later, towards evening, a startling note was received from Edwardes, written at noon near Korágh, which mentioned that people were said to be collected at Reshun to oppose him, but that he would go on and send back further information. Edwardes evidently placed little faith in these rumours, but suggested that if Moberly thought them true, Ross might perhaps move out and support him.

Moberly showed the letter to Ross, and begged him to recall the convoy at once. Ross, however, demurred (in any case, no letter could then have reached Edwardes in time), and decided to take out his full company in the morning to support Edwardes. He sent off an express to Bretherton to hasten back from Ghizr at once with every available man. All the notables of the countryside warned Moberly of danger down the river, and expostulated against more men being sent there. It is certain that Moberly appreciated the risk, but it was obvious that attempts must be made to rescue Edwardes. His plan was for Ross to hold the Nisa Gul (the Nisa ravine) and Buni, while more troops and supplies were being hurried down to him. Perhaps Ross could not bring his mind to believe that any number of draggle-tailed Chitrális dare, or could, oppose his splendidly-drilled and equipped men; but, however that may be, he declined to wait at Buni for reinforcements. It is more difficult than can be easily believed for a British-bred officer, without war experience, to conceive the possibility of meek-looking Orientals suddenly flashing out as formidable warriors. The idea seems incredible and ridiculous. Moberly seems to have been at his wits' end to know how to act. Ross was adamant in his determination to take only his hundred Sikhs. Moberly, it is said, finally wrote an official letter, which he ceremoniously handed to his senior, saying that for political reasons, he urged him not to leave the Nisa Gul unprotected, nor to go beyond Buni without a stronger force. In reply, the note was handed back to him, with the brief remark that its proposals could not be entertained.

All the local magnates were aghast, and as soon as

Ross left the fort they all fled up the Yarkhún Valley with their families; and from that moment, believing we were doomed to destruction, these Khushwaktis deserted our cause. The beginnings of a similar exodus had been stopped by the reassuring presence of the Sikhs when they first arrived. Now the people went away for good. Ross even refused to state his intentions, probably because he had not distinctly formulated them. But he did a significant thing; he insisted upon carrying with him all the men's baggage and certain hospital luxuries, which suggests that he had some vague thought of marching through to Chitrál. This, unluckily, necessitated his reducing his food supplies—the total number of porters being limited. No sooner had he started than Moberly exercised his devolved responsibility by sending off an urgent message to Gilgit for troops and guns. The following day news came of a slight skirmish at Reshun, without any loss to Edwardes; also that Ross found the villagers of Buni very helpful. No guard had been left at Nisa Gul. There is some reason for supposing that Ross believed the Mastuj people desired that place to be held from purely selfish motives and for their own safety. More rumours came on the 9th of continued fighting at Reshun. Also an overdue note from Ross, to say that letters sent forward by him on the 7th having been brought back, there was little doubt that Edwardes was surrounded. Ross added that he would try and not get surrounded also.

Reports were next received that Ross had detached forty Sepoys, under their Sikh officer, at Buni; and that the Sher Afzulites intended to seize the Nisa Gul. The noon of March 10th saw the arrival of Bretherton with one hundred Sepoys of the 4th and 6th Kashmír Regiments from Ghizr. There was an ominous absence of all news from down the valley on this and during the next day, when there was not a single baggage porter to be found in the district. If the soldiers were to move, they would have to carry everything themselves. Word came on March 12th that the Nisa Gul was certainly occupied by the enemy; therefore Moberly, leaving Bretherton in temporary command, took out one hundred men to see for himself. Although freshly fortified the position was found empty. Moberly dismantled the new works, throwing the stones used in building them down the great ravine, a useful precaution, because such material is hard to find near the Nisa Gul. Darkness coming on, the reconnoitring party trudged back to Mastuj. Unsuccessful efforts were unceasingly made to get authentic news of what was happening and to persuade messengers to carry letters to Buni.

The following morning, Bretherton, with forty men, pushed down as far as opposite Sanogher, and brought back two or three men, but they seemed to have nothing to tell. Owing to the destruction of the Sanogher Bridge it was impossible to cross the river. As the Puniál levies were said to be on the road from Ghizr, hot-footed messengers hurried out to hasten their coming. The next three days passed in great anxiety. No rumours, even, were brought in, and all attempts to get porters proved futile. On the 14th, Colonel Phula, an energetic Kashmír officer, arrived from Ghizr with sixty men. An expedition was thereupon organised for the 16th, and as there were no baggage coolies, the soldiers had to carry ammunition, blankets, rations, everything, without help. Moberly went in command, taking altogether one hundred and fifty men. As the Sanogher Bridge was broken, fifty men forded the river near Mastuj, to move down the left bank, while

Moberly, with the remainder, tramped down the ordinary road on the opposite side.   But the others were soon in hopeless difficulty, for a recent fall of snow on certain dangerous cliffs blocked their way completely.   However, Moberly's object was gained, for the Sanogher villagers, perceiving detachments marching down upon them along both banks, thought it wise to be conciliatory and restore the broken bridge.   Consequently, the fifty men re-forded the river, two and a half miles above Sanogher, and the whole party, using the rickety, newly-made bridge, camped in that village.

Bretherton, signalling from Mastuj, informed Moberly of the arrival there of fifty Puniál levies who would reach Sanogher that evening. Moberly heard from the villagers of desperate fighting at Korágh, and that a wounded British officer and forty soldiers were at Buni.   No particulars could be obtained.   After dark the promised levies marched in, and proved somewhat troublesome to manage, a reputation they had also earned for themselves at Ghizr.   Next morning, the 17th, at eight o'clock, Moberly re-crossed the river and led his men down the right bank, for he perceived how easily the opposite side could be blocked.   Another signal from Mastuj told him that a hundred Hunza-Nagar levy men would be at Buni the following day. Late in the afternoon Moberly reached that village and found there Jones, badly wounded, and forty-six Sikhs, of whom nine were seriously hurt.   He at once fortified a convenient house, and hunted everywhere for information.   There was no word of Edwardes, but all the evidence pointed to his having been overwhelmed and annihilated by a large force which was at that moment in Drásan, preparing for a dash at the Nisa Gul and Mastuj.   Jones had made various efforts to get letters through to Mastuj to explain his crippled condition, and that he could not get back without help.

As if Moberly were not sufficiently weighted with responsibility he now got a letter from Gough at Ghizr to say that the enemy held the road between him and Gupis; and asking for men. Also another from Gilgit, which showed that no troops were on their way to reinforce him. Jones, Phula, and Moberly thereupon held a council of war, and decided that their only hope was to try and elude the Drásan force by a rapid night march into Mastuj. Moberly had previously told the local headmen that he intended to return next day by the left bank; but as soon as it was dark enough, he transported the whole of the party over the river, and began his forlorn march to Mastuj. It was terribly difficult, the men being stupid from fatigue and sleepiness, while the Sikhs were somewhat de-moralised from disaster. One point told in Moberly's favour. It was the annual Musalmán fast month, consequently it was nearly certain that a Drásan intercepting force would start later, not before nine or half-past, because, after starving till sundown, they would have to cook and eat before setting out to fight. Also Moberly's stratagem about returning by the other side bore fruit. The village of Awi, directly blocking the left bank road, was seen to be held strongly by the enemy, whose crowded watch-fires twinkled like baleful red stars across the river.

Colonel Phula did wonders in keeping the men together. The Puniális, sent forward to hold the Nisa Gul, behaved admirably. Progress was slow, and at three o'clock a halt for two hours was compulsory, as the men were dead beat. The Kashmír troops, sooner than see valuable ammunition destroyed, volunteered at Buni to each carry twenty additional rounds of the surplus Martini-Henry cartridges belonging to the Sikhs, in addition to his own load, already of crushing weight, on the understanding that if he found it too heavy he was to get the nearest native officer's permission and throw it into the river. But only one or two of the men did so. The exhausted soldiers lay down in the figure of a square, the Sikhs in the middle, while Moberly organised a small search-party to go back for a straggler, the only man lost on the journey. Permission had been given that those who desired it might have one "tot" of rum before starting, and no more, the remaining liquor to be then thrown away. One Gurkha somehow contrived to evade these orders, and paid for it with his life. Finding this man drunk, Moberly hoisted him on to a pony, but, creeping along at the rear, he must have fallen off in the darkness, and been killed by one of several small detachments of the enemy who followed, cautiously and doubtingly, the retreating column. Moberly moved off again at five o'clock, and two hours afterwards came in sight of the Nisa Gul. Then all was well. Given the alternative of a long rest there, or of going straight on, the men, though stumbling from fatigue, with one voice elected to persevere, and slowly dragged themselves into the fort, after covering thirty-five miles in twenty-eight hours, with little food, no regular halts, and under excessive burdens.

At Mastuj the Hunza-Nagar levies had not behaved particularly well, and they were sent back to Ghizr, only the Puniál men being kept. The rumours of the enemy having shown himself on the farther side of Ghizr proved baseless, but, although Gough might no longer urgently require reinforcement, there was no

H

room for the Hunza-Nagar riflemen in Mastuj, which
the enemy were closing in upon.

Moberly's march was a remarkable one, admirably
carried out. His celerity and astuteness enabled him
to slip through just in time. Like all successful soldiers,
he has the knack of transmitting his surplus energy to
subordinates.

CHAPTER XIV

THE KORÁGH CATASTROPHE

JONES'S Sikhs had suffered greatly. The whole story of Ross's movement is melancholy reading, and its final catastrophe forms a lurid picture. It seems that after Ross started on the 7th March he made up his mind definitely to leave a small party at Buni, and take villager porters on with him to bring back Edwardes and Fowler. While at Buni he heard that Edwardes was in jeopardy, probably surrounded. All the messengers sent forward, quickly came back with news that the road was stopped. On the 8th the party left Buni with a large number of coolies without loads. The headman of the village went also, and gave it as his opinion that the enemy would certainly be met, and in force, although he could not guess his precise whereabouts. About mid-day they came to the hamlet of Korágh, entirely deserted. One or two men were noticed from the road making some kind of signals, and a few more were seen scudding up the hillside. Ross wrongly assumed that these people were harmless villagers, afraid of his Sikhs. The headman is said to have refuted this, and it was pointed out that simple villagers would hardly bolt from British troops without reason ; and that a most cautious advance was advisable. Whereupon Ross is alleged to have shown annoyance, and to have sternly asked the headman how he dared to tell lies, and say an enemy was on the road. Such an inexplicable speech of course disconcerted the local magnate, who is reported to have uncovered his head —the last appeal of a Muhammedan—and, throwing his head-dress on the ground at Ross's feet, to have declared solemnly that the enemy was at Korágh during the night, and that if he, the speaker, were lying the Englishman might walk upon him or kill him. He did not know any more, but if the Sher Afzulites had fled away, why—the officers were fortunate indeed. Ross, unhappily, remained incredulous.

On reaching the Korágh defile, half-a-mile farther on, the Sepoys noted with suspicion some empty sangars close to the track, also several men scattered over the hillside, but their commander remained optimistic. The defile is the result of the river cutting its winding course through terrible cliffs. A goat, scuttling along the high ridges, might start a thunderous avalanche of boulders down the unstable slopes. At the lower end of this frightful gorge the pathway begins to ascend from the river above some caves and then zigzags upwards. There the "point" of the advanced guard was fired upon, and hundreds of men disclosed themselves and set the very hillsides rolling down. Obviously the soldiers were in a trap. Everything depended on their getting out again, at whatever cost, before the exits were closed. The opposing force consisted entirely of Reshun villagers, poorly armed but incalculably favoured by their position. Nevertheless, many Chitrális are of opinion that if Ross had pressed forward with determination he might have got through to Edwardes at Reshun, though that is very doubtful, or if he had rushed back at once with all his men, he would certainly have got out. His losses in either case might have been heavy, but nothing like what they eventually became. What he did was to order Jones back with ten men to seize the Korágh end of the defile ; but what was formerly an empty sangar by the side of the road was now full of men, and before Jones reached the last shoot down which the rocks were tumbling, only two Sikhs remained with him, all the rest being killed or maimed. He sent back word of this to Ross, who thereupon withdrew his men into two caves beneath the path and close to the river, which at certain periods of the year submerges them. Jones joined them there. During the night they made another attempt to get out, and seemed on the point of success, at any rate they were getting on hopefully, when they were ordered back again. The little party seems to have been fore-doomed. All the next day the caves were occupied. A large number of Chitrális fortified themselves on the opposite bank in a sangar, whence a continuous fire was maintained against the Sikhs, who erected breastworks for protection.

That night the poor fellows tried to escape by scaling the hillside, but were brought up short by a precipice, as they supposed, where a Sikh was lost. It was thought that the man had fallen over a cliff, and that the place was impassable. Chitrális, on the other hand, say that they were within a few feet of safety, there being in front of them only a small picquet, which fired and ran away ; that the man was killed by a bullet before he fell ; and they (the Chitráli critics) never could understand how the Sikhs failed to perceive that they had actually escaped. Be that as it may, they returned to the caves once more and passed another miserable day without food. Then Ross perceived he must cut his way out at all cost. Starting at two o'clock in the morning, they rushed along, losing heavily. Ross behaved with astounding gallantry. It is related that he charged a sangar a little off the track by himself, and killed two or three of its inmates with his revolver at close quarters. Then a stone partially stunned him, and he was shot dead. Jones and seventeen Sepoys got through to the plain on the Korágh side of the defile, where two consecutive masses of charging swordsmen withered up and melted before them, teaching the Chitrális their bitter mistake in attacking Sikhs shoulder to shoulder on open ground. But three more men were killed, and the remaining fourteen, ten of whom, including Jones, were grievously wounded, crawled painfully into Buni at six o'clock in the morning, where they found the party left there by Ross. These fourteen men and one other were the sole survivors of the sixty soldiers who entered the Korágh defile.

An uncertain number of Sikhs, between twenty and thirty, failed to follow Jones, and fell back once more to their old hiding-place, where they were closely invested, small sangars being even built on the top edge of the mouths of the caves. For seven or eight days they lived there without food or water, sustained, Harley conjectures, by the opium which Sikhs usually have about them. Then three chiefs, Muhammed Isa, Yádgár Beg, and the latter's nephew, came on from Reshun, where they had treacherously seized Edwardes and Fowler and slaughtered their following. During a parley they swore to spare the imprisoned soldiers in return for an immediate surrender. These terms were accepted, and the emaciated Sikhs came slowly out, broken in spirit and with faltering steps. All those unable to walk were at once slaughtered—a terrible commentary on the trust to be placed in the word of a Chitráli. The others were shut up in a house at Kalak. Next morning, by the order of the infamous trio (two of them blood relations and the third a foster-brother of Sher Afzul), the hapless Sikhs were brought

out singly and hacked to death, one man only escaping.*
Many Chitrális refused to participate in the butchery,
for even their lax consciences were shocked at the perfidy of the chiefs. The killing was done by Broz men.

One comment only is necessary. It is this. In a
country like Chitrál the moment a small party, such
as Ross's, allows its guides to escape it is in danger.
At Korágh the first shot was the signal for all the
coolies to bolt ; yet they were of priceless value. With
their local knowledge, Ross might perhaps have escaped
either over the hills or by fording. Afterwards, his only
chance was to fight his way out of the trap at any cost
on the instant ; every moment of delay meant that it
would be more securely barricaded.

Mastuj fort, during the 19th, 20th, and 21st of
March, was set in order for a siege ; trees were cut
down, *abattis* constructed, walls strengthened and loopholed. On the last-mentioned date some of the Rághunáth recruits were given a lesson on the rifle and
its uses. But the result was not encouraging. The
following morning Moberly made a reconnaissance up
the Laspur valley, and found the enemy in position
at a place known as the Chakalwat. He was honoured
by being suspected of meditating an attack, for, upon
the appearance of his forty men, the enemy rushed
away to man their stone shoots. At the foot of a
precipitous part of the road a Chitráli lay dead, with
two others, moribund, near him. In the darkness
these, with a dozen others, fell over the drop and
were badly injured ; but the rest had been carried
away, it seemed, by their friends. This gives some
conception of the ordinary physical difficulties of

---

* This man was reserved that he might be slain by a headman at a
distance, who was supposed to desire the honour of murdering an infidel
in cold blood, but who relented.

Chitrál, which claim yearly several victims, even among the local people who know them best.

From this date, 23rd March, until Kelly arrived on the 9th April, there is little to record. The garrison was blockaded, but not closely, and no one was hurt. Sangars were built by the enemy, but the place was never seriously pressed. On the morning of the 9th a sentry reported that he heard cannon, but Moberly and Bretherton, after listening long and attentively, came to the belief that he must have been mistaken. The enemy were brisker in attack than usual, and in that way contrived to mask the retreat of Muhammed Isa's men from the Chakalwat position until it was too late for Moberly to intervene effectually.

CHAPTER XV

THE VALIANT DEFENCE OF RESHUN

WE must now tell what had befallen Edwardes and Fowler.

It was related on page 107 that, on March 6th, Edwardes wrote a note to Moberly from Korágh, which determined Ross to start out with his Sikhs from Mastuj. The reason of that letter being written was this. By Ross's orders, Edwardes and Fowler were marching to Reshun with every military precaution. But they were hampered by the length of their convoy, and by the tailing-out of the coolies. Their total force consisted of sixty fighting men—Dhurm Singh and his forty riflemen, now reinforced by Fowler's twenty Bengal (not Kashmír) sappers and miners. As there were 150 porters carrying loads, and when it is remembered that on none of the Chitrál pathways can two men walk abreast, it will be seen that the problem, how to provide advance and rear guards, as well as to properly protect the baggage and ammunition, was difficult in any case, while, if they were seriously attacked on the way, it would be a hopeless one.

While they were stringing through the Korágh defile, where dreadful scenes were to be soon enacted, the guide of the party, provided by Moberly, informed Edwardes that at Korágh hamlet a friend had told him of severe fighting at Chitrál, and that this convoy also was to be attacked. Edwardes thereupon sat down and wrote to

Moberly, and then hurried forward in search of Fowler. They decided to go on as far as Reshun. Of course, if they had marched back to Korágh, and halted there, we should have been happier in having no brave story to hear; but it must be remembered that the whole country-side was full of false rumours, that everybody on the road had been helpful and pleasant, while women and girls were working peacefully in the fields. Most important of all, Edwardes and Fowler still believed that the Chitrális were our allies, and that Umra Khán was the common enemy. Also, they conjectured that their reinforcement might be badly wanted at Chitrál. With all the evidence, as well as their preconceived ideas, tending in one direction, it would be unnatural for two high-spirited young officers to elect to retreat in the face of such plausible reasons for going forward, especially when there was a chance of "seeing service." Nevertheless, they closed up their stragglers and moved with circumspection to Reshun, which they entered at dusk. Very soon their guide brought further news that not only had there been fighting at Chitrál, but it was certain that the Chitrális themselves had attacked the British Agent's escort. Edwardes interrogated the village head-man, recommended to him by Moberly, and, after making all other possible inquiries, he and Fowler agreed to halt until they had communicated with Mastuj, and, in the meantime, to repair the roadway, which was said to be broken down a mile or so ahead. But first a camping-place must be selected. The village elders suggested the polo ground, but the political barometer was falling rapidly, therefore, a spot was chosen on the river cliff, where the party could not be surrounded. Vigilant sentries were posted, and the last peaceful sleep for many a long day fell on the little force.

Reshun is a large village—of two hundred families

or more—embosomed in steep lofty slopes. The tiny fields, and the blocks of grey houses, surrounded by orchards, are high above the Mastuj river, which flows swiftly along the base of precipitous cliffs one hundred to one hundred and fifty feet high. From the great mountain sides behind the village tumble the streamlets which irrigate the land directly or through miniature canals, and trickle past the doors of the homesteads. The surplus water finds its way through the edge of the cliff, where it has cut out two or three breakneck pathways, to the sand and stones at the river's brink. Another and easier descent, a short distance down stream, leads over a frail bridge to Párpísh and Owír on the right bank. Still lower down, a great rocky spur, nearly a thousand feet high, blocks the space between the river and the mountains, and is climbed by the tedious track which does duty for a main road between Mastuj and Chitrál. Yet, from the summit of this bold bluff the panting traveller, looking back, is rewarded by a sight of curious beauty, remarkable in melancholy monotoned Chitrál because of its bright colouring. Perhaps late autumn is the season when its charms are best displayed. Then the variegated willow leaves, yellow, russet, and green tinted, the multi-coloured fruit trees in the close-packed orchards, and the great chenars, looking as if wrought in copper, are still merely elements in a strange colour mixture. For the soil of the neat fields and the flanks of the surrounding mountains are beautifully red. The entire picture, with its rectangular boundary walls or field embankments, and its many hues, remains in the memory as a quaint mosaic, charming, but artificial looking. When a Chitráli lover sings of the ripeness of his sweetheart's lips, he compares them to the " lovely red of Reshun soil," and, indeed, the village is very beautiful.

Next morning, to see how the people would respond to his call for porters, Edwardes said nothing about halting, and by ten o'clock one hundred and fifty coolies assembled at the camping-ground. But as only fifty were required to carry loads and building material, the remainder were dismissed. When the headmen learned that the convoy was to stay at Reshun, they protested that there was no food, but Edwardes insisted that food must be provided. The camp was shifted to another position on the river cliff, where the bridge, far below, could be swept by its fire. Dhurm Singh, with thirty Rághunáth riflemen, was left as a guard for the ammunition, and to build a sangar. Edwardes and Fowler, accompanied by four local Adamzádas, with the remainder of the soldiers and the fifty coolies, then set out to repair the broken road. Immediately below Reshun is the high, steep spur already mentioned, with smooth rocky surfaces and severe gradients. There is a lower path across its precipitous river face, but the foothold there is dubious, and at certain points rough ladders have to be climbed, which precludes its use, as well for men carrying loads, as for animals. Fowler took his pony, and after the toilsome climb and the equally difficult descent on the other side to a level expanse of ground, he rode along the water's edge to see if anybody were concealed there, and to search for a ford. He only discovered one unarmed youth, and time did not permit of the ford question being properly settled.

All then went on a little way. Presently they came to the entrance of a narrow defile, completely commanded by a cliff on the opposite side of the river. As a good soldier, Edwardes, in existing circumstances, was not going into such a place without first crowning the heights on his left, so Fowler was sent up the mountain-side with

eight Kashmír riflemen, to reconnoitre. Preparatory to
going, both he and Edwardes searched the steep ascent
through telescopes and field-glasses, and discovered a
man, who seemed to have a rifle in his hand, high up
the slope. He was conjectured to be one of those
isolated scamps who were rumoured to be going about
mischievously breaking down roads. The climb was
severe, the ground rough ; but after a while, Fowler
reached a point higher than the top of the cliff on the
farther bank, whereon he discerned several empty
sangars, and, a couple of hundred yards behind it, had
a clear view of the little village of Párpísh. Still climbing, he made for the spot where the man had been seen.
He was almost there, when a rifle rang out, and two or
three hundred well-armed men streaming quickly from
Párpísh, lined the cliffs, and began a lively skirmish
across the river. Fowler sheltering his men behind
rocks, fired back, keeping an eye over his shoulder on
the place where he had seen the rifleman. A corporal
was at once killed. Fowler took the dead soldier's rifle,
and he and his men made such good practice, that for a
time the enemy was forced away some distance, for his
sangars gave him no protection, because Fowler, from
his higher elevation, looked straight down into them.
Bullets nevertheless kept pattering all round, and
Fowler himself was hit at the back of the shoulder,
though he imagined he had merely been struck by a
stone. His assailants re-lined the crest of the cliff, and,
from the direction of their aim, it was obvious that
Edwardes down below was being driven back towards
Reshun.

It was impossible for Edwardes to ford the river
and drive the Chitrális from the opposite cliff, so, if
Fowler remained where he was, his party must be cut
off, while if they descended the way they came, the only

road, it would be in the teeth of the enemy. He decided
to run that risk. The Sepoys, on the other hand, would
have been well content to stay under cover. Appro-
priating the dead corporal's ammunition, Fowler gave
the order, and down all scuttled as hard as they could
bolt, under a terrific front fire from across the river;
moreover, men now appeared upon the ridges above and
behind, and started great stones bounding and thunder-
ing down the incline. There is a special Providence that
watches over wild animals galloping over rough, rocky
ground, and protects them from the sportsman; so to-
day, Fowler, reversed in position from hunter to hunted,
received that protection he had so often grudged to a
markhor. Nevertheless, it was strange that any one
escaped. They were in a storm of bullets; one struck
under Fowler's foot, another passed through a man's
wrist, a third soldier was hit in the thigh. But their
pace was such, as they dodged in and out of the boulders,
that accurate shooting was impossible.

Arrived on the open flat ground by the river, Edwardes
was descried a few hundred yards from his former position. It was decided that a box of gun-cotton, lying in
the open, must be abandoned, because the enemy was
showing in ever-increasing strength on both sides of
the river. The soldiers were somewhat unnerved, and
anxious to be off, and it was evident there was to be
a race for life to the top of that high bluff which now
lay between them and Reshun. It was dangerous to
try the lower path, for, should the cliff ladders be gone,
escape would be impossible. The Sepoys hastened
along, followed by the British officers. Now a
charming incident happened. Fowler's Gilgiti groom,
weeping for the master he believed to be killed,
was some half-mile ahead with the pony. Looking back, he saw Fowler, and, without thinking of

his own safety — and, of course, he was neither a soldier nor of fighting stock—ran back with the mare. The man wounded in the wrist was bleeding excessively, so Edwardes and Fowler bandaged him as best they could, and put him on the pony. Hurrying up the spur, the two officers were soon spent, while high above, on the right, a party of the enemy, Patháns, raced to intercept them. Fowler seized the pony's tail, and gave his other hand to Edwardes, the groom carrying the rifle. But Fowler, as we know, was wounded, and his arm weak; still, by continually changing hands, he managed to hold on.

At the top of the spur there is a dip between two ridges, the road running over that to the left. If the enemy got on to the right one first, the story was ended. However, the pony pulled hard; the Patháns were just beaten by some of the Sepoys who "extended" to keep the right ridge clear. Nevertheless, as the game little animal crossed the summit, the enemy pressed close, and bullets flew thickly. Some passed between Fowler and the pony; one lodged in the cantle of the saddle, and another passed through the body of a poor sapper, whereupon the rider was lifted off, as he could walk somehow, and the mortally wounded man was mounted in his stead, to be taken to Reshun, where he died the same night. In descending, the pony went much more slowly than those on foot, and one or two Sepoys pluckily stayed behind to help Fowler drive it along. At the bottom they could not make straight across for Dhurm Singh's breastwork on the river cliff, because the intervening ground was impassable for horses. They had, therefore, to keep to the ordinary road, now greatly exposed, for yet another party of assailants appeared above the village, on the right; but, although the ground

was snicked up all round them, only one other man
was hit.

When the sangar was reached, all pressed together
under its walls ; but it was overcrowded, and shots kept
falling in from both front and rear. The fire grew
continually hotter as fresh bands of the enemy came
up and joined in. A short distance to the left there
was a wall along the cliff; it was decided to utilise it.
Fowler took his sappers there safely, in spite of an
excited fusilade from the hills, and then ran back
again. Next it was settled that a block of houses,
about two hundred yards distant, must be captured
before it was seized by their assailants. Volunteers
being called for, Dhurm Singh and twenty of his
Gurkhas offered themselves. Bayonets were fixed, and,
headed by Fowler, a rattling charge was made across
the open, under a heavy shower of bullets. The block
was carried, cleared, and most of it occupied ; the defenders escaping through the orchard into adjacent
houses. Rooms were searched, loopholes hastily
knocked through and the water channels dammed up,
after all available pitchers and jars had been filled ;
but the enemy, of course, soon diverted the little
canals. Edwardes, from directing the defence of the
sangar, where two or three more men were wounded,
ran over to inspect the new acquisition. To sustain
a siege in the cliff position was out of the question,
for it had no head cover, and in Chitrál it may be laid
down as a rule that, as one cannot camp near water
without being commanded on most sides by rifle fire,
and since a small detachment leaving its water supply
is, *ipso facto*, defeated, roofs impervious to bullets are
the only safeguard.

The group of houses seized by Fowler constituted a
rabbit-warren of contracted rooms, with no light except

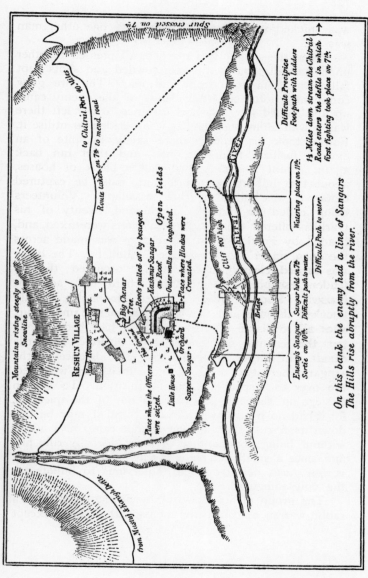

Rough Plan of RESHUN.

On this bank the enemy had a line of Sangars.
The Hills rise abruptly from the river.

Mountains rising steeply to Snowline

RESHUN VILLAGE

from Mastuj & Ghizr 8 days march

Mud Houses & Hayards

Place where the Officers were seized.

Big Chenar Tree.

Kashmir Sangar on Roof.

Roofs pulled off by besieged.

The Ground

Little House

Orchard

Sappers Sangar

Open Fields

Place where Hindus were Cremated.

Outer walls all loopholed.

Enemy's Sangar
Sortie on 10th.

Sangar held on 7th
Difficult path to water.

Difficult Path to water.

Watering place on 11th.

to Chitral Fort 30 miles

Route taken on 7th to mend road

Spur crossed on 7th

Difficult Precipice
Foot-path with ladders

1½ Miles down stream the Chitral
Road enters the defile in which
first fighting took place on 7th

Chitral RIVER

Cliff 100 ft high

Bridge

such as penetrated through the smoke-hole in the middle of each ceiling. Some yards in front lay the polo ground, a four-foot wall, with a gate in the centre intervening; beyond, at a distance of two or three hundred yards, was the main part of the village, clustered together. To the right, twenty paces away, was a garden wall—bounding an orchard with a thick festoon of vine stems, which acted as a screen. The polo ground, which ran across the front, sloped diagonally towards the left rear. At the back, the river side, there was nothing between the cliffs and the fruit trees close to the houses. Near at hand were detached hovels, sheds, and walls, which there was no time to destroy, although they would obviously give excellent cover to assailants. Every other consideration had to be sacrificed to prepare against that masterful rush which was expected momentarily. The sappers were brought in from behind their wall, and all hands started to fortify rooms, build up passages, and construct parapets on the house-tops, in almost frantic haste, but on a definite plan. One end of the block remained in the hands of the besiegers, but the connecting roofs were comprehensively broken through, so that the spaces disclosed could be fully commanded by a particular breastwork, which also prevented the enemy appearing on his own house-tops. From the hills, as well as from the houses beyond the polo ground, there was an increasing fire. To rush up the fortifications, walls were demolished to get at the sun-dried bricks they contained, and roofing timbers had to be torn out of the houses.

As the dusk deepened, the baggage and ammunition from the sangar above the river were brought in; even wounded men gave their help. Those unable to walk were carefully carried. In this category came

I

Edwardes's nice little dog, shot through the body. It seemed certain she must die, but, if so, she should die amongst friends. On the Gilgit frontier a subaltern's equipment can hardly be considered complete without a banjo and a fox-terrier. All the ammunition, such was the hurry, had to be built into the parapets on the roof, as well as much of the officers' baggage. A little house on the left flank was originally occupied, but afterwards abandoned because of the danger of isolating its garrison. It subsequently gave great trouble. Scarcely had the sun set before the moon rose; friendly clouds would have greatly helped the exhausted workers, who, because of the silver light, were obliged to labour in constrained attitudes to escape the keen-eyed marksmen, watchful for some one to aim at. No attack was made, and at dawn the worn-out garrison got some sort of rest, or rather, some cessation from high-strung expectancy. The severe nerve strain told on the men, who, during the night, kept firing excitedly—often at imaginary objects. Two of those most seriously injured died before morning. In the different houses, which were infested with vermin, a small amount of food was discovered, including one or two fowls and a few eggs, but water was the chief anxiety. All that collected was carefully ladled out by Edwardes and Fowler into the men's own vessels, to prevent caste disputes. The wounded, who showed remarkable stoicism, were tenderly helped by Edwardes and Subadár Dhurm Singh to the best of their power, "carbolic tooth-powder" being the sole antiseptic procurable.

The enemy seemed at length to realise that his profuse expenditure of cartridges must be checked, so all day on the 8th March he kept fairly quiet; and, without intermission, the garrison worked at the fortifications wherever they could do so without undue exposure. Some baggage had been left behind in the sangar, so when it was dark enough for the attempt, Fowler took out a party and brought in everything, and then prepared for an adventurous journey to get water from the river. Two great jars, lashed to poles, were carried and escorted by twelve men and accompanied by an Indian water-carrier. Silently the brave fellows filed out through the trees of the orchard and headed for the cliff. Edwardes enjoined his men to keep still; nevertheless, Fowler had not gone more than a few yards when several rifles were exploded. However, Edwardes managed to check the unsteady Sepoys, and the party resumed its risky march. Fowler and four men lay on the cliff edge as a guard, while the others, descending a steep path to the river, filled the big jars and brought them up again. The sensations of the five watchers must have been exciting. Actually, a second journey was accomplished, and, emboldened by success, even the pony was taken down and watered. It was the audacity of the whole proceeding that made it safe. The possibility of such a cool-nerved exploit could not be imagined by the enemy, who subsequently wondered why the garrison were, comparatively speaking, so well off for water.

After the moon was up, the men, especially as they were warned not to fire causelessly, could hardly be kept awake, and some slept as they stood, although everything depended on their alertness. Just before the light came, a sentry at the polo-ground wall reported a sound, as of digging, in the little house which had been abandoned. It was resolved to let a Gurkha sergeant and three of his men go out and do as they pleased, for Gurkhas are known to be clever and wary on such expeditions. But they failed badly. Advancing straight at their object, a shot was fired from somewhere, and all came running back. One Sepoy showed a slight cut on the hand, probably caused by his own bayonet. It was obvious that nothing in future could be usefully done without British leading.

The roof fortifications were in two sections, defended respectively by Edwardes and the Kashmír troops, and Fowler with his Bengal sappers. Immediately before dawn the dead silence was broken by Edwardes's voice shouting, " Present, fire ! " and at the instant, as if by magic he had unchained all the powers of darkness, the air was rent with screams, wild war cries, the discord of drums, and the incessant rattle of musketry. There was a determined assault, chiefly from the polo-ground side, from the garden wall and from the houses near the big plane tree at the corner of the polo ground. From the last-named shelter the enemy time and again tried to charge out, but were driven back, torn and shattered, by Edwardes's men, firing with deadliest precision at twenty yards' range. Behind the garden wall, when all others had gone away, a company of Patháns cursed and taunted the besieged. Fowler wished to take out a party, whip round a corner, and "go" for them, but as another rush might be imminent, it was eventually decided not to sortie. At length the Patháns also retired, shouting as they went that they would get them all before long. The losses fell exclusively on Edwardes's post, where the struggle was furious. He lost four killed and six wounded, so that only thirty-four men remained fit to fight out of the sixty soldiers who marched into Reshun. While the attack was in progress some Patháns crept round to the river side, where, daylight discovering them, several were shot. Besides the Sepoys actually hit, an astonishing number had bullets through their clothing and accoutrements. As the enemy dragged away his dead and injured before the light came, it is impossible to say how many were put *hors de combat*; but the losses were heavy, for the courage and determination of the assailants led to their exposing themselves, when the Kashmír soldiers literally mowed them down.

The beating of drums and a subdued uproar continued all day long, and Edwardes's garrison worked strenuously during the 9th March, preparing for another night attack, which, however, was not attempted, for it was neither in Pathán nor any other human nature to hazard a repetition of the slaughter. The 10th March also passed away quietly. Shots from carefully-placed sharp-shooters harassed the besieged somewhat; but the latter were principally occupied in burning six dead Gurkhas. The corpses were placed in an outer shed, with wood and straw, which were then ignited. It is always a satisfaction to their surviving friends when deceased Hindus are cremated ·in the orthodox way. During the day some of the men thought they heard distant firing, but it was not generally credited. There is small doubt, however, that it was the rifles of Ross's Sikhs in the Korágh Defile which the exceptionally quick-eared were alone able to distinguish.

As the moon would be later, there was the promise of two or three hours' darkness. It was seen that the enemy now occupied the wall on the cliff, whence came the glare of watch-fires. There was but little drinking water left, and the energetic defence formed a council of war to consider the advisability of a sortie. Edwardes, Fowler, and Dhurm Singh discussed the question. The last-named observed that the enemy could not be surprised, because of his fires. Fowler pointed out that for that very reason he would never see an attacking party, so a sally was decided upon. Twenty men, all that could be safely or even riskily spared, were to start, carrying all the spare water-bottles slung about them, Fowler to show the way. Edwardes wanted to command, but he was insufficiently acquainted with the ground, so the long, lithe Irishman, the good rider, good sportsman, and scorner of danger, tightened his belt, and looked to his bayonet and rifle, for an ornamental weapon, such as a sword, would be useless.

The soldiers paraded quietly in the orchard, and crept out stealthily one after the other. Straight in front was the reflection of the fires behind the wall, but Fowler led them softly and slowly to the left, where the old sangar was, then turning sharply, they stole closer and closer to the lights, expecting every minute to hear a sentry's challenge. The nearest glare came from a dip in the ground forty yards away. Forming in line, Fowler got still nearer. Presently, a party of twenty men, chatting and cooking round a big fire, came into view, while above the edge of the hollow appeared the head of a careless sentry. Fowler gave the word. The sentry yelled, and the soldiers, rushing to the brink of the dip, poured in a volley with awful result. Fowler jumped down and dashed at a man, but his foot tripping, he fell heavily, while the Sepoys sent a stream of bullets over his prostrate body. Only one or two of the picket escaped.

But there was the sangar ahead. There the enemy blinded by the firelight, and mistaken about the attack, sprung to their wall, and began shooting wildly in front, while all the time Fowler and his soldiers were rushing in from the flank and rear; too late the fated men discovered this, and, screaming with terror, tried to escape, but bullet and bayonet did their pitiless work, and few got away. Withdrawing his men quickly from the light of the blazing fire, Fowler had begun to search the ground, when he discovered that Edwardes was being hotly attacked; therefore, leaving all the captured arms, he hurried back, for Edwardes had but a handful of men with him. By the time the houses were reached the assault was practically over. Fowler's men, though cautioned to be silent, could not refrain from an exulting cheer as they approached the walls. However, their leader raised his voice also and warned Edwardes, so they escaped that saddest of all mistakes —to be shot by one's own friends. In the morning it was found that the enemy had returned to the cliff wall and built up strong breastworks. No single man of the sortie party was hurt, except Fowler, who sprained a thumb. His characteristic dash and levelheadedness combined were the best protection his men could have. It is true that, owing to the counter-attack upon Edwardes, made on a supposition that the garrison was trying to cut its way out, little was gained except moral effects, both upon the enemy and upon the besieged, but those were invaluable.

Hunger and thirst began to obtrude themselves on the 11th March, and there was no water to cook with. An attempt was made to dig a well, but twelve feet down solid rock was struck. The enemy built a crow's nest of brushwood and boards in the big plane-tree, about level with the fortification held by the Kashmír Sepoys. Its occupants were driven out repeatedly, but returned as often. At evening it was resolved that yet another attempt must be made to fetch water from the river, although the task was now of the gravest peril, for the enemy was furiously alert after his terrible lesson on the 10th. Unless the stars in their courses fought for Fowler, this was likely to be his last enterprise. He started with twelve men, each carrying five bottles, and a water-carrier and a Gilgit groom carrying skins. This time they bore off to the other side of the old sangar, and, with most surprising luck, hit upon a road which climbed the hundred feet down to the river, although none of them had ever been that way before. Parched and dry-tongued, the men drank greedily, while Fowler, their solitary guard, wondered if they would never fill the bottles. Then it was his turn to taste water for the first time in twenty-four hours. After that, all stole back cautiously, and, in spite of taking a wrong road for a short distance, reached the fortifications safely. Had they not discovered in time that they were going astray, they must have walked into the arms of implacable enemies. In some respects this was the most daring incident of the Reshun beleaguerment, and it was only by happy fortune that the party escaped detection—which meant certain destruction.

Such is the strength of caste sentiment amongst Hindus that two Sepoys refused to drink except from their own bottles filled from the river or direct from the water skin. Those men would have died of thirst rather than act against their religious convictions. In the middle of the night the enemy set fire to a shed immediately in front of the Kashmír rampart, and threw gun-cotton into the flames, but no harm was done, and the fire was kept from spreading by all apertures being stopped up with blankets.

Welcome rain fell heavily next day (the 12th), and was collected in waterproof sheets. Hardly a shot was fired. There was a courtyard in the block, surrounded by doors of different rooms and communicating with narrow passages. The roof defences were to-day so re-arranged that this space being entered by desperate assault the defenders could fire upon their assailants without fear of shooting one another. Edwardes and Fowler now gave up all hope of being rescued, and were merely steeled by a grim determination to fight to the finish ; but, about ten o'clock on the morning of the 13th, a flag of truce was thrust above the polo-ground wall, and a Pathán, shouting out, "Cease firing," stood forth boldly on the defence side of the boundary. Edwardes sent the Musalmán jemadár (lieutenant) of Bengal Sappers to meet him, while every one hurried to his post in case of treachery. When Edwardes's officer returned, he related that Muhammed Isa, Sher Afzul's foster-brother, with a large force just arrived from Chitrál, were come to put an end to further fighting, Umra Khán and I being now friends. Muhammed Isa sent also a polite message that he was anxious to speak with the Englishmen. In the end, Edwardes, after taking counsel with Fowler, decided to meet Muhammed Isa, who, in the meantime, had ridden up to the polo wall, where, during the ensuing interview, he was covered by Fowler's rifle.

Edwardes, after a time, returned with the news given him by Muhammed Isa, which was that negotiations were in progress between Umra Khán and myself, whereby the former was to be given the rulership of Chitrál; and that all disagreement between us was ended. He furthermore suggested that Edwardes and Fowler, with their detachment, should march back to Mastuj, whither they would be honourably and safely escorted. In reply, Edwardes, after conventionally expressing pleasure at the good tidings, pointed out that he could not move without orders from me, and suggested that the best plan was to frame an armistice for the interval which must elapse before an answer to letters could be received from Chitrál. There would be no more fighting, the garrison was to be provisioned, and the water-carriers allowed to go out and fill their skin bags.

Muhammed Isa concurred, with a great show of

friendliness, and was profuse in protestations of attachment to the Government of India.　He artfully adopted
a not uncommon Oriental stratagem, and impressed
upon Edwardes that, although he, Muhammed Isa, was
anxious to serve him, there were, nevertheless, so many
bad characters in the village that no servants should
leave the fortifications without a guard of Chitrális to
protect them.　Letters were written to me and sent
out, but shortly afterwards some men, despatched by
Edwardes to fill water-bags from an irrigation channel
beyond the polo ground, came back to say that the
water-course was broken, while the village was thronged
with Pathans and Chitrális, bristling with weapons.　A
few supplies, including a sheep, were sent in before
nightfall.　Muhammed Isa kept to his part of the agreement, and hostilities stopped, although Edwardes kept
unremitting watch and ward.　Rain fell heavily before
morning, and continued to fall on the 14th March.　It
was collected as before, and out of an artificial puddle
the pony had her first drink for six days.　Mutton soup
invigorated the wounded, and everyone got some of
that rest he was literally dying for.

In the afternoon there was further speech with
Muhammed Isa, who was now accompanied by Yádgár
Beg, a plausible scoundrel, who had more than once
conducted missions to Kashmír, and was consequently
skilled in the minor diplomatic methods of influencing
others.　He corroborated Muhammed Isa in every
particular, and, as both professed an earnest wish to be
recommended by Edwardes to my good offices, it certainly looked as if I must be in the ascendant.　Besides,
as Edwardes and Fowler argued, if it was otherwise,
why should the enemy parley at all when one determined
charge with his now overwhelming force would tread
the few remaining Gilgit soldiers into the dust?

At this time the aspect of Reshun all round Edwardes's position was as if it had been ravished by a hurricane. Trees were sliced and boughs splintered; branches strewed the ground or hung downwards half-severed. A veritable storm of bullets had desolated the place. Men occupied themselves in digging into the mud walls, which were now small lead mines profitable to work. No outsider was allowed to approach the jealously-guarded fortifications. Some food was sent in, but not enough; indeed, there was but little left in the district now, for many fighting men had gathered together, all of whom had to be fed by the villagers.

Next day, the 15th, an inch of snow fell, but the ground dried up by the afternoon, when Muhammed Isa sent in a polite invitation to the British officers to play polo in honour of peace having been made. He was courteously desired to play his game, but to excuse Edwardes and Fowler, who, besides having no ponies, were fatigued. But he was not to be denied, and begged that, if they would not take part in the sport, they would at least do him the honour of watching it. There was, he said, that other officer (Fowler) he was anxious to see and assure of his devotion. After another consultation, Edwardes and Fowler decided that it would be wise not to seem to distrust these advances, and that they could safely accept Muhammed Isa's courtesy, because those playing polo must be directly under the fire of the Sepoys on the ramparts, and they, the officers, could arrange to seat themselves under the protection of their own rifles. Therefore they agreed to go, with the proviso that all lookers-on should be removed from the polo-ground wall to the opposite side. Muhammed Isa and Yádgár Beg cheerfully assented, and, riding up and down, ordered every one

across the polo ground. Edwardes and Fowler carefully instructed and placed their men, and, that done,
went to watch the game. They were given a native
bed for a seat, and Fowler, thinking it was too near the
end of the wall, and perhaps hidden from the garrison,
pulled it farther into the open. Muhammed Isa played,
while Yádgár Beg sat between the two officers to
entertain them. For some time there were but few
spectators, but gradually the crowd opposite grew
larger. After a short while, the ponies being obviously
over-tired, the game finished somewhat abruptly, and
the British officers were deferentially asked if the
dancing might begin.

It is the custom in Chitrál always to dance after
polo, the defeated side having to caper and prance for
the amusement of the victors. They are often, in
addition, good-humouredly chaffed in a somewhat gross
way, and exposed to broad ridicule, especially if there
are any sheeted bundles seated by themselves, and
forming the ladies' gallery, to inspire the comical man
of the winning side. Not liking to seem discourteous,
Edwardes consented, and the fun began. The officers
had stood up, meaning to go; but when they agreed
to stay a little longer, their seat was pushed somewhat
nearer to the end of the wall, on the excuse of avoiding
a muddy patch. This was done cleverly and naturally.
In minor duplicities of that kind Chitrális act their
part to perfection. Muhammed Isa now placed himself
between Edwardes and Fowler to watch the posturing
and gyrating dancers. As the latter became more and
more fervid, the spectators from the other side drew
nearer and nearer, and Fowler noticed that many
were coming over to the prohibited wall. He jumped
up and told Edwardes it was time to go, whereat
Muhammed Isa, who is a tall, powerful man, threw

an arm round each of the officers, who were at once hurled to the ground by a dozen helpers, and quickly dragged under the wall which hid them from their own men, there to be securely bound hand and foot. At the instant they were seized a volley rang out from the fort, and an overwhelming rush was made against it from all sides.

The noise of the rifle-fire was terrific and continuous. Then it began to intermit, and finally stopped, when men staggered on to the polo ground, carrying dead and wounded. Dhurm Singh, that splendid boy, fought like a lion, but the enemy swarmed over the housetops, and by sheer weight crushed out his life and the life of his men. The slaughter was great. About a dozen were made prisoners—all of them Muhammedans, with three exceptions—the rest were killed ; but the losses of the attackers are said to have been astounding, although it was not until the following day, or even later, that their full extent was realised.

All this time Edwardes and Fowler were lying bound, trussed for death, as they must have supposed, for Chitrális have an odd way of tying, superfluously, the victims they are about to kill. A big Pathán, the man who began the negotiations for a truce, rushed up to Fowler and demanded to know where the money was. He was told to "go to the Devil"—a phrase never so heroically employed, I imagine. He dragged off Fowler's boots, also the buttons were cut off his and Edwardes's uniforms, upon the supposition that they were gold. All the stores and baggage in the now ghastly block of houses were brought out. Cigars and cigarettes, included in the spoil, were thrown down carelessly on the ground. Fowler asked for some, and a cigarette was placed between his lips and lighted. It was probably the only way he could show that, even with his arms bound behind him, and in death's very shadow, his soul was unconquered and scornful of the treatment he had suffered ; for he has since admitted, I believe, that he never felt less inclined to smoke in his life.

After a time, he and Edwardes were taken to Muhammed Isa's headquarters, where the "loot" was being sorted and inventories made. Next a modicum of food, and then a dark, filthy hut, shared with in-numerable vermin and by guards, who kept jerking the ropes, to see that their victims were still tightly bound, and who went over the officers carefully from time to time to make sure that no ring or other valuable had escaped their cupidity. In the morning they were taken before Muhammed Isa, and told that Fowler was to go to Chitrál, and Edwardes to Mastuj. Protests were of no avail, and the two young men said goodbye, never expecting to meet again. Fowler, with a rope tied to each elbow, was marched off in front of a Chitráli while another Chitráli and two Patháns com-pleted his escort. They crossed the dangerous foot-bridge over the river, where one careless step would have set the prisoner free for ever.

After Fowler had been taken away, presumably only as far as the river's bank, there to be murdered, Edwardes was conducted to the polo ground. As that, equally with the water's edge, is the favourite killing-place of Chitrális, he felt he was to die forthwith an ignominious death. The brave heart of this strong-framed, resolute young Englishman supported his steps, even if his knees trembled a little at the cold-blooded horror of his fate, and he whispered to his custodian to give him one minute's notice before the end came. That good fellow, glancing swiftly round, stooped, as if by accident, to press Edwardes's fingers in sympathy, as he murmured a single word, which, in the circumstances, must be the equivalent to our "back your luck." But it was not death Edwardes was going to, but to watch a game of polo! Seated once more by Muhammed Isa on a bedstead, he was again to enact the part of yesterday, and live through the last twenty-four hours a second time.

CHAPTER XVI

TWO CAPTURED OFFICERS

FOWLER and his escort had trudged no farther than Párpísh, the village so actively hostile on March the 7th, when a serious dispute broke out amongst the guards. The Chitráli couple wanted to take the prisoner to Owír; the Patháns protested, and backed their arguments by that last and strongest of all appeals, although it is often put first by Easterns among themselves—the appeal to force—sufficiently suggested by opening the breech of the rifles to show they were loaded. In the end, the whole party retired into a house for the night. What was really in question was whether Fowler was to be the prisoner and hostage of Sher Afzul or of Umra Khán.

Next morning, the 17th, the journey was resumed down the river bank, which showed that the Patháns had prevailed. The road was bad, even for Chitrál— a mere series of climbs over great bluffs faced by precipices a thousand feet sheer. Fowler, still on a rope, limped along slowly, for the soft leather boots, substituted for those stolen by the big Pathán, proved a poor protection to his unhardened feet. Besides, he had determined not to hurry himself, and his guards were complaisant. Presently, to his surprise, he was told that Edwardes was approaching, and a few minutes later the two friends were together, heartily congratulating one another. Muhammed Isa, it seemed, changing his mind about taking Edwardes to Mastuj, sent him after Fowler. One of the two Chitrális with Edwardes was that kind-hearted man already mentioned, who was so pitifully sympathetic on the polo ground. His tenderness not only included the prisoner, but the poor little fox-terrier "Biddy" also, who could scarcely crawl along the easiest portions of the track, but was nevertheless recovering from her terrible wound. This man at once untied Fowler, when all hurried forward to the next village, lighter in heart, and clamorous for food.

At the end of a good meal it was announced that a company of Patháns were approaching. This news disturbed the good Chitráli, who, taking the officers into a house, hastily barricaded it with the help of a villager. Outside there was noise and quarrelling, and the anxiety of those within grew momentarily deeper. Finally, it was agreed that the leader of the Patháns should be allowed to enter without his weapons. The door being opened, a ruffianly-looking man was admitted, with a mulla (priest), who ceremoniously swore him on the Korán to do the captives no harm, but to hand them over to Sher Afzul at Chitrál. In spite of his rascally face, the new-comer tried to make himself pleasant. Having soldiered in an Indian regiment, he knew enough Hindustáni for ordinary intercourse.

The villagers, though delighted and curious to see the two European prisoners, were naturally reluctant to feed such a large company when their own stores were so slender. At night, therefore, no one was anxious to have the captives quartered on him, and this fact led to tedious discussions and protests, which generally ended in some wretched family being kicked and pushed out-of-doors. Its home was then appropriated

K

by the numerous armed men who surrounded Edwardes and Fowler in the darkness as well as by day, and even swirled over on to the house-top to watch the smoke-hole of the apartment which sheltered them.

Next day, the 18th, after a march, too bad even for the Pathán Chief, the Mastuj river was re-crossed to the left bank, and the village of Koghazi reached. On the way a large company of Pathâns was met, whose commander declared that one of the officers must return with him to Mastuj; but Edwardes and Fowler, determined not to be separated, eventually persuaded the new-comers to sleep in the village during the night, and await further instructions from Chitrál.

Orders came on the 19th for both prisoners to be taken to the crafty Sher Afzul. Ponies, though provided, were of little use, as the wonderful hanging roads and galleries of the Baitári Cliffs having been demolished, there was nothing for it but to clamber over the steep rocks, two thousand feet above. After surmounting that last obstacle, the Chitrál Valley was gained, and the beleaguered fort came into view. Edwardes and Fowler were then taken charge of by a strong detachment of well-drilled Pathán troops, led by a colonel, who, trained in our service, gave the words of command in English. Many of Umra Khán's regular soldiers and nearly all their officers had been in our army. At least a dozen well-known British-India regiments had representatives engaged in the siege of Chitrál—men proud of their military knowledge and of the service which had given it them.

From that time forward the prisoners were always kindly treated, though closely guarded. Umra Khán's lieutenants and Sher Afzul allowed them to see the twelve Sepoy prisoners, and permitted two of the latter to cook for the officers. There was, however, much difficulty about getting food ; it was explained that all grain, not carried into the fort before the siege began, had been eaten up by Sher Afzul's fighting men or by his allies, who were already tightening their belts from hunger.   Fowler got his boots back from the brigand who had despoiled him on the polo ground at Reshun. They brought no luck to the ruffian, who was desperately wounded a few minutes later at the final assault on Dhurm Singh's defences.   Edwardes and Fowler were shown the battlefield of the 3rd of March (see Chap. xxi.), still dotted with dreadful masses of corruption, once high-spirited soldiers smartly accoutred ; and Sher Afzul's successful tactics on that eventful day were recounted.

On the 25th of March they rode to Kila Drosh, to find the redoubtable Umra Khán strong, big, intelligent, and pious ; but somewhat subtle and easily ruffled. His spotless garb, urbane manners, and kindliness to all about him impressed the British officers, who seem to have trusted and liked him from the first, notwithstanding their miserable plight in the dark verminous fort, with insufficient food.   Custom, as usual, had quickly conquered anxiety, and, although they must have sometimes reflected upon their perpetual liability to be murdered, the thought probably troubled them little.

Two days later the Lowari Pass was crossed in deep snow, a blizzard raging all the time.   Edwardes suffered greatly, and became feeble.   He and Fowler gained some protection by wrapping up their heads in Chitráli robes.   One of their fellow-prisoners, poorly-clad and hungry, could hardly be induced to persevere, the cold numbing his faculties and killing hope.   A second Sepoy, one of the bravest of the brave, died the same night.   The boot-stealing Pathán, borne on a litter, perished before the summit was reached. It was a terrible march for others besides the unfortunate captives, but Dír was reached at last, and rest, warmth, and food straightened exhausted backs and lightened leaden feet. Here they were in the country of people who crowd into forts at dusk, and never go abroad unarmed, even in the sunlight. Abject coolies, crawling under heavy loads, carried guns in their hands.

A couple more stages brought the prisoners, on March the 30th, to the top of Jánbatái ridge, whence they could see their destination, the fort of Barwar, the hereditary home of Umra Khán, who dispossessed his elder brother of life and lands by a murder carried out with all the picturesque and dramatic circumstances so dear to the Eastern mind. Barwar is at the upper end of the broad fruitful valley of Jandol. There Edwardes and Fowler remained many days, studying the useful arts of cooking, washing, breeches-making, and butcher's work.

As they had no arms, Fowler fashioned for himself a useful bludgeon, carving upon it his name, and felt happier. When lonely and in the midst of danger it is good to sleep with your fingers on a weapon. It soothes as a mother's grasp soothes a perturbed child.

The villagers all about were discussing General Low's movements in alarmed undertones, and already many had made off for secret places in the hills. Once more the officers were in jeopardy, for wild, fanatical tribesmen, in daily-increasing numbers, prowled about in sullen anger. It was necessary to go out as little as possible, and only in the evening. From the 10th of April the excitement over the whole district intensified, and the danger to the captives from retreating Patháns, furious at defeat, became still greater. On the 12th they were taken from Barwar to Mundiah, at the other extremity of the Jandol Valley. The officers rode, and their escort—twenty men in all, half on horseback—had to be quick-eyed, not for fear that their prisoners might escape, but lest some of the stranger warriors on the road should press between them to stab the captives or shoot at them from a short distance. Edwardes and Fowler wore Afghán dress, and were fairly well disguised, but Pathán eyes are keen. After an hour or two, it was decided that the risk of going farther was too much, so they hid themselves in a village till sundown.

But even then, after a mile or so, the advanced guard came galloping back in agitation, and all the party hurried forward together, the prisoners a little way behind. Alongside a stream was a group of wild fighting men, with a larger detachment beyond ; and this is the way the prisoners were got across—suddenly, the escort, aiming their rifles, covered the men at the water's edge, and compelled them to put down their arms and stand clear. With sullen brows, the others slowly stepped back, whereupon two of the guard stood over the weapons, whilst all the rest hurried through the water. Such incidents were obviously common, for no one, on either side, looked surprised.

When Mundiah Fort was neared, there was another anxious moment, and the officers were earnestly enjoined not to utter a word. All pushed their way past the gate, and through an armed crowd, into a courtyard beyond. Thence Edwardes and Fowler, with bated breath, after much jostling amongst gesticulating, excited people, reached the keep and found Umra Khán seated in a small room with priests and secretaries. "Biddy," the faithful fox-terrier, lost in the crush outside, where a whistle might have cost the prisoners their lives, had hardly been mourned for, when a stalwart

Pathán appeared carrying the wriggling creature in his arms. Already, it had been borne in upon the Jandolis, that however unclean a dog may be to a religious Musalmán, yet, if you wish to please an European, you must also cherish his four-footed adorer. Consequently, the little slut was hardly less considered than her master.

In an inner apartment, gained by a ladder, was discovered a Peshawer official, a charming Muhammedan gentleman, sent to Jandol by Major Deane, General Low's political assistant. At midnight he took away Edwardes (only one officer was allowed to go) carefully disguised, leading him over the hills by secret paths to the camp of the British troops marching to the relief of Chitrál. Before leaving, the young officer was given back his sword, which Umra Khán had contrived to obtain from Chitrál, thereby adding one more to his numerous kind actions. He deserved the warm thanks which Edwardes gratefully gave him.

For the next four days Fowler had to be kept hidden, so that he might not be seen by the unruly mountaineers who had collected to help Umra Khán. After dark he was taken for exercise upon the roof of the house. While it was light he remained secluded in the apartments which had formerly been the harem. The noisy auxiliaries were a constant anxiety. At the time for serving out rations they behaved obstreperously ; guns were pointed, and naked steel displayed as protests against short weight. On one occasion a serious conflict was narrowly avoided.

There was bad news on the night of the 15th of April, for a letter came from Major Deane to say that all negotiations with Umra Khán had been broken off. Everything, then, depended on the honour of Umra Khán, and how he would behave on hearing that he was irrevocably ruined. But, although some of his thoughts and methods jar upon western nerves, he has never been accused of unnecessary cruelty, so now his only thought seems to have been how to get Fowler away safely. About noon, on the 16th of April, he sent him forth dressed as a Pathán, and protected by a few horsemen and some tatterdemalion foot-soldiers, all light-hearted, and as gay as if they were marching to the sack of Indian cities. Umra Khán pressed Fowler's hand, and wished him well. He was dejected and nervous, but a high-bred Musalmán gentleman to the last, than whom there is none in the world more admirably courteous. Fowler promised to do everything he could to help him out of his scrape ; and so they parted, each kindly disposed towards the other. I suppose there is no British officer in India who would not think himself lucky if, by making sacrifices for the brave Khán of Jandol, he could help that picturesque individual, who, at one point of his career, not long ago, was a kind of Napoleon in miniature.

Fowler and his companions, pleased with themselves and one another, cracked jokes and indulged in playful badinage. The troopers allowed no one to come near. Many deeply-suspicious groups of fierce hill-men were passed on the way. At length the British outposts were seen, and the cavalry, after cheerful farewells, rode back, only the sturdy armed scarecrows remaining with Fowler, who tied a white rag to his cudgel and waved it over his head. Finally, all his companions, except two, whom he persuaded to accompany him unarmed, halted six hundred yards from the outposts, and said goodbye, leaving their late prisoner fervently hoping his good-natured friends might not send a volley after him—for the Pathán idea of a good joke differs somewhat from ours. Soon he came upon a party of Sikhs, who ordered him to halt, and in reply to his questions, said in an offhand manner, that they had an officer somewhere near. Then, as he dismounted, they realised that it was not a Pathán they were addressing but a British officer, and they crowded to him in excited joy, setting up a shout which told all within earshot that one of the bravest of Her Majesty's soldiers had come back to duty, out of the very jaws of the grave.

CHAPTER XVII

KELLY'S MARCH THROUGH THE SNOW

ON the 22nd of March, Colonel Kelly was instructed, by telegram from Calcutta, to take entire command of the Gilgit district, and co-operate with another force marching direct from India to Chitrál. His regiment, the 32nd Pioneer, had been at work making a road from Bunji to Chilás all the winter; but, owing to the course of events, and the fevered state of the political atmosphere, four hundred of the men were already collected at Gilgit. Of this number, two companies — that is to say, one-half — were ordered off, under Captain H. B. Borradaile, to Gupis on the 23rd of March; the remainder waiting until one-half of the mule mountain battery had been hurried in from Nomal, eighteen miles away on the Hunza road, when they followed, a day later, as a guard to the two seven-pounders. On the 27th, Borradaile, who took over command of the Pioneers, replacing his colonel, who had left regimental for general authority, set out from Gupis fort together with Colonel Kelly and his staff officers, while the mule guns, and their escort of two companies of Mazbis under Lieutenant F. H. Petersen, followed this advanced party, as before, at one day's interval. Officially, it is held that the famous march to Chitrál began on the 27th of March, and that Gupis was its starting-place. Lieutenant C. G. Stewart of the Royal Artillery had been for a short time the commander of Gupis fort. He relinquished that duty to Captain de Vismes, and thenceforward led this section of the battery which he had so untiringly trained.

At that time all the troops between Gupis and Chitrál were either at Mastuj, which was blockaded by the enemy, or at Ghizr, where Gough now held a detached post, except that Lieutenant Oldham,* and forty Kashmír Sappers and Miners were marching to the latter place, where orders had been sent for them to stop until Colonel Kelly arrived.

Mastuj was defended by forty Sikhs, the survivors of Ross's ill-fated party, 120 men of the 4th (Rághunáth) Regiment, and 115 men of the 6th Kashmír Rifles. Moberly had long before won his spurs on the Gilgit frontier, and under him was the gallant Kashmír Colonel Phula. There were also within the walls, fifty men of the Puniál local levies, and, in addition, the wounded Lieutenant Jones and Captain Bretherton. If small, the fort was not badly placed, considering that it, like all fortified places in Chitrál, was designed against matchlock fire only. As Moberly could always count upon the active help of Bretherton, as well as on the advice of Jones, he, comparatively speaking, was safe enough.

Gough's command at Ghizr comprised but sixty trained Kashmír soldiers and a hundred Hunza-Nagar undrilled riflemen. These local levies in the sequel did admirably, but like all men of that class, they must gain confidence in the regulars associated with them, and they require one or two successful skirmishes to brace their nerves. Though not well placed, the Ghizr post was the best available. Rumours were abroad that it was shortly to be attacked ; also that the Dárel and Tángír tribes, from beyond the southern

* Lieutenant L. W. S. Oldham, R.E.

watershed of the valley, meditated a raid to cut its communications with Gupis. The position was a difficult and an anxious one, but its commander's patronymic was a pledge that an enemy would find him a hard nut to crack, for wherever fighting has been hardest in India, a Gough has usually contrived to be there and increase the family renown.

By the 31st of March, Colonel Kelly's tiny expedition assembled at Ghizr. Four hundred men of the 32nd Pioneers, two mountain guns, and Oldham's forty Kashmír Sappers, constituted a force small enough to satisfy the youngest subaltern in Her Majesty's army; but it was of first-rate material, and exceptionally well officered. The infantry, the half-battalion of Pioneers, were in hard training from their work in the Indus valley. Between Gupis and Ghizr the intervening stages, four in number, had been easy enough for foot-soldiers, although the last march was uncomfortable by reason of about a foot of snow on the ground, with intervals of mud and slush. Indeed, the chief interest had centred in the mule battery, and in the possibility of its getting along. Slowly and laboriously it climbed over the difficult hill-track, which was the sole road, without loss, although at one place, where the path was buried in a great snow-slip, a couple of mules—one carrying a gun and the other a pair of wheels—tumbled over and over down the steep incline for some fifty yards, and stuck at the very edge of a five hundred feet drop sheer to the river. Stewart, and an equally bold driver, slid after the struggling animals and knelt on their heads. Girths were loosed, and the heavy ordnance saddles got rid of and carried up the hill-side. Long powerful straps were then buckled together, and slipped, with several tarpaulins, under the frightened beasts, which were simply hauled by main strength on to the road. To handle terrified mules, plunging in an avalanche at the brink of a precipice, demands sturdy nerves. The battery finally arrived without further mishap, except that the Major, a Dogra, and many of his men were beginning to get snow-blind.

Ghizr is a terribly exposed place, 10,000 feet above the sea-level. It is an ancient lake-bed of wide extent, the upper end converging to a mighty gorge flanked by wild rocks, which can be confidently held against a hostile force advancing from Langar. Upon these rocks, Gough had stationed his Hunza-Nagar irregulars. Even in April the cold is considerable, and to add to Kelly's difficulties, there were three feet of soft new-fallen snow covering the earth. On the 1st of April he made a start, but it was discovered that seventy baggage coolies had decamped, or gone into hiding during the night. This was serious, for without them, how were the guns to be carried over the Shandúr, if the pass proved hopeless for the mules? Stewart, therefore, eagerly volunteered to ride hard, search the roads, and force back any runaways he could catch. Kelly agreed, and told Lieutenant A. S. Cobbe of the Pioneers, who had charge of the rear-guard, to wait behind at Ghizr to help. Some Kashmír riflemen were also sent down the road after Stewart, to secure any men he might stop. Fearful of being left behind with his guns, Stewart rode furiously along the break-neck paths, overtaking and driving back with imperious gestures, supplemented by occasional revolver shots over their heads, forty unlucky villagers. War is a grim slave-driver, and the gentle and innocent who cannot fight have to travail for those that do. By this time the poor pony was driven to a standstill, but a passing traveller needed no second bidding to change horses with a broad-chested Irishman, late, perhaps, for a fight. So Stewart returned to Ghizr

betimes, and he and Cobbe tramped after the main
column, yet they had gone but four miles when they
met the whole of the force returning.

Colonel Kelly had forced his way through the deep
powdery snow for eight miles, but the farther he went,
the greater were his troubles. At length, on a big plain
which begins about three miles beyond the wind-swept
hamlet of Teru, all the animals were pounded hopelessly;
they could do nothing but plunge and flounder in the
snow. Since there was no help for it, the "retire" had
to be sounded, and the little force, turning in its tracks,
trudged to Ghizr again in dejection. The younger
officers, especially, were inconsolable. It was just like
their luck, they said; everybody else would get to
Chitrál except them, and so on, over and over again.
Had there been some one to blame, some individual for
them to hang morally in secret, it would have been a
consolation; tired hearts fretting in disappointment
instinctively demand a scapegoat. Blinding snow began
to fall, and Kelly determined to wait at Ghizr till the
skies should clear, or until porters could be collected
to replace the useless transport animals. Tired and
depressed, blundering along the treacherous path, some
vaguely imaginative person compared the scene to
Napoleon's retreat from Moscow, and everybody became
crosser than ever.

The moment was opportune for an indomitable
spirit to exert itself, and, as always in our service, the
occasion produced the man. Borradaile asked leave,
cheerily, to halt at the bleak Teru hamlet (three miles
from Ghizr) with his 200 Pioneers, and to try, on the
first opportunity, to push over the Shandúr Pass and
seize Laspur, the highest village on the other side.
Permission was given him, and also extended to Oldham
with his forty Sappers, and to the Hunza-Nagar levies

as well. Colonel Kelly, his staff, and the rest of the force then resumed their march to Ghizr. All the available coolies were handed over to Borradaile, who placed guards upon them. These poor people were now more precious than ever, for the day's experience demonstrated that it was impossible for the mules and baggage animals to get through the snow. It was arranged that if Borradaile did manage to reach Laspur, he was at once to send back all his transport to take over the rest of the force. He and Oldham got their men under shelter, and with Surgeon-Captain Browning-Smith,[*] and Cobbe, who came in later, made themselves as comfortable as they could in a dirty and leaky hut; but what are a sieve-like roof, hunger and wet clothes to men buoyed up with great resolves?

All that night and all the next day the skies were pitiless, and the snowfall never stopped. At Ghizr, Stewart and Gough went into committee with the latter's Kashmír adjutant, to decide how the seven-pounders could be taken over the pass. " Upon sledges," said the British officers; " By road digging," argued the other. Next, the possibility of carrying the guns was discussed, and it was soon perceived that it could only be done if the Pioneers would volunteer for the work, and Borradaile could let them undertake it, for it was obvious that they would have plenty of trouble in getting through the snow themselves without the added burden of these great loads. With the help of the battery carpenter's tools a rough sledge was completed on the 2nd of April, the runners being made of young poplars coated with the tin linings of old commissariat chests. Down an incline, where the snow was only a foot deep, the machine was found

---

* Surgeon-Captain S. Browning-Smith of the Indian Medical Service, the medical officer of the 32nd Pioneers.

capable of carrying eight ammunition boxes (1000 lbs.)
but up hill it dragged badly. Nevertheless, its enthusiastic designers pinned their faith upon it, and the
ingenuous Stewart reported to Colonel Kelly his conviction that the problem of transporting the mountain
guns was solved. In the afternoon he, with Gough
and all the gunners, besides forty of the Ghizr Kashmír
garrison, started for Teru—where the real difficulties of
the road began—to make experiments. They carried
with them entrenching tools, and also wooden spades
from the village. Oldham, as soon as he heard their
story, showed the impracticability of the adjutant's
plan of digging a road, because such a scheme could
not be carried out under several weeks. Thereupon
the sledge, the child of so much hope, was proudly
produced, tried, and found, alas, to be useless in deep
snow. Stewart gazed with tragic wistfulness at Borradaile, longing, but fearing, to ask that the Pioneers
might help to carry his guns. Just then the senior
native officer came up and earnestly asked that his
men might attempt it, as they did not want the cannon
left behind. Borradaile went into the question, and
having satisfied himself that the suggestion was a
practicable one, agreed to have it tried. It was then
found that the old subadár of the Kashmír Sappers
and Miners had just previously made a similar request
to Oldham on behalf of his men.

Early on the morning of the 3rd of April, poles
were shaped and devices planned for carrying the two
seven - pounders, with the ammunition, all of which
Colonel Kelly sent up from Ghizr at eleven o'clock.
The snow had stopped. Baggage coolies were very
scarce, so everything except the barest necessaries,
even four pairs of ammunition boxes, had to be left behind at Teru. Eight sledges had been also constructed

and proper reliefs of Sepoys were organised for each load. For the first two miles the going was easy, then the deep snow was met. The mules sank in to their shoulders and struggled frantically. Even un-laden animals could not be driven forward. Certain half-bred yâks, which are peculiar to this district, were sent for in the hope that they might be able to tread a moderately firm path in the snow ; but they could not be kept in single file, and even when that object was occasionally attained, each animal stepped so exactly in the tracks of its predecessor, that the result was a series of deep holes at equal intervals, instead of a beaten track.

As yet another resource the mules were forced down and into the river, the idea being to wade up its margin ; but close to the bank it was three feet deep, and big stones and sudden drops caused blunders and stumbles. The cold was so intense that even these hardy brutes could not stay in the water, while exact and painful experiment proved that a British subaltern could only withstand the icy temperature for four minutes at a stretch. It being hopeless to persevere, the mules were sent back to Teru, and the sledges were tried. Thirty men dragged at each, but the labour was terrible, for the haulers every instant sank into the snow to the waist, or even as high as the armpits, and the machines proving too broad for the narrow tracks, they turned over continually. Therefore this plan also was abandoned, and the anxious Stewart's last hope put to the test ; the loads were slung from the poles, and pioneers, gunners, and Kashmír soldiers staggered along, straining at the weights with hard-set teeth.

No wonder the march seemed interminable. Every moment a man fell, when his end of the pole would drop and the balance shift; then the whole of that group would tumble over together. Many of these eighty-two devoted fellows were already in the agony of snow-blindness. The best pace, over the easier bits, was three-quarters of a mile an hour. Eight o'clock came, the darkness was as intense as the cold, while Langar camp, which Borradaile had hurried on to occupy, was several miles away. Moreover, everybody was worn out. It seemed clear nothing more could be done that night, but a battery havildár (sergeant), as a last effort, took one of the little cannons, two hundred pounds in weight, upon his shoulder and actually carried it some distance with merely one man behind to keep it from wobbling. Stewart went to help them, but he could hardly stand from fatigue, and the three, with the gun, fell exhausted into the snow. That settled it; so guns, carriages, wheels, and ammunition boxes, wrapped in tarpaulins, were stacked and left, the soldiers being sent on to camp.

Young Gough, after strenuously carrying loads all day long, had been sent on to see if Borradaile could give any more men, but with only just enough strength to stagger into camp, he fell down unconscious. It was long before he could be restored. Everybody, indeed, was near the snapping-point of nerves and tendons. Browning-Smith, the doctor of the Pioneers, a fine fellow, helped Stewart to set up the poles to mark, in case of a fresh fall of snow, where the loads were left. Those two also brought on the rear-guard, and got into Langar about midnight—a camp 11,000 feet above the sea-level and unsheltered.

One might suppose that officers ending a march so painful might fairly consider their day's work ended and think of food and rest; but it is so important that the soldiers be taken care of, and there are so many details

L

to be seen to personally, that in critical times a British officer often seems to work from day to day without any intermission. So it was in this instance; all the men who arrived late must have their feet inspected for frost-bite, and, when necessary, rubbed with snow to restore the circulation. Then they were literally put to bed. Two soldiers' kits were spread upon the ground and six men made to lie closely on them, wrapped in two more double blankets, while the remaining two sets were put on top. Such duties cannot be safely delegated to Oriental subordinates, for everything, the very existence of the force, depends upon their proper performance. Borradaile's advance party had not reached camp till long after dark. Happily, the night was fine. Many of the Pioneers, old soldiers, cheery, though frozen, passed the night sitting round the fires, which could hardly be kept alight because their only fuel was green scrub-wood. They talked gaily, and made jokes of all past and future difficulties, but the younger men were too exhausted to take part in this seasonable bravado.

Borradaile resolved, guns or no guns, that he would take his two companies over the Shandúr the next day to Laspur; so he now decided to leave Gough's Kashmír rifles behind, as well as the battery detachment, in the hope that they might get the guns in and then bring them after him. Also, by dropping three days' food, he was able to hand over thirty baggage-carriers to Stewart; and he further promised to send back as many more as he could spare, after he had established himself at Laspur.

On the 4th of April, with an "*au revoir à Laspur,*" to Stewart and Gough, Borradaile set out with his two companies of Pioneers, the Kashmír Sappers and his irregulars, to cross the Shandúr. He had with him,

Cobbe, Oldham, and Browning-Smith. The little party might form some estimate of the physical troubles in store for them, but they could not guess what the Chitrális would do, whether they would hold the Laspur ridges in strength, or fight on the pass. First went the levies, who knew the way, to make a track across the snow, which was carefully kept by all the soldiers and porters. In time, this path became fairly firm for those in the rear, though, at short intervals, great holes indicated where the leaders had tumbled and fallen through.

The Shandúr pass is really a mountain plain, somewhat rough, and indented by a couple of lakes; its highest point is but 1200 feet above Langar. During April its difficulties are great, especially when the seasonable meltings are accelerated by a hot sun, or when a strong wind blows over its dreary expanse Cobbe, an athletic young officer, led the advanced guard, but before the descent to Laspur was reached, only half of his men were with him; the others kept dropping through the snow, up to their chests, because of the weight of their accoutrements, and because they became nearly helpless from fatigue. The leader, of course, was obliged to keep well forward, but the indefatigable Browning-Smith kept all stragglers on the move and cheered them to further efforts. Happily, there was a fair proportion of glare-glasses; consequently, most of the men escaped the pangs of snow-blindness, but all alike had blistered faces, and suffered horribly from thirst. Excessive work for two days, and the unrestful night at Langar, told on the whole force, and many fell out and lay like logs in the snow; but Borradaile and his officers, by firmness and encouragement, brought everyone over at last. A kindly stream, immediately beyond the pass, gave new life to the flagging. The levies crowned the heights on each side of the steep descent, and ten hours from the start the detachment reached Laspur, so delighted with themselves that the soldiers forgot their sufferings, and declared themselves to be less tired than when they started. Although many of the baggage men gave up altogether, most of them carried their loads into the village.

At the top of the pass, the advanced guard had seen two or three of the enemies' scouts, who made off at once. When Laspur was reached, the villagers in a body met the troops to beg they might not be fired upon, to the amusing indignation of the younger officers. What people, however uncivilised, they asked, could imagine British soldiers capable of shooting unarmed men? There was comparatively little snow on the ground, and all were hutted except the pickets, who had to camp out. Next morning, April 5th, Borradaile and Oldham set to work and fortified a group of huts. During the afternoon, word came that the enemy was in force in lower Laspur, whereupon Borradaile took Cobbe and eighty of the Pioneers to reconnoitre. About a hundred men were seen running away, and there the incident ended.

We must now go back to Stewart and Gough, who were left behind at Langar. Making two trips, they brought the guns and ammunition boxes into camp, finishing the task late in the afternoon. The dead-tired coolies declared, with conviction, that one more day's work would kill them; but the Kashmír Sepoys, under Gough, pegged away with unflagging spirit. Yet every one now doubted if the seven-pounders could be got over the pass. Axles were removed from the carriages to lighten the loads, and it was decided that no ammunition, except one pair of boxes for each gun, and one box of star shell, should be taken. By kind words, lavish promises, and much petting, the carriers were induced to forget their gloomy thoughts for the time and go to sleep. Everything depended upon the weather, which proved disappointing, for on April 5th a bitter wind was blowing; nothing could be more unpleasant or even dangerous on a long, flat expanse like the Shandúr. Nevertheless, at half-past seven the guns and carriages moved off, nine porters to each load, carefully escorted by Sepoys, and an hour later the rest of the convoy was under weigh. Smoked glasses being few in number, most of the soldiers, including Stewart and Gough, became snow-blind. To ensure there being some one who could see to lay a gun, four men, who had protective spectacles, were ordered not to take them off for any reason whatever. Before mid-day, half the journey was over, and the porters sent back by Borradaile began to arrive. Late in the afternoon, Laspur was entered amidst the enthusiastic cheers of its garrison. The track made on the previous day froze hard during the night and greatly helped the march. Borradaile had more cases of frost-bite than Stewart, while the latter had many more men blinded by the snow, the glare under the blazing sun being terrific; all those without tinted glasses suffered acutely.

When every allowance is made for the determination and energy of the British officers, there is still room to admire the dogged persistence of the troops, the way they toiled and strove right up to the exhaustion point, and then again and again resumed the struggle in spite of rarefied air, over-strained muscles, and, in many instances, the excruciating pain of inflamed eyes. Anyone who has traversed the ground under more or less identical conditions, is astonished at the rare endurance and fortitude shown by these Eastern soldiers, the great majority of whom were men born and reared on the plains of India.

The effect produced by this passage of the Shandúr was invaluable. The Chitrális doubted if regular infantry could cross, while they were certain that guns could not ; and to precisely the same degree that they grew disheartened, were the local levies from Puniál, Hunza, and Nagar astonished and encouraged. From this time forward, there are no longer half-complaints of their behaviour or conjectures about their loyalty ; nothing is heard but a chorus of praise concerning their devotion and bravery, and at the end of the campaign Kelly wrote of them officially in terms of unstinted panegyric. In estimating the fighting value of irregular, undisciplined troops, such as levies, who throw in their lot with us for pay or from fear, or because it may advance their material or sentimental interests, but rarely or never because of any sympathy or affection which we inspire, it must not be forgotten that these men can only be relied upon to play a winning game. They are alien in religion, in customs, and in modes of thought, and know nothing of military discipline, that bond which tightly binds the British-Indian soldier to his British officers, and induces, as well as maintains, a habit of unquestioning obedience in Musalmán or Hindu to his Christian leader.

CHAPTER XVIII

A SMALL PITCHED BATTLE

A REQUISITION of all ponies and saddles in the Laspur district being made, in order to replace the battery mules and harness left at Teru, the levies collected and handed over to Stewart as strange a variety of animals as was ever offered to a smart artillery officer for military purposes. The assortment ranged from a raw-boned, half-starved creature of fourteen hands, with a pitiful sore back, down to six donkeys not more than thirty-two inches high; in fact, of all those brought in, only five were of the least use. With their owners, and forty villagers, impressed as porters, these five animals were shut up and carefully guarded, for upon their safe custody depended the mobility of the mountain guns. On the other hand, some of the miseries of war were lessened to the poor men, because they were well cared for and properly fed.

Although there were alarms which compelled no precautions to be omitted, the night passed away quietly, and on the morning of the 6th, Borradaile made a reconnaissance in force, to discover if he could communicate with Mastuj. He pushed down the valley with one hundred and twenty Pioneers, the levies, and the two seven-pounders, as far as the village of Gusht, and two miles below that place found the enemy strongly posted on both banks of the river, at the Chakalwat position. Having seen what he wanted, Borradaile returned to Laspur after dark. All the gunners, even the "layers," wore bandages over their eyes, while Stewart and Gough, now quite blind, were led along the roads. The same afternoon, Colonel Kelly and his staff arrived, having crossed the pass from Langar, where they spent the previous night. Wednesday, the 7th, was a halt, for the men were worn out after such hard work at high altitudes, and a large proportion of them required medical treatment, especially for their eyes; it also gave time for coolies to be sent back to Langar for the ammunition which Stewart was forced to drop there.

On the 8th the whole force camped at Gusht, when the enemy was found to be still at Chakalwat, which was reconnoitred and carefully sketched, preparatory to an attack on the following day, while urgent messages were sent back to Laspur for the Puniál levies, who had been left there. The Chakalwat is one of the many easily defensible places to be found on this frontier, and is well known to all the people as a *darband*. A Chitrál general has not to sit down and meditate upon the best place to make a stand, for the capabilities of every good position in the country have been tested on numberless occasions by actual fighting. From a military point of view, Chakalwat is a powerful defence against an enemy trying to seize Mastuj, which is round a spur in its rear; but the peculiarity of its being fortified and held, in this instance, lies in the fact that Mastuj, though blockaded by the Chitrális, was strongly garrisoned by our troops, who could sally out at any moment. Muhammed Isa, the general in command, had therefore to fight with a continual glance over the shoulder, to see that his retreat was not imperilled by the appearance of Moberly behind him.

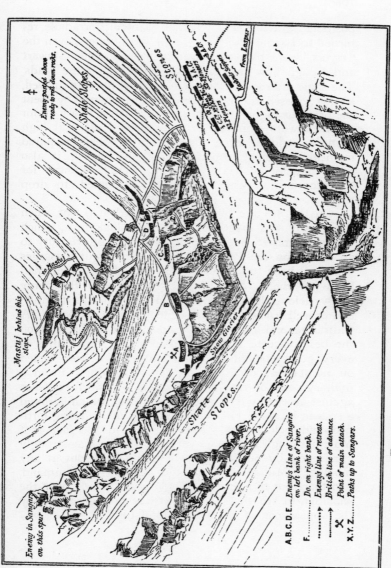

RECONNAISSANCE SKETCH OF CHAKALWAT POSITION.

A.B.C.D.E....Enemy's line of Sangars.
F.................Do. on right bank.
..............Enemy's line of retreat.
............British line of advance.
✕..............Point of main attack.
x.y.z..........Paths up to Sangars.

Mastuj behind this slope.

Enemy in Sangars on this spur.

Enemy parties above ready to roll down rocks.

Shale Slopes.

to Mastuj

Stones

from Laspur

Nagrul Spurs

Snow Glacier

Shale Slopes.

The Chitrális held Chakalwat strongly on both banks. There the Laspur torrent takes a couple of bold curves and is shaped like a reversed S. Each concavity of this reversed letter is filled by a broad turtle-backed plain, ridged and furrowed, and across the river, opposite to each, is a mighty shale slope; that on the Gusht side (on the left bank), with its linear outcrops of rocks and its frozen snow-slip, being altogether impassable, while that on the right bank is indeed crossed by a narrow track leading to Mastuj; but it can be blocked at pleasure by stones rolled down the terrific incline from the ridges high above. Everywhere it is difficult, and in most places impossible, to descend to the water's edge. The shale slopes, for instance, end abruptly in a continued series of low precipices. The crossings between the two banks are at the up-stream end of the whole position, a little below Gusht, where there is usually a bridge, and at a point near the juncture of the double curves, where, with caution, the river may be forded from one enormous convex "fan" to the other. To stop Kelly, the enemy destroyed the bridge, and built sangars, which commanded the ford from the left or Gusht bank. In line with these, and on the same side of the river, along the top of the steep river cliffs, were three similar fortifications, whose fire could sweep the Mastuj road on the opposite bank. That path, blocked farther on, by a long loop-holed barricade, was also threatened with destruction at any moment by small companies of men stationed on the rocks above to start a thunder of stones and débris rushing and plunging down to the river. Sharp-shooters were posted on the Gusht side on the rocks jutting out from the shale. Their business was to harass anyone on the great rugged plain across the river. The whole position is well shown in the military sketch opposite, made officially by Beynon, Colonel Kelly's staff officer.

At 6 A.M. on the 9th of April, Colonel Kelly sent the Hunza and Nagar men, under the guidance of his own staff officer, straight up the hills on his left (that is to say, on the left bank of the river), to turn the right flank of the enemy from above, while the Puniál men, just arrived from Laspur, were despatched across the torrent to climb the hills forming the right boundary of the valley, and dislodge the Chitrális posted there to roll down stones. Three hours later, Kelly moved out of Gusht with all his force, except a small baggage guard, to make a front attack. A mile below the village, Oldham, with his Kashmír Sappers, improvised a temporary bridge for men on foot, upon the site where the other had been demolished by the enemy. The mountain guns taken through the water on ponies, were afterwards carried up to the big fan by villagers, carefully guarded.

The advance was led by Cobbe, with a half company, one section of which formed the advanced party. His men were commanded in dumb show, or by the whistle —for their British officer was still speechless from exposure during the Shandúr march. Next in order came Oldham, with his Kashmír Sappers, then the main body under Borradaile, one and a half companies of the 32nd, and Stewart's guns. Perhaps it is not surprising that the bullets from the rocks across the river fell harmless amongst this little band. Spread out on the huge, rough, and undulating fan, it must have been difficult for the Chitráli marksmen even to see Kelly's drab-coloured men. As the river was again neared, the fire grew hotter. Cobbe's second section was brought up in line with the first, and began with it alternately to discharge steady volleys at the greater of the two sangars protecting the ford. Borradaile next sent forward the guns, and another half company of the Pioneers, while the Kashmír Sappers moved over to the left.

The seven-pounders were carried into action by the gunners, to the great mental relief of the unhappy villagers. The range, 600 yards, was discussed by Cobbe, who could scarcely whisper, and Stewart, who could barely see, but the third shell broke a hole into the sangar nearest the snow-drift, when its defenders at once began to bolt. Soon the enemy's fire grew slack, whereupon the infantry and artillery advanced to within 400 yards and attacked the next work, which made no response. At the proper moment, the Hunza and Nagar men, who had already made themselves heard, showed above, the river was forded without opposition, and all was over. The flying enemy was chased down the left bank for a couple of miles, but pursuit was hopeless. Native Indian troops might as well try to catch a wild goat as fugitive Chitrális, whose energies on this occasion were spurred by the knowledge that round the corner the Mastuj troops were probably already on the move to intercept them. Luckily for the runaways, the guns had not been heard by Moberly. Not much loss was suffered by either side in this little affair. Kelly had four men wounded, but only one badly hit; while five or six bodies left on the ground, alone gave any clue to the extent of the enemy's casualties.

The attack was nicely planned, and well timed. If the resistance of the Chitrális was not strenuous, it must be confessed that they showed effrontery in fighting at all, with Mastuj so close in their rear. Muhammed Isa retired with neatness. To distract the Mastuj garrison he opened a lively fire upon the fort;

then by the time it was decided that retreating horse and foot were not merely falling back for a stratagem, and Moberly sallied out to discover what it all meant, the quick-moving enemy was beyond reach. After a halt, Kelly, fording the river again, marched into Mastuj. The Sikhs, saved from Ross's disaster, threw themselves at Stewart's feet, and "salaamed," with dust on their heads. Sighing, they declared that now the guns had arrived all would be well.

Three days were passed at Mastuj, but not in idleness. Much had to be done, many points to be decided. First and foremost, could the Gilgit force press on to the relief of Chitrál, or must it wait for supplies and until transport was collected? After careful reflection, and discussion with Borradaile, his second in command, Kelly decided to advance; so Oldham set to work knocking down houses and built a bridge over the Mastuj river with the timbers thus obtained.

On the 10th of April, the second detachment of the 32nd Pioneers, two companies, marched in under Lieuts. Petersen and H. Bethune. They brought with them the battery gear and ammunition which had been left behind, and on the 11th Stewart, having collected ponies from all the country round, tried a hill parade. The result would have disappointed any one but a subaltern of a mountain battery on field service, for the small, weak creatures could hardly crawl under their burdens, several fell, and all were doubtful. However, good food and care revived them somewhat, and the enthusiastic Stewart actually started on the 13th for the Nisa Gul fight, with an imposing string of animals carrying the guns, carriages, wheels, and ammunition boxes in orthodox style, each led by a local driver pressed for the service. Only twelve of these poor beasts reached Chitrál.

Muhammed Isa was known to be at the Nisa Gul with a strong force prepared to dispute its passage. The whole position was thoroughly reconnoitred on the 12th, and a sketch made of it by Beynon, the staff officer. Next morning Colonel Kelly explained the plan of attack to his officers. All recognised the fact that if the sangars were obstinately defended there would be sharp fighting; but the troops were in splendid heart, as much elated at the prospect of action as they were relieved to learn that they were not to remain at Mastuj; every man was furious at the news of the treachery practised upon Fowler's and Edwardes's party. Oldham devoted much care to making ladders; he also collected ropes to deal with the enormous ravine which constituted the chief strength and defence of the enemy. Kelly, on the 13th April, marched to the attack.

The position held by Muhammed Isa was extraordinarily strong. It was always asserted by Chitrális, that to force a crossing from the Chitrál side, to attack Mastuj, was impossible, and that the only way it could be carried in the opposite direction (the one taken by Kelly), was by a determined advance along the ordinary road, and by battering down all barricades with cannon. It is certain that no one in Chitrál would have believed it possible to force the Nisa Gul in the way it actually was forced.

For five miles below Mastuj there are two paths, one a hill track running dangerously across rocky slopes on the right bank; the other blundering over boulder-strewn stony patches, and through an endless series of eccentric water channels, which wash round those pebbly islets. This latter road can only be used when the waters are low. It, after innumerable fordings, makes a last plunge into the main river to join the hill

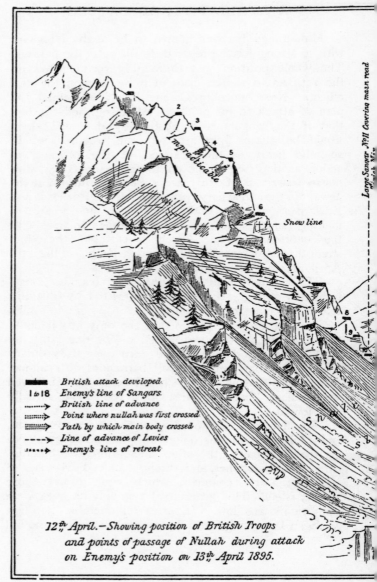

Large Sangar Nº11 Covering main road through Nisa

Snow line

	British attack developed.
1 to 18	Enemy's line of Sangars.
	British line of advance
	Point where nullah was first crossed
	Path by which main body crossed
	Line of advance of Levies
	Enemy's line of retreat

12ᵗʰ April.—Showing position of British Troops
and points of passage of Nullah during attack
on Enemy's position on 13ᵗʰ April 1895.

RECONNAISSANCE SKETCH OF

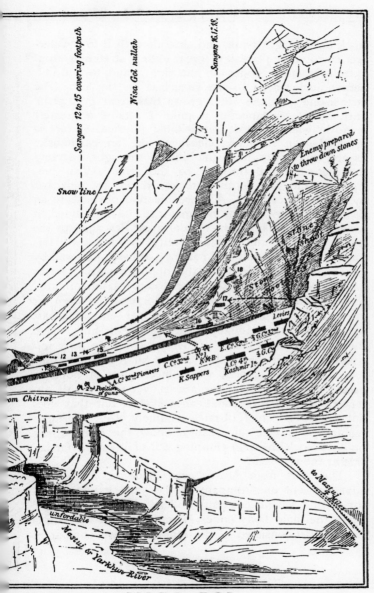

POSITION AT **NISA GOL.**

track on the right bank, and ascends with it to a water-
less corrugated plateau of great extent, stretching from
extremely steep slopes on the right hand, to end in a
perpendicular drop to the river bed on the left.   The
farther one gets, the wider grows this great grey plain,
until at the distance of a mile it attains a greatest
breadth, when a most remarkable physical feature is
revealed — an immense cleavage, like an earthquake
fissure, which runs from the hills on the right, bisecting
the plateau right through to the river.   With precipitous sides, its depth is reckoned not by tens, but
by hundreds of feet.   A more effectual obstacle to an
advancing army cannot be imagined.   Undefended, it
would cause delay.   The regular road descends to the
river's edge at the left extremity or outlet of this
mighty cleft by a difficult narrow pathway, followed by
an equally stiff climb up the opposite side.   Horses
have to be taken over with great care ; a few minutes'
work would make the crossing impracticable, even for
men on foot.   At the other or upper end, this vast
square-cut gully gradually loses itself in the hills, where
the unstable slopes, loosely covered by shale, look impassable for an ibex.   To journey all round along the
top of the watershed, would necessitate a hopeless
détour.   Kelly's difficulties are shown to a small extent in Beynon's reconnaissance sketch, but that does
not show the chief obstacle—namely, this enormous
rectangular ravine—nor can it show the fortifications
built to block the road climbing out of it on the farther
side at the river end.

The start from Mastuj was made at 7 A.M.   In
advance went one company of the 32nd, led by Peterson, with a second company under Cobbe, as a support.
Then the main body under Borradaile, with whom was
Bethune ; it consisted of the remaining two companies

of the Pioneers, Oldham and his Sappers, Stewart with
the mountain guns, and one hundred men of the 4th
Kashmír Regiment, commanded by Moberly. At 11
A.M. the plain was reached, when the two leading
companies advanced in line, but some distance apart—
Peterson's on the left. Together, they constituted the
firing line, and support. No sooner had they extended,
than the enemy opened fire, and a native officer with
the main body was hit by a Snider bullet; a piece of
bad luck, when the long range is considered. The
Pioneers marched on steadily without firing, the configuration of the ground preventing their seeing the
sangars in front, at the same time, that it protected
them greatly from the enemy. Peterson first bore off
a bit to the left threatening the right of Muhammed
Isa's central defences, which were designed to sweep
the ordinary road for about 450 yards, while Cobbe
attacked the same four sangars straight in front, advancing eventually within 250 yards of them, almost
to the edge of the ravine.

By this time the guns had been brought up on the
right, and beyond them, Borradaile's two companies of
Pioneers were busy silencing the small hill sangars,
and scattering groups of Chitrális on the slopes at the
extreme left of Muhammed Isa's line. The levies were
posted still farther away; their orders were to try and
cross the dangerous shale on the steep inclines which
border the upper end of the mighty ravine, and then
attack the sangar marked No. 17 in the sketch. At
first there was some difficulty in getting the guns up,
for bullets were dropping everywhere, and the drivers
refused to budge an inch. The man with the leading
pony bluntly declared he would be shot if he did.
Having no escort, Stewart drew his revolver, put the
muzzle to the man's head, and explained, that though

he might escape the enemy's rifles, he could not possibly escape the officer's pistol. The poor wretch saw the force of this grim logic, and the guns were brought into action about 400 yards from No. 17 sangar, when the unlucky driver was at once shot through the stomach. It was very hard, but war is hard and cruel, and there is no poetic justice in the billeting of a bullet. The rest of the animals, and the spare ammunition were then sent back a short space to shelter in a dip of the ground. Stewart began pounding at No. 17, which was Kelly's chief point of attack, with shells filled with sand. Those with bursting charges also break up against stone fortifications, but the live variety burst with the fuse outside a thick wall, thereby weakening the blow perhaps, while sand-plugged shell seem to concentrate the whole of their energy in smashing themselves stolidly against it.

This particular sangar, admirably built, was hard to demolish, but being placed on a sharp declivity, every stone that fell off in front rolled clear, and was finally got rid of. In that way, it was eventually cut down to about two feet six inches. In the midst of the showers of shot and shell, a splendid-looking dog ran out to play. He dashed delightedly at the dust knocked up by the bullets, for a few moments, then bolted away, poor fellow, with his tail between his legs and a shot in his body. Peterson's and Cobbe's companies silenced the central defences, while Borradaile on the right, not only kept in check No. 17, as well as the other hill posts, but drove the groups of Chitrális high up the slopes. The enemy's fire everywhere was slackening, so the guns were limbered up, and the trembling villagers with their ponies were sent for, to transfer them to a spot opposite sangar No. 12. But the battery in moving to the left excited such a heavy fusillade, all sangars waking up to join in, that the Pioneers chaffingly called to one another to give the gunners a wide berth. It came into action again on Peterson's left, at not more than 150 yards in front of No. 12.

While the pieces were being laid, only the top stones of the sangar wall could be seen. The battery havildár-major (sergeant-major) was already wounded, two ponies were hit, and another driver shot through the chest. Very slowly the guns were run forward. The range was desperately close. Gradually the line of loopholes rise into view. An anxious moment and —whew! no faces, no rifles, no smoke! It was lucky this sangar proved empty, or the brave gunners, little more than 100 yards away, would have been terribly slated. No. 17 now began to stir again, and had to be quieted with a couple of shell; also, two "case" were fired, just for the look of the thing. Then another havildár was hit, a corporal shot dead, and a gunner wounded in three places; altogether, 50 per cent. of the men on the two guns were *hors de combat*. As there was no more work for the guns at that moment, Stewart retired them again some yards while he went to Colonel Kelly and obtained permission to search for a road down the precipitous face of the ravine.

The military sketch shows a long gap between the enemy's hill sangars and their main defences. It was, in fact, considered so certain, that in this interval no one would dream of crossing the ravine, that it would be absurd to build works there. But Muhammed Isa was wrong. Noticing this absence of fortifications, Oldham and Beynon also asked leave to hunt for a spot where the ladders and ropes, which the former had brought from Mastuj, might be utilised. The two eventually found a place, not very promising indeed,

M

but where it was thought an initial attempt might be made. Then Oldham hastened back for his Kashmír Sappers, and Beynon went to report the find to Colonel Kelly; Oldham quickly returned and set to work. For the first forty feet the descent was comparatively easy, so that a man, by holding on with one hand to a rope made fast above, could with the other contrive to cut rough steps with a pick; but then there came a vertical drop when the ladders were the only hope. The adventurous little band was all the time under a galling fire. One Sapper was soon mortally wounded, and a havildár shot through the groin. No time was to be lost. The stalwart Oldham scrambled down the rope, placed the ladder with his own hands, and descended. He was followed by a dozen brave fellows. By dint of care and coolness in cutting footsteps, all reached the bottom; the lower they got the safer they were. The undaunted thirteen next attacked the opposite slope and found, to their delight, a goat-track, only moderately bad, by which they climbed up the enemy's side of the ravine. It was a rare deed for one British officer and twelve Kashmír Sappers to cross that awful place to meet above them unknown ground and an unknown enemy; but the man who did it (an unsung hero) is a member of that famous corps which gave Gilgit an Aylmer to blow open Nilt gate, and a Fowler to cover himself and his comrades with glory, even amidst the slaughter at Reshun.

Looking back, Oldham found that Cobbe had lined his side of the ravine with Pioneers, so he stood up, waving a handkerchief, lest his party might be fired upon by friends, and shouted himself hoarse for them to hurry over. The enemy in No. 17, scared at seeing that a lodgment had been made on their edge of the great Nullah, now tried to get away. They raced, singly, over the steep hill-side, but, it is said, only one man escaped. At this instant the levies appeared, and occupied the deserted work. In some miraculous way, they had crossed the stone shoots. Naturally enough, they were in no hurry to make the attempt; but were finally induced to do so by Moberly, whom Borradaile sent to urge them on. The men in the sangars, on the enemy's extreme right, now also tried to bolt, but many were driven into the works again by horsemen placed ready for that contingency. Suddenly the flying Chitrális paused, and began to crowd back in jubilation. A very odd thing had occurred, which completely deceived them, and might easily have ended tragically for Oldham's isolated party.

It seems that Oldham brought with him a few slabs of gun cotton, in case of need, which were placed on the ground near where the descent was made. A chance bullet struck these slabs, but as they were not detonated, they merely began to blaze a yard or so in front of Cobbe's men. The Kashmír Rifles were close at hand, preparing to follow Beynon and Moberly, now in the bottom of the ravine with a couple of orderlies. As there might be other explosives near, Cobbe retired his left half company some fifty yards, to a depression in the ground, and ordered the rest of the men to lie down. The Kashmír Infantry were also told to fall back, which they at once did, in stolid, Oriental fashion, marching slowly away, as if executing a drill manœuvre, to the distance of a quarter of a mile or so, when, by good luck, they came across an army surgeon, who suggested that they should return. They at once wheeled round, with great equanimity. It is, perhaps, idle to speculate how far they would have gone if they had not met the English doctor, for the Kashmír officers evidently appreciated the military virtue of obeying orders. These retrograde movements were misunderstood by the enemy, who believed they had won a victory in spite of themselves. But not for long. Borradaile hurried up and sent Cobbe over with his company ; but the enemy by this time perceiving their mistake were in steady retreat again, followed by Oldham, Beynon, Moberly, the two orderlies, and the twelve Kashmír Sappers, who pursued, firing volleys as they went, and enjoyed themselves thoroughly. The retreating Chitrális stopped behind every big stone to take steady aim at them. Soon Cobbe and a few of his Pioneers appeared, breathing hard—for the ropes and ladders were anything but easy of descent—but the ground suddenly falls away to the west, so Muhammed Isa's men got hidden by it, and escaped with small loss. Kelly led the rest of his force by a road, shown in the sketch, down into the ravine, and then up again on to the captured position.

So ended the fight at the Nisa Gul, a brilliant piece of work. The loss of the Gilgit force was comparatively small, but the troops had, nevertheless, been under an extremely heavy fire. It would hardly be credited how difficult it is, even for careful marksmen like Chitrális, to hit drab-coloured men, scattered over a great dust-coloured plain. Most of the casualties occurred where men were grouped from necessity, as, for instance, about guns. Only one British officer was touched, Moberly, whose hand, resting at his side, was grazed by a bullet. The undulations of the ground gave sufficient cover against the direct fire from the defences at the edge of the big ravine. Nothing is more uncomfortable than to be subjected to a heavy dropping fire from an invisible enemy, and many of the groups and small parties of Chitrális on the hills were completely hidden. It tries the best troops. The Pioneers were admirably steady and confident, and their discipline was perfect ; in short, they maintained the reputation they have long held, as one of the best regiments of the Punjáb. Good fighting was expected from them; but the behaviour of the Kashmír gunners and sappers surprised everyone, for they are not British-India troops, with scientific training long continued, the possessors of proud traditions, and many of them, the gunners particularly, were recruits. Stewart's thoroughness, his tireless energy, and the power he has of inspiring confidence in Orientals, are the true causes why the battery was so good, while his daring, physical strength and determination, are precisely the qualities which impress Eastern soldiers, and delight their imagination. Young Oldham, too, with his splendid dash and go, carried his twelve men across the ravine simply by the force of his own brave energy. They followed him trustfully, as children obey the voice of one they admire and feel to be strong. Great as were Kelly's achievements, it must be confessed—and he would be the first to admit—that his officers were of wonderful fibre. From Borradaile, the man of unswerving mind and iron resolve, to the youngest subaltern, all were of the finest quality.

The force bivouacked uncomfortably on the plateau a little beyond the enemy's captured works, and opposite to the village of Sanogher. In answer to signals, the baggage was brought on from Mastuj, under a guard of the 14th Sikhs, and the same escort took the wounded back next morning. Stewart had to deliver a funeral oration to his decimated gunners, and then this fighting Irishman, with the big tender heart, devoted himself to soothing the dying moments of a poor young Kashmír artilleryman, wounded in three different places. He was only a boy, and looked sadly out of place in such a scene. Next morning, before starting, Colonel Kelly spoke a few appreciative words to the battery, and gladdened the hearts of the men. The one fear the wounded had was that they might be left behind.

The march from the Nisa Gul to Chitrál, after a visit to Drásan, was most toilsome. All roads had been destroyed by Muhammed Isa, and bridges broken. Rain, and misery at the camping-grounds, followed exhausting days; while the track of the battery was dotted with dead ponies—the requisitioned animals being too weak to replace the powerful mules still on the wrong side of the Shandúr Pass. Drag ropes had continually to be fixed to the guns, and then the men pulled for all they were worth, as the saying runs, to prevent the overloaded brutes pitching headlong off the path. In spite of all efforts, a gun would occasionally fall off the road, and have to be laboriously hoisted up from the carcass of a broken-backed pony. Oldham's Sappers were unceasingly at work mending the damaged pathways.

On the 17th of April the jaded force found itself by the water's edge opposite the village of Baranis, the road in front demolished to the last vestige, and the bridge over the Mastuj river reduced to charcoal. There was nothing for it but to ford. The stream ran strong. Soldiers and coolies were sent through in parties of not less than four or five, but so heavy was the current that several men were washed away—to be rescued skilfully by some of the levies who were stationed midstream, on horseback, for the purpose. The battery detachment stuck to their guns pluckily, amidst the rushing water, while the British officers, mounted and ballasted with six or eight rifles apiece, blundered slowly through the torrent with a straggling line of Sepoys stringing from the ponies' tails. All landed safely in the end.

Most of the 18th was devoted to foraging, so the

march was a short one; but the Sappers, as usual,
worked nearly round the clock. On this day, in back-
waters of the river, ghastly remains of mutilated bodies
were seen, doubtless those of the Sikhs murdered at
Kalak. At the halting-place of Maroi, news came that
Muhammed Isa was holding both banks of a gorge, a
short distance ahead, called the Gulan Gul. He had
been falling back steadily one day's march in front of
Kelly, waiting for reinforcements promised him from
Chitrál. When they arrived, he believed he would be
able to attack with certainty of success.

The Gulan Gul, where he was now posted, is a
stupendous defile, whose wild waters race between precipitous rocks to hurl themselves into the Mastuj river.
Near the point of juncture, there used to be a mere
spider's thread of a bridge; the Chitrális had burnt it
down and entrenched themselves on the farther side.
Kelly consequently directed Bethune to recross the
Mastuj river with a detachment, and enfilade the
position from the opposite bank. To facilitate this
movement, at daybreak of the 19th, Oldham started
with his Sappers, supplemented by some of the skilled
artisans of the Pioneers, to find if the remains of a
bridge seen on the 17th could not be utilised for the
erection of another. They found its near cantilever
gone, the farther one smouldering, and the masonry
red-hot. Indeed, in the middle of the abutment
there was excellent white lime burnt in this self-
constituted kiln. Two of Bethune's soldiers, and some
of the Hunza men, first swam the strong river, and
then Oldham, finding it impossible to make them hear
his instructions, plunged into the water. His header
was applauded by the levies, who always jump in feet
foremost, but the stream was icy cold, and the un-
acclimatised Englishman paid for his unavoidable swim

by two months of fever. At the moment the bridge was completed, word came that it was no longer needed. Muhammed Isa, it seemed, instead of receiving reinforcements, received an urgent summons to Chitrál, so the passage of the Gulan Gul was unprotected. The whole force crossed as soon as the bridge could be repaired, and camped at the village of Koghazi, one march from Chitrál.

Cobbe made a reconnaissance during the afternoon. He had gone about four miles, when men were met coming from Chitrál, spluttering with good news, and bringing letters in my handwriting.

Only one day more, then, and if there were no fighting on hand, perhaps some of those arrears of sleep and rest which Nature was pressing for, might be paid —and how gladly! In the meantime, back to camp to hear the first despatches sent out of Chitrál, with mingled feelings of delight for the safety of the garrison, and pain for the loss of Baird, everybody's friend, and for those who had fallen with him.

THE EAST TOWER

WATER TOWER   NORTH TOWER   THE CHABUTRA

CHITRAL FORT FROM THE ENEMY'S UP-STREAM SANGAR

KELLY

ROAD TO
CHITRAL BRIDGE

SPOT
WHERE
BAIRD
FELL

OLD
MISSION
HOUSE

THE
BAZAAR-
SERAI

HAMLET
ATTACKED
MARCH 3RD

LOWER ROAD

CHITRAL FROM THE VILLAGE OF DANIN

WHITCHURCH

EAST TOWER   STABLES   FLAG TOWER SITE OF SIFAT'S ENCLOSURE
    GUN TOWER   NORTH TOWER
                             WATER TOWER

CHITRAL FORT

SHEWING THE MARBLE ROCK, THE WATER TOWER TUNNEL, AND THE REMAINS OF CAMPBELL'S COVERED WAY

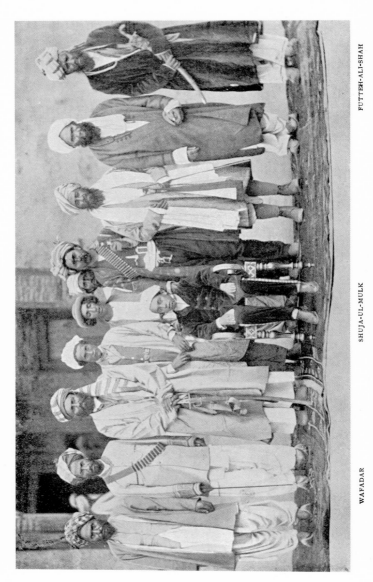

WAFADAR   SHUJA-UL-MULK   FUTTEH-ALI-SHAH

THE LITTLE MEHTAR AND THE CHIEF OF OUR ALLIES IN THE SIEGE

THE EXPLODED MINE

H. K. HARLEY   B. E. M. GURDON   C. V. F. TOWNSHEND

G. S. ROBERTSON

CHAPTER XIX

LOW'S ADVANCE FROM THE SOUTH

WE must now, to weave in all the threads of the story, explain, with brevity, what was happening in India. On the 15th March, a division of troops was ordered to mobilise on the Peshawer frontier by the 1st of April; and a pronouncement to that effect appeared in the *Gazette* of India. The Government commenced to hire camels for transport a week earlier, without saying why, and naturally the Indian Press became greatly excited at being kept in the dark. After a council meeting at Calcutta, the object of the expedition was set forth. Major-General Sir Robert Low received the command of this force, which was to march straight to Chitrál from Nowshera on the Kábul river.

On the 3rd of April the Malakund Pass was stormed, all three infantry brigades taking part in the fight, one regiment only being kept in reserve. It was skilfully planned. There are three passes leading over that rocky range of hills which must be crossed to reach the Swát river from the frontier military station of Mardán. All three were defended against General Low. He made a feint before the Shahkot, the middle one, with the 1st brigade, at the same time that the 2nd and 3rd brigades menaced the Malakund, the most westerly. Finally, concentrating the whole of his force, he rolled it over the Malakund before the enemy could parry the manœuvre.

The Malakund is of vast strength, a place pleasanter
to hold than to attack under a burning sun. Yet,
although it was occupied by seven thousand Patháns,
they were powerless against the tactics of the British
general. An artistic handling of sixteen mountain
guns, firing crushing salvoes wherever the enemy
massed, kept the defenders scattered and embarrassed.
The Guides infantry, with the 4th Sikhs, were sent up
the steep hills to the west, but it was quickly seen that
they could not fully carry out their flanking attack in
time. So the Gordon Highlanders and the King's
Own Scottish Borderers were *loused* by their Brigadier,
Waterfield, a well-known Indian officer, affectionately
nicknamed "the bear" by native soldiers. Racing for
the honour of their regiments, the men swarmed over
the rugged declivities at a wonderful speed, and breathless but triumphant, had crowned the pass by two
o'clock, the 60th Rifles being close up. Considering
their poor armament, for General Low estimated that
only between a third and a fourth were armed, the
remainder simply rolling down rocks or hurling stones,
the Patháns fought splendidly, and therefore suffered
much loss. The British casualties were comparatively
few, eleven killed and forty-seven wounded.

Because of the narrow roadways, the transport
animals jammed, and time was unavoidably lost in
shifting the places of the 2nd and 1st brigades, so
as to get the latter in front. After this was done, the
1st brigade, the following day, had a small but "regular"
engagement with the enemy, including a cavalry charge,
to the north of the range, and camped for the night at
the village of Khár. General Low reconnoitred as far
as the Swát river on the 5th, and a special correspondent,
the late Major "Roddy" Owen, indulged his adventurous
heart by splashing over to the right bank. He was

probably the first European to pass the great stream undisguised. On the 7th, a crossing was effected after a brisk skirmish, ended by a picturesque flounder through the rapid water, and a spirited charge by the 11th Bengal Lancers. Next day, General Low moved his headquarters to Chakdára, on the farther bank. A *contretemps* at the Panjkora river, on the night of the 12th, owing to a sudden rise of flood-water which brought down heavy timbers and carried away a newly-erected bridge, delayed the force four days. At the time of this accident the Guides were on the farther side, and remained for a time in jeopardy, losing their colonel, one of the devoted family of Battye that sacrifices a son in every frontier war. For three days the water continued to rise, as did the Swát river also, whose pontoon bridge was likewise in danger. As General Low depended upon that bridge for his supplies, it was an anxious time.

The Jandol valley was attacked on the 17th, and occupied without further resistance the next morning. General Gatacre set out on the 19th with a couple of battalions, some guns and twenty days' food, for Dír and Chitrál. He is a man whose exploits, based on an almost superhuman energy and power of endurance, may some day become fabulous. After making a record, he sets himself to break it as a point of honour, while he was champion road-maker of the expedition. He crossed the rugged and tedious Jánbatái ridge, and had only moved one march beyond, when there came bad news from Chitrál. Up to the 17th, so ran the messages, the tired garrison, though still holding out, were beaten to their knees. Mines had been burrowed within a few yards of one of the towers, and the portentous gloom hanging over the fort might at any instant be broken into by the flash of an explosion—the signal that all was over.

Between Gatacre and Chitrál there were at least five days' journey, with places where the troops must quarry a passage for the mules, and more than one spot where a dogged enemy could defend himself bloodily. How were the besieged, in such urgent case, to be succoured? Time was not only short, but beyond estimate, for any moment might date the crash of disaster at Chitrál, and let loose men, drunk with victory, to rush madly upon the other infidels directly in the line of retreat. These, and minor considerations, must have shown themselves to the Brigadier without disturbing him. What were frontier generals for, but to overcome the impossible; Kelly had vanquished the Shandúr, why should not Gatacre remove mountains by faith and will, and make the Lowari Pass merely the chief incident of a day's long march? So he signalled to Sir Robert Low for permission to take five hundred British soldiers, two mountain guns, and a few Sappers to rush for Chitrál at all cost—to save, if it were to be so, and to leave nothing undone if it were otherwise decreed. The same tidings which had fired Gatacre, equally fired his chief, and an answer flew back, that the former might cast himself off at once with the assurance that troops and supplies would be pressed after him, under the very eye of Sir Robert Low, who would himself conduct them.

Gatacre and his five hundred lean, hard-bitten Buffs were already stripped and girded for the great race, when fresh messengers brought word that the cloud at Chitrál had passed away. So there was no more need for hurry, and Gatacre carried his brigade over the Lowari Pass on the 25th April, with difficulties that were trifling in face of his cheeriness and "go."

CHAPTER XX

THE STORY GOES BACK TO CHITRÁL

IT is now the time to hark back to Chitrál itself, and
pick up the story where it was abruptly left at
Chapter xii. with the safe retreat of the Gáirat detachments into the fort on March 1st.

On the 2nd March all the troops were in good heart,
and worked hard in carrying inside certain supplies
which had been stored in a large apartment just outside
the main gate. Thanks mainly to Gurdon's cleverness
and vigour, we had collected rations to last the soldiers
for three months. But more food stores were wanted,
because our only hope of defending the fort successfully,
if events forced us to that last resort, lay in our associ-
ating with us in the siege, willingly or involuntarily, as
many Chitrális as possible. This unknown number must
also be provided for. A certain young prince, named
Asfundiar, a cheery boy, and a good sportsman, had
gone over to Sher Afzul. His house at Chitrál, full of
grain, we determined to seize. Amír-ul-Mulk's men
were told off for this work, but, acting under their
master's secret orders, they delayed so long that, in the
end, the supplies were lost. Whereupon the Mehtar,
with maddening simplicity, excused his conduct to me
by saying that he did not want, needlessly, to multiply
his enemies in Sher Afzul's camp.

Eventually, he with all, or nearly all, the remaining
headmen decided on a plan of action. My chief native

Indian assistant was invited to a conference, where Mian Ráhat Sháh, the individual referred to on page 85, acted as spokesman throughout. He began by producing two letters from Sher Afzul—one addressed to his daughter, a widow of the murdered Mehtar, Nizám-ul-Mulk, and the other written to himself. In both of them it was declared that the future relations of Chitrál with the Government of India were to be on the basis that the latter must pay the former an annual subsidy, and that no Europeans were to live in the country. Mian Ráhat Sháh went on to explain that they had unanimously decided that Amír-ul-Mulk and all the Chitrál headmen present, were collectively to inform me that I was in a critical position, and must accept Sher Afzul's terms. There was no alternative. How could we be reinforced, he asked, seeing that all the bridges and the worst pieces of road had been broken down? If I were certain of getting more troops, we might, perhaps, try to hold the fort, but such a plan was not really feasible. I might, indeed, go with some of my men to Mastuj, travelling up the right bank of the Mastuj river, and there collect troops preparatory to returning in force, while the rest of my escort remained behind in the fort with Amír-ul-Mulk; but the best plan was for me to start without delay for Mastuj with all the soldiers. This was the real gist of the proposals; it was the old plan, warmed up, to catch the Gilgit troops on the Baitári cliff. Amír-ul-Mulk and his friends, having resolved to make their peace with Sher Afzul, thought they could not make a nicer peace-offering than a British force, helpless and hopeless, neatly caught on those terrible galleries five miles from Chitrál!

It was arranged that my answer should be spoken to the chiefs assembled in durbar. They were accordingly received, ceremoniously, in a large inner room of the fort, Amír-ul-Mulk being seated upon a large arm-chair at my right. All the British officers were present. Every precaution against treachery had been taken. In front of Amír-ul-Mulk and us British officers the head-men knelt in rows, after the Oriental fashion, on a spread carpet, and the conference began.

After reviewing the existing state of affairs, I went on to remark upon Sher Afzul's apparent alliance with Umra Khán. His obvious hostility to the Government of India also came in for comment. I then showed that Amír-ul-Mulk had been given every chance to prove himself capable of ruling the country. Though helped in many ways, and even officially accepted as Mehtar as far as my powers permitted, it was clear that he could not maintain proper authority, and it was equally clear that he had been listening to the promptings of ill advisers. By this last act he prac-tically resigned the Mehtarship in favour of Sher Afzul, but I had determined to make his younger brother, Shuja-ul-Mulk, the head of the state, condi-tional on the approval of the Government of India.

By a gesture, Amír-ul-Mulk was directed to leave the arm-chair, which was treated as emblematic of a throne, and I then ceremoniously placed the little Shuja-ul-Mulk upon it, and formally entrusted his personal safety to Captain Townshend, the officer who immediately commanded the Kashmír part of my escort. The silence of profound surprise fell upon the durbar; even Mian Ráhat Sháh lost his presence of mind and could only stare fixedly, his face lengthen-ing with astonishment. After a time they recovered themselves sufficiently to profess acquiescence in the arrangement, and to offer homage to Shuja-ul-Mulk A further dramatic element was infused into the scene when Amír-ul-Mulk, rising from his lowly seat

approached timorously and with a deprecating manner
to salute his brother. I then explained that as the
Mehtar was very young he would require experienced
advisers, and that I looked to the princes and headmen
before me to instruct him in the duties of government.

For the present, Amír-ul-Mulk must remain within
the fort, for outside his life was no longer safe. This
was strictly true. It was merely the divinity that
hedges round a Mehtar which preserved him from the
still, but implacable, hatred of Nizám-ul-Mulk's relations. Bereft of this sanctity, he was so generally
despised and disliked that only by compulsion could
a menial servant be got to attend upon the late ruler
of Chitrál.

Present at the durbar was a murderous scoundrel,
the wretch who had actually slain Nizám-ul-Mulk.
Campbell arrested him ; his carbine was found to be
at full cock, but he had been most carefully watched
all the time. Shuja-ul-Mulk, at the instigation of his
uncles, made a first experiment of the reality of power,
by asking that the assassin be handed over to him to
be dealt with justly. This was done, and eventually
the unhappy prisoner was marched to the river bank,
where he was executed with sword strokes.

In the afternoon, Shuja-ul-Mulk held a durbar in the
square yard of the public part of the fort. Drumming,
piping, and rejoicing, of a not very enthusiastic kind,
announced his succession to the Katúr throne, and
many people came to make their obeisance to the boy
sovereign.

Sher Afzul, at half-past four, was known to be at
Aiún with a strong force. All that had passed was
explained to him in a letter, and he was warned that
if he did not come in he must, in the end, be the
sufferer.

CHAPTER XXI

OUR DEFEAT

ON the 3rd March, a fateful day, a reply came from Sher Afzul, and also a document alleged to have been sent by the Chitráli headmen with him. In both it was demanded that Sher Afzul be made Mehtar, and that his stipulations be agreed to. These letters were brought by the prince now infamous as Yádgár Beg. As my illness was severe I received him in bed. He was both intelligent and influential, so I tried everything in my power to make him speak out frankly, and to find what was actually going on at Aiún. After a time, by the help of presents, the Chitráli euphemism for bribes, and by friendly and sympathetic talk, he gradually softened and told me, confidentially, that these letters had no real meaning, as everything turned on certain negotiations which were, at that very moment, being discussed by Umra Khán and Sher Afzul. If those two chiefs came to terms, which seemed inevitable, the latter would immediately press on to Chitrál.

During the afternoon of the previous day, an alarm had gone forth that Sher Afzul's advance guard was on the great Chitrál fan, and not more than three miles away. A trustworthy Chitráli, appropriately named Wafadár (faithful), rode out with a few horsemen and proved the rumour false. Now, a seemingly truthful report declared that a dozen of Sher Afzul's

N

riflemen were actually in the Chitrál bazaar, a serai-like enclosure about 750 yards from the fort walls. It must be understood that we were by no means in a good defensive state. On the west, the main gate side, there were large guest apartments and guard-rooms, where the grain had been stored, and to the south and south-west numerous detached buildings, comprising the temple, pleasure houses, and stables. The advisability of clearing away these structures had been admitted ; it was, indeed, beyond dispute, but until all hopes of peace were gone, it was resolved that they should not be touched, because, in Chitráli eyes, these royal adjuncts of the fort were almost sacred.

Obviously, it was of the first importance that Umra Khán and Sher Afzul should not get their men into these buildings covertly, or under any pretence, for, once there, with our parapets commanded on every side, the fort could be assailed at a terrible advantage, and easily fired. The fact of armed men being in the bazaar looked as if the fuse were lighted and an explosion imminent. Time was badly wanted, not only to clear the precincts of the fort and to level dangerous walls, but also for loopholing and other measures of inside defence. In short, it was necessary, above all else, that the advancing enemy be kept at a distance. Sher Afzul's designs had been truly gauged, and have been already explained, while our main object was to keep him as far from the walls as we could, until troops marched to our relief, or until he and his followers gave up their adventure in despair.

So I now asked Campbell to take out a sufficiently strong party for safety, and make a reconnaissance across the Chitrál plain, to see if it were true that Sher Afzul was there with an armed force. This was at a quarter to four, and in less than half-an-hour two

hundred of the Kashmír Rifles, more than half of our
garrison, fully equipped, marched out under Captains
Townshend and Baird, Campbell being in chief command, and Gurdon accompanying him as a "political"
officer. I was ill and in great trouble, but my anxiety
became so strong that Sher Afzul should not get close
to the fort in its unprepared state, by any crafty Oriental
stratagem or plausible excuse, that I got up, put a
horseman's cloak over my night-clothes, and rode after
the party.

Campbell detached fifty Sepoys to hold the serai-
bazaar, and Baird was sent away forward with an
advance party, leading up some slopes on the right,
to confront about one hundred and fifty men of dubious
intention on the farther side of a great outlet through
the valley boundary of hills to the west, and about a
mile south of the fort. With Baird thrown forward
high up on the left bank of that big ravine, the main
body under Townshend covering my old mission-house,
and between these two a connecting support for Baird,
and with the serai also held in the rear, there was time
to discuss matters. All wayfarers were stopped and
interrogated. Some travelling priests were carefully
questioned. There seemed little, if any, doubt that
Sher Afzul, with an armed party, was in a house or
hamlet hidden from view on the right bank of the
stream, whose outrush through the hills Baird was
overlooking. What numbers were thus concealed could
not be determined. It was 200 or 400, certainly not
more, according to the guesses of our informants. The
whole of our force, save those men in the serai, was now
on the edge of a sinuous curve of high ground, which,
after walling in one side of the polo ground, stretches
to where Baird was posted.

One or two horsemen, all we had, were sent scouting

across and beyond the polo ground. They, however, showed no disposition to push their investigations farther than half-a-mile or so. They rode backwards and forwards, looking very gallant with their long spears, but doing little good. The men over against Baird were differently described as Lutkho men, ready for the fight, and as timorous villagers who had fled for safety to the hills. A balance of opinion amongst the native Indian officials, the brave Rab Nawáz Khán and others, was that they were simple folk terrified at the sight of armed forces. In the end it was settled that it was not too late for a further reconnaissance. Campbell thereupon ordered Townshend forward with a hundred men ; and in an extended double line they marched upon a house which Campbell indicated. Unfortunately, this movement necessitated a descent from the edge of the plateau to the lower level. Perceiving this, Campbell sent a mounted messenger after the detachment with the written order, " left shoulders forward," which would have brought it to the upper ground again, but unhappily this note never reached Townshend, who, following out his original instructions, eventually came upon the enemy somewhat at a disadvantage.

Gurdon was now reverted from " political " to military duty, and placed at Campbell's service, who sent him off with a letter to Baird which embodied my wishes that a single shot should first be fired over the heads of the men at the farther side of the ravine, when, if they proved to be enemies and not simple villagers, they were to be steadily volleyed at and driven back. The note itself has been lost, but there is no doubt that it conveyed exactly what was intended. Unluckily, the written word of the English language is not always incapable of misconception, and the mood of the reader at times influences his grasp of its meaning.

Baird read his instructions, and fired a single shot, which was at once answered by a volley. He then decided that a phrase Campbell had used to the effect that the men across the ravine were "to be turned out" of their position, if they proved hostile, could only mean that he was to descend from his place, cross the bed of the mountain stream, and attack with the bayonet up the opposite slope. No doubt, he was chafing at inaction, for with all his kindliness and gentle manners, there was no braver or more dashing officer in the army. Then, he was fond of military apophthegms, for instance, amongst his papers was found the following—"When you meet an Asiatic go for him"—a sufficiently comprehensive formula. This, perhaps, shows his chivalrous fighting disposition. Gurdon, who always grows cooler as his clear head sees danger, ventured, as a junior, to hint that Baird had not read the letter correctly, and begged he might, at anyrate, be allowed to fetch up the men of the support, who were some little distance away, before the assault was made; but Baird answered that the orders were clear to his mind, and that Gurdon had better remain with him. So they hurried down together, crossed the bed of the stream, and soon found themselves climbing the spur on the other side with but thirteen companions, for the remainder of the men had taken cover. Immediately this move was made the attacked Chitrális retreated a little higher up the hill, then scrambled down into the gorge, to climb and seize the very ground Baird had left.

Taken thus in the flank, as well as overwhelmed from above, by riflemen who were invisible because of the unevenness of the steep slope, Gurdon, a Gurkha officer, Subadár Badri Nár Singh, whose name deserves to be remembered in spite of its outlandish sound to English ears, and three Sepoys were soon all that were left, the

remainder of the party being shot down. Even a small
fox-terrier was amongst the killed. Gurdon started off
a man for Whitchurch, the doctor, and leaving a couple
of Sepoys with poor Baird, who was mortally hit,
actually climbed still farther up the hill, with Badri Nár
Singh, to a spot giving a view of the riflemen above, and
where he could try also to keep down the fire from the
side which Baird had first held, whence the enemy were
now shooting with great skill. In this way alone could
Baird be protected. Time passed, and then Gurdon
saw Whitchurch carry off the stricken officer in a
"doolie," but he still kept his faithful post for some
time longer, until the convoy might fairly be supposed
to be out of danger. Then he hurried down the slope,
energetically collected as many of the laggard men as
he could find, and, with Badri Nár Singh's help, got
them into some sort of order on the bank of the torrent.
Gurdon looked after the right, and the Gurkha posted
himself at the left of the little line thus formed to offer
a cool front to the Chitrális, and to await developments.

No bugle had been heard to blow the retreat, but
that question was decided by a mass of the enemy who
had ascended the right bank of the stream from Sher
Afzul's main party, and now burst through the middle
of the line; by sheer weight they forced Badri Nár
Singh and half the Sepoys down the road Whitchurch
had taken, while Gurdon and the rest of his men were
pressed uphill. With the enemy above, they were thus
completely surrounded. By great fortune the darkness
had grown deeper; and the imperturbable Gurdon,
never losing his nerve for an instant, led his men
quietly back in the very throng of the Chitrális, who
were panting to cut his throat.

Fact is often more surprising than romance. Gurdon,
with his little party, silently, their steps unhurried, but

all hearts beating hard, passed, unrecognised in the
gloom, between the Musjid and my old house, already
crowded with shouting Sher Afzulites.   Thence he
crept to the bank of the Chitrál stream, and ran his
party down the steep incline to the water's edge.   Now
was the time to be quick; and without the loss of
another man, Gurdon hurried along the stream some
quarter of a mile, waded through, and climbed the left
bank, when a straight dash across fields brought him
to the fort, flushed and breathless, but with the pleased
look of one who takes exercise of an interesting kind.
Immediately, at my request, he hurried away with a
fresh detachment, hastily collected, to cover the main
gate of the fort, and at the same time help in the
retreating column, which proved to be close at hand.

We left Townshend's party moving over a long
slope of the convex Chitrál plain, towards a house
pointed out to him by Campbell, as the place where
Sher Afzul probably was.   Campbell himself stayed
with me for a short time on the higher ground to the
right, but soon afterwards, when the firing became
heavy, he went forward, as will be seen, to direct
Townshend's attack.   Townshend found the house
empty, but in front, and a little to his right, lay a
hamlet enclosed by a wall.   There men were noticed
dodging amongst the tree-trunks which clustered
thickly round the houses.   Just then the sound of
sharp firing came from Baird's side—our extreme right.
So Townshend decided that those in front of him must
be the enemy.   Consequently—his detachment volleying, by sections—he continued his advance.   The
hamlet replied furiously.   Townshend had only a
hundred soldiers with him, and of those he kept back
a couple of sections as a support.   About 200 or 250
yards from the enemy the men found fair cover behind

a low stone-reveted bank, but the Chitrális shot carefully, and soon there were several casualties. Townshend
decided to keep his ground, and engage the little village
steadily. His idea was that Baird would eventually
come down from the high ground on the right, and
attack the hamlet from above; when, if the enemy
bolted, he, Townshend, would be admirably placed to
catch them as they ran.

But time went on, and there was no sign of Baird,
while small groups of the enemy began to move around
his left flank, and enfilade him from the direction of
the river. On his right, also, one or two of the enemy's
skirmishers were creeping up; the day was closing, and
it would soon be dark. Campbell was now near enough
to shout to Townshend that he had better rush the
village. Townshend answered that he was trying to
get his supports up. Campbell ran across to him and
then went back and brought up as many men as he
could find. To rejoin Townshend, he had to climb
over the débris of a fallen wall. As he paused on the
top to use his field-glasses, a bullet struck him in the
knee.

The charge could not be carried home. An attempt
was gallantly made, but two brave Kashmír officers and
several men were at once killed, when the remainder
began to lie down and hunt for shelter. As it was
hopeless to persist, Townshend brought them back to
their old position, and reported to Campbell, adding,
as his own opinion, that seeing it was rapidly getting
dark, we ought to retire. Campbell, badly wounded as
he was, sat down and wrote a message to Harley to
bring out the Sikhs to cover his retreat, and told
Townshend to wait a little and then fall back. Of
course, Campbell's intention was to go slowly, but the
instant the enemy perceived the retrograde movement

they came on with ardent yells; their shooting was
terribly galling and well-aimed. Closing in, they yet
offered no mark to our riflemen. Training and heredity
have made them adepts at this kind of fighting, while
their marvellous activity, and the suppleness of their
sinewy bodies, enable them to find cover everywhere.
Occasional gleams of white clothing, head-dress, or
banners, were alone to be seen; even those were rare.
The position of a hostile rifleman was merely indicated
by a little puff of smoke.

Campbell and Townshend tried hard to stave off
the imminent panic. Four men were assigned to the
former, but they hurried him so, that he packed them
off and hobbled along by himself, leaning on his sword.
From the left rear the bullets came thick. A devoted
Brahmin hospital assistant, who had been tending the
wounded with singular devotion, fell groaning to the
earth, with several other men. The poor Indian doctor
offered large rewards to anyone who would carry him,
but he was a heavy man, and mortally hit, and there
was none to aid. A Gurkha seized Campbell's left
hand and refused to leave him. He had to be shaken
off, however, at a wall, which his wounded officer needed
both hands to surmount, preparatory to rolling down
the other side, where his faithful little comrade picked
him up again. Grown bold now, white-robed Chitrális
were running in like wild dogs round a failing deer, but
Campbell managed to keep them off with shots from
his revolver; a quarter of a mile farther on he came to
the little enclosure which I held with a few men.

I had kept along the edge of the high ground to the
right with Campbell, until he went over to Townshend's
party after the fight developed. Eventually my little
party stopped near a small orchard, full of trees, a low
lateral wall running eastward from it at right angles

There the enemy's sharpshooters were so brisk and clever that our horses had to be trotted away sharply to a safer place, while we crouched down under the low wall.

My few followers consisted of Gilgit Rajahs, Rab Nawáz Khán, the little cavalry man, and some Muhammedan clerks and orderlies, as well as two or three Chitrális, who together formed a kind of rough escort for me. On the way a shocking accident nearly happened. A moving group of men was noticed low down on the spur opposite to that where Baird had originally gone, and beneath the Chitrális who were shooting rapidly from above. None of the Gilgit troops being thought of in such a position, it was concluded that this group must be the enemy. Someone suggested a volley; I agreed. Distances were calculated. Already a settling of shoulders on rifle stocks had begun, when a sharp cry of "Stop" was raised. I had recognised Gurdon's long legs. Just in time; shortly afterwards poor Baird was seen stretched on the slope, and was identified by the fox-terrier at his feet. Messengers were sent to Whitchurch, who, mounted by Campbell, galloped uphill, meeting on his way the man Gurdon had sent to find him.

After the horses were hurried away, the fire on our party grew extraordinarily sharp and accurate. The only cover was the low stone wall, and it had to be strictly kept. Bullets went "ishing" just over it with curious monotony, as if a machine gun were working. Raising my head, very occasionally, to look over, I had my fur cap cut; my companions had not to be advised to lie low. As a matter of fact, our only half combatant little company was the object of excessive attention on the part of the Sher Afzulites, who thought us the real attacking force. We could enfilade them to a small extent, and, quite unconsciously, we kept them back until they found out their mistake.

I was desperately weak and suffering, and was alternately doubled up with pain, and made to tingle with pleasure as the cavalry man shouted reports of the progress of the fight. " Now they fly," he would call. " No, they don't." " Yes, yes, they do ; hurrah ! " So it went on almost to the end, each cry growing more and more optimistic. Suddenly the little man, with staring eyes and mouth fixed open, pointed to the right and ejaculated, " They are on us." Startled out of my pleasant feeling of success, I glanced to the left and saw a little party of Sepoys racing back. They must be Townshend's men, then ! But where was their leader? Turning, I begged Rab Nawáz Khán to fire one or two shots, just to steady those rolling in on us from the right, while I got hold of the retreating Gurkhas. It was known afterwards that the brave man did exactly as he was told, and was cut down, hacked in many places, and left for dead, after he had killed a couple of men. He actually stopped the advancing Chitrális for an instant by his pluck, when his rifle jammed and he was at once overwhelmed.

Running across to intercept the men, my weakness was so great that I had to sink upon a stone in the open. It was like a nightmare. " Alas, you are hit," said a voice in my ear, as Sifat Bahádur, the brave Puniál Rajah, ran up with a protecting arm. " No, Sifat, not hit. For God's sake, try and get my pony." Then a strange incident occurred. A Gilgit groom, usually the most timid of men, was seen determinedly bringing up my big galloway, an animal possessed of a tremendous stride, and now snorting with terror. The enemy's fire was wonderfully hot, the earth being thudded into as at the beginning of a mighty hail-

storm. It was a marvel how horse or groom, or anything else, for that matter, escaped. Half-maddened
with fright, the brute was hard to approach, and after
I had been mounted by the two Orientals it seemed
impossible for me to keep on his back. When we
caught up the retreating Sepoys I could not stop him,
but only force him round and round by hauling with
both hands on one rein. In the end I had to throw
myself off, just as the Gilgit groom, cool and most
earnest, ran up and seized the bridle. Near by was
a small enclosure a few yards square. Into this I
hurried all the men that could be got together. Leaning their rifles on top of the rough walls, the Kashmír
Sepoys behaved beautifully; only one or two flinched
from exposing their heads above the breastwork. My
suspense for the next few minutes may perhaps be
imagined. What had become of Campbell, Townshend,
and the others? Baird was not thought of; he, of
course, had been carried back, and was safe in the
fort.

The enemy was firing, seemingly, all round. One
or two Sepoys, who at first could not be stopped, were
now running back towards us, hard, which showed that
there were hostile Chitrális in our rear, and that we
were more or less surrounded. However, our sole duty
was to wait, keep off the enemy, and hope that more
men would come in to the poor shelter. After a little
a Sepoy, on the long south side of the enclosure, raised
a cry, at the same time firing his rifle into the middle
of a mass of men emerging out of a gloom enlivened,
intermittently, by fire sparks which fell from the muzzles
of the matchlocks, which had now joined in with Sher
Afzul's riflemen. Heaven send that that soldier's shot
went harmless!

In another instant Campbell and Townshend, with

the remainder of their party, were in the enclosure.
Campbell was the last, or very nearly the last, to arrive.
Even at such a moment his picturesque appearance
stamped itself on my memory. Without head-covering
of any kind, he had literally thrown away his scabbard;
a roughly - bandaged knee showed he was severely,
probably dangerously, wounded. As he limped in, chin
in the air, with a wrathful glance over the shoulder—
the rigid tension of his right arm and wrist made the
sword vibrate, and told graphically all that was passing
in his mind—he was the ideal of a man brimming over
with fight. A great crisis seems to accentuate a man's
characteristics, and on this occasion Campbell, who
has naturally a somewhat jaunty bearing, looked the
type of an Irish cavalry soldier, though from his name
he is probably a Scotsman.

In answer to me he said he was merely hit in the
knee, and went on looking after the men. Three horses
had now been brought into the shelter of the walls, and
I bawled to Campbell to mount one. Thinking this
meant he was to leave his men, he demurred, and
begged to be allowed to stay with them. He was
almost forced on to an animal in the end. In a rapid
conversation with Townshend it was decided that the
latter should bring along the detachment quickly, while
I was to try to get to the fort and bring out Harley
with his Sikh company, for neither of us knew that
Campbell had already sent an order to that effect.
Yet once more, quite calm and unruffled, my Gilgiti
brought up the horse, and with Sifat Bahádur's help
got me into the saddle. This was the last piece of
energy that groom ever showed. He got back to the
fort safely; then he collapsed. For weeks afterwards
he sat motionless and dazed. He could not even be
induced to bring water for his horse by the covered

way. As he believed himself ill and unable to work, no one interfered with him. His limited stock of manhood had been too severely trenched upon, but his devotion on the 3rd March was not forgotten.

My frightened animal started off with big bounds, while Sifat Bahádur, who had protested all the time against my going, yelled for me to come back, as the low boundary walls were already dotted with the enemy's swordsmen; but the horse was now practically uncontrollable, however much I might have wanted to stop him. With a great leap he cleared both the walls of a narrow lane, and then strided down a series of small drops from one terraced field to another. Finally we landed on the polo ground. There a group of Chitrális on foot, flourishing their swords, charged, but the pace was too good, and one abrupt swerve avoided them altogether. Now from the left and from the ridge above, a lively fire was opened by Chitráli matchlock men, but they also did not allow for the speed we were going, and most of their bullets fell behind. The firework-like effect of the sparks belching out from the ancient weapons at close quarters was both exciting and confusing.

At the upper end of the polo ground, near the Chitrál torrent, I was able to take a pull at the horse preparatory to a rush through the hamlet, just below the house of a useful friend of ours, Futteh Ali Sháh. There I found two faithful Chitrális mounted, and armed with long spears. We three splashed through the torrent, heads low, and crouched in our saddles, to gallop hard and run the gauntlet of the narrow lanes between the hovels, when we saw, to our great content, that the place was empty, save for a few old women seated on the housetops, who seemed too aged even for astonishment.

Farther on, near the fort, we came on Harley advancing at the head of his Sikhs, in line. At the moment that Campbell marched out with his reconnaissance party Harley was outside on duty. When he got back and took charge he brought in all his men, posting them, and the remainder of the Kashmír infantry, on the parapets to await events. A few long shots were fired from across the river, one man being hit, but there was no serious attack. Shortly before six o'clock he was handed Campbell's orders to take out his men and cover the retreat. The messenger, a soldier of the Central India Horse, Campbell's orderly, undertook to show the way. He was evidently a little at fault, but a hundred yards from the walls they came upon me, and I sent them up to the serai.

I was debating how to ensure that stragglers following along the road I had come should not fire into Harley's men, marching in the serai direction. No one would volunteer to go, although two men started obediently enough, when ordered to warn all detached soldiers how things stood. To make quite sure, I was thinking of riding back myself, but first shouted after Harley to ask how many men were left in the fort. "About forty, sir," called back that ever-cheerful Irishman, as he trudged on in front of his Sikhs. He under-estimated the number considerably, but his reply made me catch my breath. The bridge and the towers commanding it were luckily still held by Gurkhas, but an enterprising enemy might easily get round through the trees on the west, and attempt, perhaps, to rush the fort. I hurried inside. There was indeed a scene of confusion.

Harley had formally handed over custody of the place to a Dogra officer, who was paralysed at his own responsibility, aided, no doubt, by a vivid imagination.

He could merely reply to my orders by a graceful bow, somewhat oddly combined with a military salute. In consternation and doubt some Sepoys were trying to close the gates. A rather dull-witted, but brave Gurkha officer came to the rescue. Men were rapidly collected and pushed outside to the west to cover the main gate, while other guards were sent to the parapet above it. A sharp lookout was enjoined everywhere. These arrangements occupied some time, and then Gurdon arrived. He at once hurried to the south-west corner of the fort to support Harley, if necessary, but he had gone but a few yards when the retreating force came in together, followed by the steady Sikhs. Soon all were inside the walls once more.

Campbell and Townshend, who worked most zealously, brought the defeated Kashmír troops along the east side of the polo ground, with much skill, exposing them as little as possible to the enemy's skirmishers. They rallied the men just before they crossed the bridge over the Chitrál stream and entered the serai, but the soldiers were a little out of hand, so when Harley in the darkness saw a confused-looking crowd tumbling out of the bazaar enclosure, he concluded that it was the enemy.

Now comes an undoubted incident. The Sikhs were in line. Shots were falling all round and between them, and wild matchlock work was going on in every direction. Any troops in the world might have been a little excited, as they were several hundred yards from the fort, with no supports as far as they knew, and were being shot at on three sides. When the mob-like mass of men rushed out from the bazaar, Harley gave his Sikhs the word, " Present." Campbell, fortunately, heard it, and raised a warning shout at the very moment that Harley recognised the grey horse he rode. It was a close shave, but so absolutely cool and in hand were the Sikhs, that not one rifle was let off; and Campbell's party passed between the Sikhs, standing grim and silent with fixed bayonets. Harley gave Campbell 200 yards' start, and after firing two or three volleys, which effectually drove back the more adventurous of the pursuing enemy, retired to the fort slowly, and in that way gave numerous stragglers, coming by the lower road with my messengers, time to reach its protecting walls.

No sooner was everyone inside, than an informal roll-call showed that Baird, Whitchurch, and their party were missing. A sorrow too heavy for thought fell on our hearts, but there was work to be done. Campbell was peremptorily sent off to hospital, and Townshend, as the next senior officer, succeeded him in immediate military command. He and I decided that we must try and give the defeated troops a few hours' repose to recover themselves, for the effect of a disaster on soldiers is rarely temporary, and is too often hard to remedy. The parapets and towers were manned, the trustworthy Sikhs keeping a sharp eye on the main gate and on the river front. Now poor Campbell and the other wounded had to be attended to, and I went to see what amount of skill the native Indian dispensary doctor possessed. Campbell was found to have his knee-cap shattered by a bullet, while deeper and graver injuries were suspected.

Desperate emergencies sometimes justify drastic action. Thus, finding that medical skill does not mellow and improve by being put aside for years, I nevertheless, trusting to my old surgical principles as a substitute for recent experience, seized a bottle containing carbolic acid dissolved in water, and poured the strong mixture relentlessly over and into Campbell's

o

wound. The resulting pain was hardly less great than his indignation at such rough treatment, and it required all his politeness and self-control not to say what he felt. It may be here mentioned, that although convinced I had done right at the time, I never reflected upon this episode without something like remorse, until I was assured long afterwards, by the most famous surgeon in London, that my prompt, if vigorous, action probably saved Campbell his leg, and enabled him, less than two years afterwards, to make one of the champion polo team of the Indian cavalry.

Hardly was this work done when the astounding news was brought that Baird and Whitchurch were outside the fort at the garden entrance. It was quite true. How we scrambled to unbar the door! We British officers pressed outside to find Whitchurch, tired, breathless, and white, with his hands clasped under Baird's arms, his labouring breast supporting the drooped head of his dying friend, who had a moment before received yet another bullet wound in the face. Several Gurkhas completed the group. They had helped Whitchurch to carry in the kind, brave, little soldier who was obviously death-stricken. We were most anxious about taking down the names of these Sepoys, and did so hurriedly. It is, therefore, possible that one or two included in our list had no right to be there, for the lantern was dim, and the excitement considerable, but it is certain that no man entitled to a place in that honourable band went unrewarded.

Next I had to indite despatches, and with Gurdon's help send off messengers to Mastuj, and then perform the most pleasant act of that unhappy day, and thank Whitchurch formally, but with a full heart, for his devoted courage.

One chief reason why the retreat had been made with

so much comparative success was that the bridge and the towers commanding it were all the time held by our soldiers. Although swarming on the opposite bank the enemy could not cross the river. It was clear that this guard must now be recalled and the post abandoned, for it could not be rationed. The question was how and when should this be done? Campbell and Townshend wanted to try and get the men in during the night, while I was of the contrary opinion, on the ground that in the daylight we could give effective help if it were needed. However, the orders sent out were misunderstood, and the men came back in the early morning, while it was yet dark, and without loss. The enemy occupied the deserted position at once, shouting with delight. For an hour afterwards they beat their drums in triumph. This retirement, though absolutely necessary in the circumstances, was, of course, a confession that we were completely defeated, and that no Kashmír soldiers could any longer remain outside the fort, so perhaps there was reason for the extravagant elation of the victors. A certain number of the Chitráli princes and headmen of doubtful loyalty had been quartered outside in the summer-house. Seeing this final turn of events, they now fled and went over to Sher Afzul. They were as sure as he was that the fort was untenable, and wisely, according to their lights, joined the winning side.

About eleven o'clock and consequently before this conclusive event, the sentries reported that a dying man, in a litter, was at the main gate. It was found to be Rab Nawáz Khán. Left for dead, and stripped, he had been found by one of the illegitimate princes, who, while decently covering up the body, discovered that it still had life. With the help of his servants, he brought the wounded man to the gate. He himself refused to enter, but remarked that if in the end the British were successful, he begged that his charitable action would be remembered. Thus he was able to hold the position most loved by Chitrális—that of a man who does not stand to lose anything whichever side wins.

The dead had been left on the field. Inquiry showed that out of the men actually engaged the casualties amounted to thirty per cent., while the number killed was especially heavy—half of the total. Perhaps an extract from my private diary may fitly end this chapter. It runs : "The true reason of our defeat was that we found the enemy too strong and too well-armed for us. There were other reasons also. Our men behaved well on the whole. A large number behaved splendidly ; an almost equal number behaved indifferently : the one party counterbalanced the other. But it was quite clear that the Rághunáth (the name of the Kashmír regiment) Sepoys had not the faintest idea of musketry. Their shooting was terribly wild— atrociously bad. They fumbled with their rifles, let them off at all manner of unexpected times, dropped their ammunition about, and behaved, many of them, as if they had never before fired a shot. There is too much reason to fear that some of our men, at any rate, were hit by the wild, unaimed shooting of their own comrades. Some of the men were capable of being rallied ; others no man could have stopped. One humorously smiled at me, and said, 'All right, Sahib, but I am wounded, see!' and he exposed a shattered arm. Others excitedly exclaimed, 'Barút nahin' (meaning they had no more cartridges), and twisting their fingers with the Eastern gesture which means 'I have nothing.' Then they rushed on with wide open eyes, and pupils dilated like those of a hunted animal. I feared to seize such men and examine their

pouches, lest others equally panic-struck might seek to
justify their conduct by throwing away the precious
ammunition. Still, on the whole, considering the circumstances, and considering the noble behaviour of
some of the men, the Rághunáths did not do badly.
They were hampered by their greatcoats (it was a warm
afternoon), and by their other clothes, while they had
to fight a numerous, better armed, far more skilful, and
far more active enemy. The way Sher Afzul's men
took cover during the advance was wonderful. I hardly
saw one of them until the swordsmen came at me.
They hid behind rocks, trees, and walls with such skill,
and dashed from one cover to another with so much
agility, that in the deepening gloom they were practically invisible."

The above extract was written at the time when all
facts and impressions were fresh in my mind. It remains to be added that the Kashmír Sepoys were armed
with Sniders having the grooves worn away—such as
are known, flippantly, as gas-pipe rifles. Perhaps it is
not surprising that the Chitrális, with us in the fort,
avowed that Kashmír troops were not only no better
than they were in the old times, but that it would
be impossible ever to improve them.

CHAPTER XXII

BAIRD'S DEATH

THE following day, the 4th March, the siege began.
A dropping fire was kept up on the fort all day
long from the village of Danín, across the river, and
from the high ground all round us. Campbell had to
be removed from the durbar room, where he was first
placed, into a somewhat dark but safe apartment to
the south. Although convinced that he could not be
hit where he lay, he had to confess that it was poor fun
to lie in bed with bullets striking the walls. His new
room was utilised as the store-place of the officers' mess,
because, as he could never leave his couch, he was able
to watch, unceasingly, over the precious pea-flour, the
few tins of tobacco, the scanty condiments and pro-
visions, and the four bottles of brandy, which comprised
our whole stock. So, though badly wounded, Campbell
was helpful from the first, and later he became, as will
be seen, a kind of special intelligencer for me. Vigorous
efforts were begun to knock down the old stables and
other buildings on the garden side, both to prevent the
enemy approaching too near the walls, and to procure
firewood and timber for interior defences.

The Kashmír troops did the demolitions, but only
with partial success. Willing they undoubtedly were,
but a certain unhandiness made them slow and clumsy,
while it also attracted the enemy's notice, and one man
was badly shot through the thigh. It was clear some

change was necessary ; so, a few days later, I organised a special corps from horse-keepers, officers' servants, and low-class Chitrális in the fort, and placed them all under the command of the strong-willed Sifat Bahádur, who has an instinct for dominating frontier men of that rank. From that time forward, one of the very remarkable sights of the siege was to watch Sifat's men at work. Walls were pulled down, or defences run up, heavy timbers adjusted, or wooden pillars dragged from the condemned roofs they supported, with the maximum of speed and effectiveness, and much more quietly than would be readily believed. From first to last, none were seriously injured while thus employed. Night was the time usually chosen for such work, but if it had to be done in the daylight, there was never any hesitation.

Perhaps the most curious point about their working was the light-hearted gaiety of these people. An abject Balti, one of a race remarkable for its absence of manly virtues, a poor wretch who at ordinary times would throw down a load and sit trembling or dart about mad with fear, even at the suspicion that he was being shot at, might be seen, under Sifat's rule, skipping across the open, full of fun, grinning at the dust kicked up by the bullets, and dodging from cover to cover as though he were a child playing a merry game. With energies seemingly as everlasting as their good spirits, that nimble labour-corps proved invaluable. Not only was the heavy work skilfully done, but the troops were saved the fatigue of uncongenial tasks, conserving their strength for military duties.

But to return to the record of the 4th March. On this day Baird died. During the morning Whitchurch informed me there was no gleam of hope, that the poor fellow had but an hour or two of life, and that he

particularly wished to see me privately. I found Baird
propped up into a sitting position with pillows, his right
arm round the neck of a Kashmír servant, who had
knelt in one position for several hours holding his dying
master's hand, from which the thumb had been severed,
with that kind patience and womanly tenderness so
often found amongst Orientals. A pad and bandage at
the waist showed where the mortal wound was, while
a third bullet had struck him at the fort gate, as has
already been told.

In low tones, but with perfect clearness, Baird began
to speak. He knew he was dying, he said. His breathing space seemed to grow smaller and smaller. But he
did not mind dying. It was a soldier's death (here the
faded eyes lighted up for a moment), but he wanted to
tell me about Whitchurch. Then he related the brave
things that all the world knows now. How Whitchurch
stuck to him always, never leaving him for an instant
except when compelled to place him on the ground
while he, with Badri Nár Singh and his few Gurkhas,
charged and dispersed hostile bands of Chitrális. Could
even Whitchurch deserve a higher panegyric than that
spoken in interrupted words by the comrade he had
brought in, with so much scorn for his own safety, to
die amongst friends? Baird urged me "not to forget
Whitchurch." · Speech was then difficult for me—it
is hard now to recall this scene with undimmed eyes—
but I put my hand gently on the bloodless forehead, and
gave a solemn promise. He made one or two further
requests of a sacred character, for he was as piously
filial to his widowed mother as he was urgent about
his brave friend. Just then a message came that I was
wanted at the main gate. I moved towards the door
and looked back. The pallid lips slowly framed a half
smile, the kind eyes grew soft, while, with a voice weak

but almost cheerful, Baird murmured, "Goodbye, sir; I hope all your plans will come right." What could be answered? I automatically uttered a wish I knew to be impossible, that Baird would yet help me to carry them out, and then hurried away.

On my return a little later, Whitchurch, standing by the door, reported that Baird was unconscious. He expired shortly afterwards. A fit and proper ending to this story was Whitchurch's remorseful account to me, a few days later, of his "brutality" to Baird. He told how, as he was carrying Baird in the litter across the polo ground, the enemy closed round. Three of the four carriers were shot dead and the other mortally hit. Of course, the doolie dropped to the ground, and, naturally enough, the Gurkhas fell back for a moment and left Whitchurch. Although of short stature, Baird was thick-set and muscular. Whitchurch could not lift him, so he pulled his right hand over his own shoulder, and circling his waist with his left arm dragged him along the ground for some distance, when Badri Nár Singh brought his men back again. It was touching to perceive that Whitchurch evidently thought he had used his dying friend roughly, and was unconscious of the steadfast heroism which his narrative disclosed.

It would be gratuitous to moralise on such facts, yet one cannot refrain from exulting that in this· practical fame-seeking age, when a soldier's glory is as marketable a commodity as any other, British officers can nevertheless be found ready to die for purely unselfish sentiments of comradeship, or to devote their last moments to securing the just recognition of another's merits. Baird, gentle as he was brave, and possessed of that sublime tact which springs from innate kindness of heart, lies buried on a distant frontier and among an alien people; but his memory will linger for awhile even in India, that land of forgetfulness, and his story may perhaps remain in the minds of others than those who knew him in life. Whitchurch's name is enrolled in the list of the Queen's heroes, and is indelibly stamped on the hearts of those who were his brother officers at Chitrál.

Poor Baird, wrapped in his soldier's greatcoat, was buried the same night, in a building immediately in front of the main gate. Harley, who undertook to dig the grave, at first led some men quietly into the garden on the opposite side of the fort, but found the soil there a mere network of tree roots, and, after several trials, had to give up the attempt and return. Before they did so, the alarm sounded, and there was firing from the west. The Kashmír riflemen guarding the east tower, seemingly did not know what was going on in the garden, and fired a couple of volleys at Harley's party, but, as that officer subsequently remarked, " Luckily for us, on this occasion, the Rághunáths were in the habit, when they fired from the parapets, of holding their rifles at an angle of elevation instead of depression, and the bullets lodged in the tops of the chenar trees!"

CHAPTER XXIII

BESIEGED

A THOROUGH consideration of all points connected with the defence took place on the 5th March. There was sufficient ammunition, but none to spare—namely, 300 rounds a man for the Martini-Henry rifles of the Sikhs, and 280 rounds for the Sniders of the Kashmír troops, with a little over. Food was scantier than we expected. The Bengali Commissariat Agent had returned as in stock a certain quantity which he only expected to receive in return for advances paid to local dealers. However, the little Mehtar Shuja-ul-Mulk handed over to me all his private stores, and finally, it was ordered that each man was to receive one pound of flour a day as the basis of his diet. This poor allowance would enable the garrison to hold out for three months. It was to be supplemented by rations of ghi (clarified butter), the eastern soldier's delight, and condiments, as far as the limited supply of those articles would stretch. There was a little rice available for the officers' table, but the few sheep had to be reserved for the sick and wounded in hospital.

To grind the corn properly was a difficulty which was never completely overcome. Harley had amongst his Sikhs an invaluable man who seemed able to do anything and everything which required skilful hands. But the only stones for him to shape into hand mills were of a wrong kind and soft, consequently they were continually wearing away, and the flour was always mixed with gritty particles. As a result, the men got dysentery and other internal ailments. We soon found that the Commissariat Agent was a fair organiser, and able to relieve us of all details connected with the payment of the mill-workers—the odds and ends of people about the fort who laboured well and cheerily for liberal wages. The Bengali himself proved interesting in many ways: in the first place, he thoroughly knew his business, and issued the daily rations quickly and without causing a grumble. Next, he was a frank coward, but lost no man's respect thereby, for his avowed tremors never interfered with duty. A man shot dead alongside of him at the scales probably added no additional shakiness to the figures in the checking book. He crossed dangerous places looking sea-sick, but never thought of shirking the risk. Indeed, his timidity almost attained the dignity of one of those physical infirmities which excite admiration when an afflicted person triumphs over it, or at any rate does not permit it to interfere with his vocation. How we should have got on without this feeble-bodied, weak-nerved individual, it is hard to guess.

All unnecessary mouths — that is to say, useless prisoners and so forth — were sent away, but there remained inside the walls no less than 550 persons to be fed. We had just over 340 riflemen, but, excluding those in hospital, only 83 of them were Sikhs—good shots and trustworthy soldiers. Fifty-two Chitrális were included in our numbers—people not to be trusted; indeed, they were always carefully guarded, with one or two exceptions, whenever there was an alarm. On the other hand, they were necessary. Without their help, and without their peculiar knowledge of local

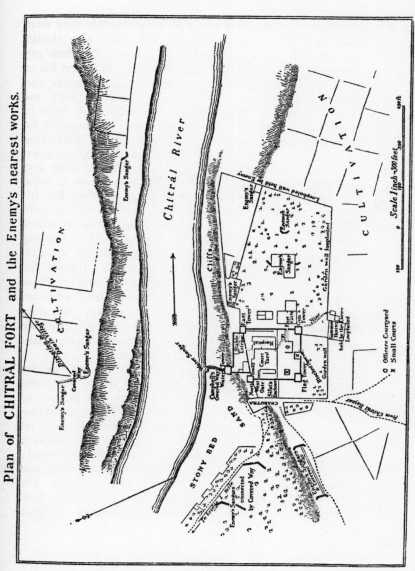

Plan of CHITRÁL FORT and the Enemy's nearest works.

methods of assaulting and defending fortified places, we should have done badly.

As will be seen, we had no real fighting after the 3rd March, except when the Gun Tower was fired, and on the day of Harley's sortie. We merely stayed on the defensive, exhausting our ingenuity and our limited resources in making the place impregnable. For such work the Chitrális associated with us were invaluable. They also gave a certain limited but useful moral support, including, as they did, the little Mehtar and his brother, Amír-ul-Mulk, as well as six or seven others of the most important men in the country—princes and chiefs.

The sufferings to be borne during a protracted siege are not to be measured entirely by the number of men killed and wounded, or by the semi-starvation and sickness the garrison may have to endure. There are other miseries as well, minor, no doubt, but real. Perhaps the worst are anxiety, confinement, bad sanitation, over-crowding, and fœtid smells especially, for although the nose, like the mind, becomes intermittently deadened to prolonged sensations of the same nature, yet it is long before it grows callous to really bad stinks. Imagine what it must be for five hundred and fifty persons to be cooped up in a space eighty yards square for forty-seven days! It was at first proposed to dig latrine trenches in the open space of the courtyard, but I finally settled they must all be outside the walls on the river side—a happy decision, as it proved.

During the 5th March, under the protection of a white flag, a messenger brought two letters, one from Sher Afzul, the other from two chiefs, kinsmen and lieutenants of Umra Khán, lately arrived in Chitrál, with a thousand men, a large number of whom were said to be armed with good military rifles. The purport of the two communications was identical ; they demanded that Sher Afzul be formally recognised as Mehtar of Chitrál, and that I should at once march back to Gilgit, under the safeguard and guarantee of the Jandol Kháns. A brief acknowledgment of these documents was sent back by the man who brought them. This individual was by no means unfriendly in manner, but inclined to talk freely. We discovered that the Chitráli losses in the fight on the 3rd March had been small, less even than was imagined, and that they probably did not exceed ten or fifteen casualties altogether, while the only man of mark killed was that ill-mannered envoy of Sher Afzul who came to me at Gáirat. After getting as much news from our informant as we could, he was dismissed with gifts of money.

This was the initiation of a consistent policy. It was clear that the enemy was too strong for us. The greater part of our troops were still demoralised by defeat; fighting was, therefore, to be avoided when possible. All we could do was to lie low, strive to counter all devices or stratagems of the besiegers, and hope either that they would in time be disheartened and grow hopeless, or be driven away by a relieving column from Gilgit. The bad site of the fort, commanded as it was on every hand, and the grave danger there was of its being fired, owing to the large amount of wood used in its construction, made it of supreme importance that our opponents should, if possible, be kept from attacking us determinedly. To accomplish this, the obvious method was to induce a belief that food was scarce. My Indian clerks played up to this plan ably, and their occasional small lapses caused no suspicion, for the Chitrális in the fort gave us great, though unconscious, help. With a very few exceptions, they were all Sher Afzulites,

and, consequently, each was anxious to be the sender
of good tidings to that prince. They therefore
seized every chance of whispering to messengers with
flags of truce, or of sending word in any other possible
way to Sher Afzul, "that So-and-So bids him be full of
hope for the Feringhis have no food, many are sick
and hurt, and all must soon surrender." Many of these
men fully believed what they said, for it was obvious
that from the first no one had enough to eat.

Another important aid in furtherance of our design
was to encourage flags of truce, to get armistices as
often as possible, and to prolong all negotiations.
Messengers, therefore, were made much of, and bribed
to smuggle the food we knew they could not bring.
Our end was gained when they related how hungry we
must be.

To cheer up the garrison, on the 6th, fourteen men,
including Badri Nár Singh, were formally put in orders
as proposed for the *Order of Merit* for their pluck and
steadfastness in remaining with Whitchurch on the
3rd March. This Indian decoration for native soldiers
is divided into three classes. It is the reward of
bravery, and carries with it a life-pension. A gallant
and lucky Sepoy may, by successive acts of courage,
ascend from one grade to another, the perpetual allowance increasing at each step. Probably a more popular
or more useful institution for Eastern soldiers could
not be devised. As hinted before, it is possible that
more men were included in this list than strict justice,
apart from sworn evidence, would have admitted,
for the total number with Whitchurch was certainly
fewer. He himself could only identify Badri Nár
Singh and three others, while Badri Nár Singh, when
asked who were his companions on the famous occasion, sent in the name of every man in his section

However, the prompt publication of the recommendation did a great deal of good, and served to enliven, as well as to stir the ambitions of, the Kashmír detachment.

On the same day an envoy of importance came to see me, protected by a flag of truce. This was no less a person than Umra Khán's "Diwán" (which may perhaps be translated in this instance as financial minister and confidential adviser). He was an astute-looking man, dressed as a Pathán, but actually a Hindu. A large hooked nose gave a somewhat predatory character to an intelligent if impassive face. There was a long preliminary talk, which ended in our agreeing upon the polite fiction that Umra Khán's private secretary was incompetent, and could neither write Persian correctly nor lucidly translate it into Pushtu, and that, therefore, Umra Khán and I might possibly have been at cross purposes for some time past. In this way the path was cleared for the Diwán *Sáhib* to tell his master's story in his own way.

He began by protesting that I had imprisoned Umra Khán's messengers, which was quite untrue, but gave the speaker the moral superiority of accepting gracefully, and with dignity, the necessary explanations. Then he observed, without the shadow of a smile, how sorry Umra Khán was that Gurdon should have gone so near to Drosh fort on the 18th of February (see page 88), and yet have departed again without seeing him. As Gurdon's invitation to stay was a well-directed volley of musketry, this point also was soon dismissed. Next, it seemed that the Jandol Khán was hurt at my suddenly leaving Gáirat without publishing my intention. Probably there was sincerity in this remark, for a further delay there might have caused the capture of our little force by Jandol men brought along the side

valley by its faithless Chitráli guards, and interposed
between us and Aiún. " But," proceeded the Diwán
Sahib, " Umra Khán is still the friend of the British,
and had positively warned Sher Afzul not to fight with
the 'Colonel Sáhib' (the British Agent)." Not only
had he done this, but he had actually sent his two
kinsmen and a thousand men, not to support Sher
Afzul, as the vulgar might suppose, but to serve as
a kind of police, and to prevent any collision, even if
they had to employ force.

Nothing irritates an independent frontier man more
than to be convicted even of the most glaring and
obvious lie. Such a coarse and rude action is un-
pardonable in his eyes. Therefore, the Diwán was
not asked if the steady fire daily poured into the fort
by the Patháns was also an act of covert friendship.
His remarks were simply met by a kind smile, which
he returned in a pensive manner, and continued.
Somewhat inconsequentially he hinted that the Amír
of Kábul was helping Sher Afzul, and then openly
declared that all Muhammedans were united together
against the English to drive them out of Chitrál.
Finally, he played his best card in alluding to the fate
of poor Cavagnari, slain at Kábul in 1879, and explained how that brave officer had been killed simply
for want of such a friend as Umra Khán desired to be
to me. As a disinterested person he urged me to leave
the fort and return to Gilgit, or to Asmár if I preferred
the latter road. Umra Khán would be answerable for
our safety in either direction, and was even prepared to
explain matters personally to the Peshawer authorities,
if the "brave Colonel" were afraid to take upon himself the responsibility of retiring from Chitrál without
orders from the Government of India.

I gravely thanked the Diwán Sahib for his advice,
P

and expressed my gratitude to Umra Khán for sending me an envoy of his rank and ability. It was gratifying to hear how anxious the Jandol chief was about my safety. At the same time, as a soldier, Umra Khán would reflect that it was impossible for us to evacuate the fort; and perhaps, on the whole, it would be better if he addressed himself in future to Mr Udny in the Kunár Valley, as, in the circumstances of a siege, it was difficult to receive his representatives properly. Not till six o'clock in the evening did the Diwán Sahib take himself and his inscrutable countenance away.

All the 6th and 7th there was much to be done in the way of making volley loopholes, and in arranging log head-cover on the parapets. Some of this work had to be altered subsequently. Volley loopholes are good against an enemy that attacks with a masterful rush, but they are useless against marksmen who cannot be seen, and who never forget that, because of the cruelly hard restrictions imposed on the frontier contraband trade in stolen ammunition, a poor Chitráli can nowadays get no more than five or, at most, six cartridges for a rupee. Therefore he aims his rifle from an improvised rest, and carefully; also, as a reminiscence of matchlock shooting days, he likes to get near his object. Consequently smaller loopholes had to be substituted for the larger and dangerous variety at first made. A dropping fire was kept up desultorily by the enemy while daylight lasted. Each night there were slight alarms, when the garrison, still wanting in experience, responded with unnecessary commotion and much sounding of bugles.

CHAPTER XXIV

LIFE UNDER FIRE

EVER since our defeat on the 3rd March, it had
been a chief object to send news of what had
happened to Mastuj. Four days in succession men
were induced to try and get letters through the cordon
which was tightening round us, but on the 7th of
March no one would make the attempt. We were
anxious about that convoy of ammunition which
Moberly had been told to send down to Chitrál for
the use of the local levies ordered up from Gilgit. It
was thought probable that the convoy had not started,
for there was no urgency about it, and we were to get
two days' warning before it left Mastuj. Nevertheless,
bearing in mind the singular power of duplicity which
the Chitráli possesses, there was danger of the truth
about recent events not having reached the ears of the
commander of Mastuj, and that therefore the cartridge
boxes, and their guard, might be in jeopardy.

On the 7th I sent out a spy, carefully instructed in
his part, to find if my former messengers had been caught.
Supposing all went well, he was to creep back at night
to the marble rock by the river edge, at the end of the
covered way, where the sentries would be warned about
him. During the night the enemy made a demonstration
against the north-west corner of the fort with matchlock
men, and shortly afterwards a fire was discovered in that
part of the waterway which runs under the river tower. It

blazed up gaily, but there was never much danger. A couple of water-carriers constituted the entire force necessary to cope with it. Afterwards, we learned that my spy had gone straight to Sher Afzul and told him everything, whereupon a man under sentence of death was offered a free pardon if he would play the *rôle* of the returning spy and fire the water-tower. He jumped at the chance, and, after setting light to his combustibles, got away uninjured, but he was too flurried to do the work properly. The sentries on the walls allowed him to enter and begin what it only perhaps required coolness to turn into a successful enterprise. The nights of the 8th and 9th were comparatively quiet. Men were seen amongst the trees to the north-west quite close to the walls. What their object was could not be discovered. A few volleys were fired and they ran away.

On the 10th March the first week of the siege was ended.

Nothing remarkable had occurred; Sher Afzul seemed to be taking matters easily, possibly because he expected in a few more days that the fruit, rapidly growing overripe, would fall of itself into his mouth. Also, it was noticed, on the 9th, that large numbers of men were moving up the valley. They marched along the highest ridges to the west, far out of range. We conjectured that their object was to block the road against reinforcements from Gilgit. Townshend reported to me on the same date that the Kashmír troops were still depressed, and evidently had not recovered from their bad shaking on the 3rd. All, including Campbell, agreed that it would be hopeless to rely upon them for a sortie or other offensive measure just then, and that any action of that kind would certainly result in the loss of one or more of our few British officers. Great strides had been made during these seven days in making the fort secure.

Sifat Bahádur's corps had done wonders. The stables on the river front had been loopholed, and made into a good flanking protection to our covered water-way, and both ends of the stables enclosure were properly blocked up with strong walls pierced for rifle-fire.

Patháns and Chitrális alike seem to have no experience in making direct assaults on a fortress. Even the current stories of Umra Khán's prowess and originality —how he battered with cannon and then stormed hostile positions—were of doubtful truth ; while everyone knew that if its water supply were cut off, no garrison could hold out. Therefore, it was clear that the enemy would press the attack against the water-tower, and the covered way to the river, when they began to fight seriously. It followed also that our best energies must be devoted to the protection of those vital points.

Chitrál fort, and its attached buildings, are on the verge of the river bank, so scarped away at that particular place as to be practically inaccessible, except at one narrow gully where a rough rocky path, of surprising steepness, has been partly converted into a tunnel by the isolated water-tower which encloses and roofs it in, and is then carried, in two floors, above the plane of the stable enclosure, but not quite so high as the north-east parapet. According to the seasonal meltings in the mountain-born river, the distance between the lower end of the tunnel and the water's edge is lengthened or contracted. During the early months of the year it is at its greatest. Over this intervening space, as already mentioned, Campbell, previous to our beleaguerment, constructed an invaluable passage more than five feet high. On account of the inequalities of the ground its direction was as irregular as its floor was uneven. Several great boulders, including the marble rock half-in and half-out of the water, were utilised in making the walls, and gave them strength. From lack of time and material no roofing had at first been attempted. One night the enemy ran up a crafty work, showing no loopholes, on the opposite bank, whence their marksmen found the short range so helpful, that out of the five men wounded during the first week four were shot in this passage. By the marble rock and at the foot of the tower were the dangerous spots. Wood for properly closing in the narrow way was now obtained by the demolition of the store-rooms and other apartments just outside of the main gate, under one of which poor Baird's body lay buried. This head cover was hastily and rather clumsily made, but fulfilled its object.

From the fort side of the water-tower there is a steep but short climb to the narrow level space separating the stables from the parapeted wall. The last two or three feet of this sharp ascent always remained exposed, but a couple of quick steps to the left gained good shelter. Water-carriers, however, could not be persuaded of the risk in pausing for breath just at the top of the slope. Fatalistically, or fatuously, they invariably rested a moment at this dangerous edge, and it was not until two of the poor fellows were shot dead within a short interval that the remainder could be induced to halt two yards short of the top, take breath, and then scramble up the last few feet and dodge smartly to the left for the protection of the stable wall. By this method, they gave no time for that deliberate shooting which the Chitráli marksman, properly parsimonious of ammunition, loves so well.

Campbell's waterway constituted the rigid south boundary of a bay of white sand, which is covered in the melting season. Its curving northern limit, the only accessible place, was the comparatively low bank of a marshy flat covered with big trees. This flat, held by the enemy, was considerably lower than the level of the fort, which it reached by a steep path debouching in front of the main gate. Between path and gate an oblong enclosure intervened, thanks to Sifat Bahádur, who, by his demolitions, had converted a mass of buildings and passages into that simple form. The sand itself, being the open way for a direct assault upon the loopholed waterway, had to be sedulously protected, and one of the chief problems of the defence was how to converge from walls, parapet, and towers, such a fire upon it as would crush the masterful charge of a furious foe.

And now, a word about the structure of the fort. The walls are made of coarsely-squared timbers, some 4 inches by 4 inches, laid horizontally between layers of stones embedded in mud mortar. In thickness the walls vary, being especially strong near the main entrance, which is on the west side, and feeblest on the flank looking down the valley to the south. The long timbers are strengthened in position by short cross pieces, similarly made of inflammable pine wood, which stick out some few inches from the wall like stumpy almonds from the surface of a plum pudding. At the corners of the towers, where the long lateral timbers overlap, they are often fixed together by a clumsy tenon and mortise, and jut forth several inches beyond the uneven walls. Projecting knobs are, therefore, to be found all over the fort, but particularly close together upon the towers. A monkey would find them convenient steps to climb anywhere, while a lithe Chitráli could follow him in most places.

The immense amount of wood in the towers, where the intervening layers of masonry are only a few inches thick, is not all disclosed to the view. For there is an inner pine-wood frame corresponding to that seen from without, and separated from it by about a foot of rubble.

In very dry weather it would be almost sufficient to light one of these structures with a torch to make it blaze like a blast furnace.

A transverse block of buildings divides the fort into two unequal oblongs, that on the river side being the larger. This part is used by the public generally, and it is provided on three sides with a maze of living rooms for the garrison, servants, and guests. One room of great size, with a good verandah, was the old durbar hall. We used it as a hospital. Many of the rooms have a central smoke-hole large enough for the passage of a man, as poor Gurdon found one night when going his rounds to visit the sentries on the banquette. He fell through one of these apertures on to the floor below, happily with no worse damage than bruises and a bad shake. On the other or south side of the great partition is the private half of the fort and the women's quarters. None but a very select few of their subjects ever visited the Mehtars of Chitrál in that dignified and secluded place. It has one large and three smaller courtyards, the rest being covered in; and it was on its flat, continuous roofs that promenades were possible at night when the firing was slack. While there was light all business there had to be transacted at a trot. It was interesting to watch the different modes of hurrying across this exposed place in the daytime. Most did so at the double, as above described. One or two walked with prodigiously long rapid steps, which took them faster than another man's run, and with a nervous grin, almost amounting to a frozen smile, in the direction whence a shot might be expected. A very few ambled along, gurgling with facetiousness, and making occasional jumps over imaginary bullets. These were the wags among the native servants.

After the 10th March we, so to speak, settled down

regularly to the business of standing a siege. Before
that date various experiments had been made in dividing the night guards between Townshend, Harley, and
Gurdon, but with indifferent results. Two hours stretches
were no good, and a couple of officers going round
together still less so. It was decided that the experience of sailors should be followed, and thenceforward
regular watches, similar to those of seamen, were
organised. This plan worked well ; but after the attack
developed, and alarms multiplied, it might almost be
said that all three officers were on duty continuously
during the dark nights. When there was bright moon-
light no demonstrations were made, and there was rest
for all.

At first the Sikhs, our chief reliance, had been put to
guard the south wall because it was so weak ; subsequently, it was recognised that the north tower and the
river parapet together constituted the post of honour.
Cut off from the water our case would be hopeless ;
therefore the Sikhs were transferred to that side of the
fort and not again moved, although small detachments
were taken away from time to time for particular duty,
as will be seen. Whenever there was an alarm raised
Harley commanded the parapets occupied by or near to
his men, while Gurdon looked after those defended by
the Kashmír troops on the southern portion of the fort.
Townshend, the senior officer, placed himself at the head
of the inlying picket, which, after the first few days
of our investment, always collected at the inner end
of a broad passage leading from the great courtyard
to the main gate. They were perfectly sheltered and
could act readily in any required direction. Happily,
no direct assault was ever made, so they were
never wanted. They constituted our reserve. Whitchurch, the silent doctor, on these occasions fell in with

Townshend. He was the hardest worked individual in the place. All day long he toiled in the dreadful atmosphere of the hospital, and when the men at night rushed to their posts he, armed with a double-barrelled rifle, waited with the inlying picket until all danger of an attack had passed away.

It was my chief occupation to devise plans, with the help of Sifat and Wafadár Khán, for strengthening our defences or protecting the soldiers from reverse fire, or for screening them by what may be called dodges, such as putting up portions of tents to hide ladders or paths frequently used ; the careful enemy did not fire, as a rule, without somebody to aim at. There was one exception to this. Curtains were designed to conceal men at the loopholes under the banquettes of the south wall, but those curtains were regularly bombarded from across the river.

My small room looked down from the back of the dividing block into the largest of the small courts in what was described as the private part of the fort. By daylight the apartment had the appearance of a little armoury, as in the corners were rifles, certain packages of cartridges, and some eastern swords. At first, as before said, every summons to arms was sounded on the bugle, but after a time that was changed, and the men scrambled rapidly but silently to their assigned places.

Half-awake, one shot would set me listening; two—three—four—in rapid succession might bring one foot to the ground. Then perhaps there was silence, and I fell back again on my pillow, very likely to be lifted clean out of bed, a moment later, by a heavy rattle of musketry. My faithful little servant would appear in the doorway, fumbling with an Alpine Club lantern, and help me, for I was miserably weak, into a coat.

Already a shuffling rush of soft-shod feet made the narrow staircase creak and vibrate, and Sifat and the Gilgit Rajahs would silently bustle in with some of their men, followed by Wafadár Khán, and one other of the Mehtar's advisers, who snatched up the rifles in the corner and buckled on the swords, for all the Chitrális had been disarmed on a transparent pretext. So these two trusted friends kept their weapons in my bedroom, that we might not appear to unduly favour them. There was no fear of their fellows seeing them after *retreat*, for the former were so carefully protected, to speak euphuistically, from any possible danger, that four great Sikhs compelled them, at night, to remain in the two rooms put aside for their use.

With my scratch inlying picket I used to make rapid tours, at intervals, along the south wall, examining the drains by which it was perhaps possible, though unlikely, that men might enter, and using the sharp eyes and keen hearing of my companions to investigate all weak spots. Between times we went wherever the excitement seemed greatest, but kept, as a rule, near Gurdon's parapets, for his men were still doubtful both of themselves and of their rifles, and could not be trusted completely.

Being still anxious for more exact knowledge of what was going on in the enemy's camp, I accepted, on the 10th March, the offer of one of the Chitráli headmen to go out and learn what had become of the body of General Báj Singh, who was shot dead on the 3rd, while helping to lead the abortive charge immediately precedent to our retirement. My messenger on this occasion was a terrible rascal, in which respect he did not differ materially from his brother magnates. He was the son of an lilegitimate prince, which gave him the right to affix a title of honour to his name. As he was intelligent, and could undoubtedly get me the information I wanted, he was sent forth on a horse in a stately manner. We ran up a white flag, and sounded the " Cease fire."

When it was discovered who approached them our besiegers began to cheer lustily. The sending out of such an important man was looked upon as an indication that we had decided to surrender. Shortly afterwards learning the truth, they anathematised me heartily. However, the game was theirs, for I had unwittingly lent them the best military engineer in the country. He did not return, and in vain we listened all that night for the word " Rajah " to be shouted from the garden, the signal agreed upon to let me know that some one had brought news. After dark, none the less, Sifat's brigade did first-rate work in demolishing outside houses and carrying in the timber. Only a few shots were fired at them.

We now began our second week of siege.

All day on the 11th March, there was an interchange of letters between the fort and Sher Afzul. The Diwán Sahib also came with a letter from Umra Khán, enclosing a note I had entrusted to another agent of his to forward to Udny. Umra Khán declared that the Afghán Commander-in-Chief would not allow any Jandoli messengers to approach the British boundary commissioner. Sher Afzul sent three letters altogether. There was something different from usual in their tone. Writing politely about poor Báj Singh, he suggested that I should send a Sepoy to identify the body. He protested that he really desired peace ; and Umra Khán also seemed to sing to a gentler tune. It was all very strange, but, in reply, Sher Afzul was told that if he sincerely desired peace, he should make his submission. For answer, he said he did not understand how he could submit unconditionally ; and repeated his

old terms about being subsidised, and that no Europeans
were to remain in the country.   Then he suggested that
two Chitráli headmen in the fort should be sent out
to discuss peace proposals ; but as my first emissary
had not returned I demurred about sending them, or
my head clerk, who had also been asked for.

At length, as it was getting dark, and, in the hope
of having another quiet day, while negotiating, I excused
myself to Sher Afzul's letter-bearer until the following
morning.   This man had really given me the key to the
unusual anxiety shown by the enemy to come to terms
quickly.   He asserted—but he was not believed for one
second—that there had been disaster to two British detachments, one at a place called Reshun, three marches
from Chitrál, on the left bank on the Mastuj river, the
other a little beyond that village ; that of the former,
forty Sepoys and one British officer were killed, and
sixty boxes of treasure and twenty loads of cartridges
captured, while ten men, the sole survivors, were defending themselves in a fortified house.   The other
party was declared to have fared still worse, sixty-two
men being crushed to death by rocks hurled down the
cliffs ; the bare dozen remaining were said to be
entrenched in a cave by the river's edge.

I looked upon this story as not only false, but as
showing small power of invention.   The touch about
the sixty boxes of treasure, in particular, was considered
unworthy of even an average Chitráli.   Yet its substance
was lamentably true.   We also learned that three of the
men I had sent to Mastuj with letters had been captured
and put in prison.

There was a beautiful full moon, which always
meant a cessation of the enemy's fire.   Tirich Mír,
the mighty mountain to the north, which the Chitráli
imagination peoples with fairy folk, flung up its twenty

thousand feet against a clear sky. In the morning Sher Afzul's man did not return, but there was no firing into the fort till ten o'clock. As a rule, daylight was ushered in with a light sprinkling of bullets. Over the river, at the village of Danín, there was a marksman—or perhaps two, for the method of doing it was never clear—who always before breakfast discharged a series of shots in couples, not simultaneously, but one a fraction of a second after the first. The interval never seemed to vary, and the performance was as monotonous as it was futile, but it recurred every day, starting when our bugles clanged *reveillé*.

During the quiet of the preceding day, Townshend had busied himself with making an epaulement for a gun on the south side of Sifat's enclosure. We had found in the fort two seven-pounders and eighty rounds of ammunition, with solid projectiles. The little cannon were in fair order, but had no sights—a graduated piece of wood, and a small pyramid of heaped-up flour being used by the Chitrális instead. Only one man in the fort knew anything about artillery, that was the Kashmír colonel of the Rághunáth regiment, who formerly served in one of the Maharajah's mountain batteries. His knowledge, however, was limited, and he had all the infantry man's lack of enthusiasm for ordnance. On this date, the 12th, it was decided to try a shot, but by some unfortunate mistake, the detachment told off for the duty carried the gun into the garden to the south-east instead of to the epaulement made for it on the west. Being right in the open, they had only a couple of rounds fired when they had to bolt back into the fort, with one man *hors de combat*. The shooting was not at all bad considering; indeed, it was afterwards said that my old mission-house, occupied by Sher Afzul, was hit at the corner.

A week or two later, another attempt to utilise a gun was made through an aperture dug during the night in the west wall of Sifat's enclosure. But the morning light revealed that the port was completely blocked by a big tree trunk; so another had to be made. Then one of our solid shot hit the top beam of the nearest hostile sangar, but without doing much damage as far as we could learn; whereupon the military officers decided it was useless to continue the experiment, and the little seven-pounders were relegated to purely ornamental duties in the big yard. A knowledge of artillery cannot, unfortunately, be evolved from the precepts of common-sense, nor acquired on the spur of the moment. It was during the experiments with this gun that Wafadár horrified me by bragging that in the old time, when salutes were fired in my honour and he officiated as battery commandant, so expert did he become, that not more than three or four men retired to hospital on each occasion with burnt hands!

I have mentioned that the window of my small, first-floor room, which had a south aspect, looked down into the biggest of the four inner courts. For some reason, not to be explained, its sliding open - work shutters were never once hit by bullets, though, towards the end of the siege, it used to be constantly hammered with stones slung by men hidden behind a wall thirty yards from the parapet. Beneath me was the little Mehtar's treasure, with a sentry guarding the door. To the east, on the same floor, and separated from me by the staircase, which led from below to the roof in two flights, divided by a landing, was a long, dark apartment, inhabited by Townshend and Gurdon. Their only window, a mere ventilation hole just under the ceiling, opened high above the great yard of the fort.

On the other side of me Harley occupied a chapel

with a separate stair running downwards to our court. A passage led from his room to another one behind, whence I had been expelled by the sharp-shooters across the river, and then through an ante-room into a largish durbar hall on the west, whose big open casement also looking north, could be seen, throughout its length and breadth, from Danín. Consequently, it was often hit by the enemy's marksmen. We used one corner of it for bathing. Behind a barricade of Chitrál saddles, old boxes, and carpets, we were quite safe.

The ante-room mentioned communicated with our commissariat office underneath, and a high range of roofs above, by two huge deeply-notched poles. It had been a favourite murdering-place of the Mehtars of Chitrál. There was in it a wooden screen, behind which executioners could lie concealed until the victims emerged from the durbar, expecting, of course, to descend to the apartment below, and thence reach the great yard; no Oriental of good manners would be so wanting in etiquette as to apprise a doomed man of what was in store for him. Afzul-ul-Mulk had three of his brothers slain there one evening, but they probably anticipated their fate when they were coldly dismissed from the Mehtar's presence. It is said that even he showed signs of agitation, and turned pale, when the sickening sound of mortal blows was heard through the closed door. But the whole of the fort was blood-stained. A lover of gruesome stories could there drink his fill of horror.

The partition between the two halves of the fort contained, therefore, within itself, so to speak, an upper and a lower floor of apartments, some of which I have enumerated. Looking north-east into the great yard, it had no windows or other openings on the ground level, only three doors. One, already mentioned, led into the commissariat store, whence the rough stair-pole climbed to the slaughter-house ante-room. A second door to the west was of minor importance. The third and chief was in the corner by the hospital. It was one end of a high, twisted passage which passed under a prison chamber, and was therefore completely closed in. Nevertheless, it became deplorable in wet weather, when a slip from one of its stepping-places soused one over ankles in muddy water. The inner extremity opened upon a tiny court, across which ran a way from our quarters to the strong, high garden door, protected, at this time, by a backing of water-worn stones many feet in thickness.

The common road for everybody moving about the fort was along this tortuous dark passage, and no British officer passed through it after dark without being challenged by a sentry hidden away in the gloom of the long roofed-in passage leading from the garden entrance. He generally allowed his fellow-soldiers to go unnoticed, but although he must have known us as well as he knew them, and we were certainly less likely than they to be mistaken for an enemy within our gates, yet he greeted us each time of our appearance with an exuberant "hukm dár?" (who comes there?), and demanded the password in the sentinels' orthodox catechism. On lively nights, the same man must have challenged me a dozen times.

Being only an ignorant civilian I accepted this ceremony as esoteric, but, no doubt, an essential foundation of military discipline. Whenever, from hurry or forgetfulness, my responses were cut short or I shouted "Colorado" when "Timbuctoo" was the word, I felt a sting of conscience afterwards. My feelings will therefore be imagined when, soon after Colonel Kelly arrived, I was told that his staff officer had observed that passwords were "all rot," and were never used in

Q

his force. So military had one grown then, that it was hard to refrain from saying that the service must be going to the dogs. The officer who repeated the iconoclastic speech to me was bluish-red with indignation.

The inner court, which our sleeping-rooms, on the upper floor, bounded on one side, was surrounded on the other three by a high, wide verandah supported on strong wooden pillars. At one end Harley at first screened off a portion for a bed-chamber, till some stray shots, a little slanting rain, and similar inconveniences drove him into the chapel. He was a melodious person of gregarious instincts. Looking back, one reflects how churlishly his songs and shuffling accompaniments were sometimes received, and how badly we should have missed them. I think that Harley, even after an all-night watch, always lay down to sleep with reluctance, and would never have rested at all had there been anyone equally companionable to talk to. His unquenchable good spirits stimulated us greatly without our knowing it.

The middle length of verandah was our mess-room. A rough table, with two camp chairs and some improvised seats comprised its furniture. Our viands were a scanty supply of tinned beef and a vast deal of mustard ; but, by blessed fortune, there were many tins of pea-flour ; so every day, from the beginning to the end of the siege, we had pea-soup for dinner. Little Shuja-ul-Mulk presented us with a few ornamental birds which his brother Nizám had collected, but they only lasted a few days. There was bread, made half of flour and half of stone dust, for the bold ; and a little rice. To me all these articles seemed luxury, for I was starving on a milk diet—Swiss milk (the last tin) and hot water. A little later my weakness became great, and brandy was given me from our store of four bottles. At one corner of the mess-verandah was the kitchen door ; at the other the entrance to Campbell's room, which he shared with his devoted nurse and surgeon, Whitchurch, who having already so much to do, naturally superintended our victualling also.

Amongst my engineering contrivances was one failure of the most dismal kind. The stable space outside the walls was dreadful to the nose, and small pools of horrible water were dammed back all along the floor of a long low chamber, with doors at both ends, which connected the stables with the big yard within, and served both as a guard-house and a thoroughfare. Sifat and I had a miniature surface canal dug, with much attention to levels, to carry off this liquid sewage. The outlet was a short distance down Campbell's water-way, above the tower, through a scupper piercing one of the side walls ; and it acted very well. But we could not see the configuration of the cliff slopes outside, and, next day, we discovered that all the drainage had found its way back within the covered passage close to the river, into the small rocky basin where buckets and water-skins were filled !

Upon this date the Fort Commandant's diary has the following entry :—" The British Agent desires me to let off thirty rounds a day from the towers on to Sher Afzul's house." This represents an amiable wish on my part that Sher Afzul also should experience the dis-comfort we felt from " sniping."

No messenger appeared, and the 13th of March passed away. Sifat Bahádur and his companions, in-veterate cartridge wasters, were allowed to amuse them-selves with some old Enfields we found in one of the rooms. Probably the Chitrális with us conceived that our other ammunition was running short—a valuable piece of news for the lucky man who could convey it to Sher Afzul

A bright day, sunshine and clear sky, was followed by a dark, clouded night. One or two of our Chitrális, under Wafadár, were sent out at eight o'clock to prowl round the walls, and see if they could find any signs of a mine. They came back quickly with a report satisfactory enough as far as it went. It became darker still, a dense blackness falling upon us like something palpable. At half-past ten there was an outburst of firing from the Sikh parapets, near the North-tower. Then followed wild cries from the garden, where a regular British bugle sounded the charge, and Gurdon heard a voice cheering men to an assault on the East-tower. We threw down a fire-ball, and responded with volleys which reverberated through the fort. Our bugles blew the *Cease-fire* at half-past eleven, but the rifles rang out again, independently, from time to time until midnight. Afterwards there were only the few occasional shots of the sentries.

The total result was that the enemy completed a good sangar, one hundred and fifty yards or so up-stream on our bank. It was this noise which started off the Sikhs in the first place. A plausible feint was thereupon made against the East-tower, perhaps with the idea of its being developed into a real assault if we were caught napping.

On two successive nights, fresh works had been built close to us. But even now, after full consideration, I do not see how this could have been prevented. If we had been strong enough and enterprising enough to sortie, we should have destroyed one of the enemy's defences, no doubt; but a second attempt might easily have landed us into a trap, for, unless there were the element of surprise in our attack, we might have found ourselves in a dummy sangar, exposed to a terrific fire from hidden riflemen—and we dare not risk a second reverse.

Practically, we had only the Sikhs who could be relied upon absolutely, and not more than eighty of these were fit for work. There were splendid fellows among the Kashmír soldiers, it is true, but in the gloomy, downcast looks of most, one could read that they still suffered from their former defeat. Again, heroic as were two or three of their officers, the majority were of a distinctly inferior class. We had no British officers to spare, so there was nothing for it but to allow the enemy to develop his plans, and content ourselves with keeping a sharp outlook for an occasion when a forcible blow might be struck with all the odds in our favour.

Gurdon was most anxious for an adventure against the last built sangar, but it was felt to be premature.

To stop the stealthy approach of the Sher Afzulites, in any other way than by sorties, was impossible. A sangar was bullet-proof before it was discovered. Their method was this. First, a number of fascines, of fresh branches tightly withe-bound, was made. All Chitrális assert that one such bundle, if sufficiently green and properly tied, will stop a Martini-Henry bullet. Provided with these faggots, two or three men would creep silently along the ground some dark night, and heap them up on a spot previously chosen. Others, behind, passed forward more fascines from the rear, and in a few minutes there was a useful barricade formed. Next, stones were handed along, and, finally, timbers. At this last stage, the noise of hammering could not be muffled, but as the workers were behind a bullet-proof screen they were safe. When heavier materials had to be brought from unsheltered places, a false attack on the opposite side of the fort was generally sufficient to divert the attention of our sentries, because of the terrific noise inside the walls, caused by the echoing volleys.

CHAPTER XXV

MISFORTUNE

IT has been said that to stop any attempt upon the East - tower we threw down a fire - ball ; this requires explanation. One night, during the Hunza-Nagar expedition in December 1891, the Nagars imagined we were attacking a position they held at a Ziárat (shrine). With much outcry and firing of guns, they rolled fire-balls down the steep river-bank, and lit up the scene effectively. I afterwards learned that the chief component of these novel contrivances was a special kind of pine wood which blazes splendidly, because it contains much turpentine. There was plenty of this material in the fort, so we set to work to make, with pine chips and straw, balls of about a foot in diameter, and stuffed inside a casing of coarse canvas. We had a small quantity of kerosene oil, and each ball was saturated with a wine bottleful of this before it was set on fire. Our supply of oil being scanty, it was further ordered that the lighting, as well as the throwing, must be done by British officers. On the whole, the experiment was successful, especially on the night of the 13th, when the East-tower was brilliantly illuminated for nearly half-an-hour. But everything depended not only on the care with which the balls were set on fire and made to blaze well before they were hurled, but also on economy in their use. I was feeling qualms about the rapidity with which they were being expended, and at the shrinkage of the kerosene, when a much better expedient was suggested by Wafadár Khán, which will be described in the proper place.

All day long on the 14th there was a great deal of sniping. A new sangar, which had not been discovered by anyone, was shown to me by Wafadár Khán, and made me rub my eyes in surprise. This will indicate how quickly and silently these approaches could be thrown up.

In the military diary of this date the following appears :—" Rághunáths steadier and better in hand last night—no wild firing. British Agent pleased with them." The Kashmír riflemen were improving under the immediate care of the British officers, their volleys had been fired steadily ; hence my commendation.

It was getting dark, about six o'clock, when the approach of a flag of truce was reported. A long interval—three whole days—having now passed without a letter from Sher Afzul, there was some curiosity to learn what he had to say. His messenger proved to be a poor old woman, who mumbled out that Sher Afzul would hold himself responsible for the arrangements of my journey, if I would only leave the fort and go back to Gilgit. All troops and stores might go with me. He would also consent to be friends in future, if the Government of India agreed to revert to their line of policy during the reign of Amán-ul-Mulk. Having delivered her message, the old woman told us, as news, that all the peoples of Yághistán (the rebellious country—*i.e.* the independent frontier land) had decided to rise against the British, under the leadership of Sher Afzul and Umra Khán. My picturesque little friend, Muhammed Wali (see page 38), had been sent for, she said, with his relatives, and even Gilgit and Puniál were beating the drum of revolt. Our informant went back without any reply being given her.

The stables were further fortified during the day, and placed under the guardianship of a section of the Kashmír Rifles, who were to be changed each night, for the stench there was otherwise insupportable. Twelve Sikhs were also sent into the loopholed water passage every evening. As the tower over it was also strongly held, it was now well protected, even without help from the fort. If this covered way were seized, we should have to re-take it at any price. While Harley was superintending the work in the stables, with me as a spectator, a little incident occurred, illustrative of the accuracy of the shooting from Danín. The walls were old and crumbling, so that a loophole often suddenly enlarged itself in an embarrassing way, and required to be partly filled up again. On one such occasion, the space left was about a foot square, and a man was about to block it with a big stone which he had on his shoulder, when a bullet, from over the river, came through the aperture and whizzed between the stone and his face. He flinched a little, and again advanced. This time the stone was hit plump, but the man, luckily, finished his task unhurt.

During the night there were frequent alarms and excursions. A couple of fire-balls had to be thrown out ; and Pathán yells in the garden added to the disturbance. It was again pitch dark. Much of our firing was probably at some animals turned out in the afternoon, because our stock of straw was almost ended. All ponies were driven forth with the exception of eight, kept in case we wanted them for food, but the poor beasts lingered near the walls all day, and when no longer distinguishable in the blackness outside, several were killed from the walls. It must be admitted that, sorry as one felt for the unfortunate ponies, the fact of their being shot in the garden, from parapets not held by Sikhs, showed that the Kashmír Rifles were beginning to aim low when they volleyed—a cause for satisfaction indeed.

We were now growing used to the Pathán war-cry. It is a kind of loud note increasing very quickly, both in sonorousness and in shortness of interval, till it grows into one swelling roar. They gave us continued opportunities of studying it.

The morning of the 15th March revealed that the enemy had been busy improving his sangars; but all day long no single shot was fired at us. Rain fell without ceasing. We took advantage of the calm to convert the river end of Campbell's covered way into a small but strong little fort. Sifat had recommended it, and his men worked with a will. It was to be held at night by eight additional Sikhs. Our besiegers were not altogether idle, and long after dark we heard the sound of another approach being constructed in the garden. In the afternoon the rain changed to sleet, but at six o'clock snow covered the ground to a depth of four inches.

Another letter was brought from Sher Afzul. Each day seemed to produce its daily letter. This began in the customary manner by saying that the writer was anxious for peace, but insisted upon his own terms being conceded. An accompanying missive was addressed to the Chitráli notables in the fort, telling them to go at once, and make submission, when their past faults would be forgiven. Sher Afzul also wrote that he had a letter from a British officer, a prisoner at Reshun, to me, telling of the capture of Sepoys at Reshun, Buni, and Mastuj. He offered to send the document, provided I would allow two headmen, specifically named, to fetch it.

I disbelieved the story; indeed, the possibility of its being true never entered my thoughts. But Sher Afzul himself seemed to me enigmatical; his persistent complaints against me, personally, were strange even for a Chitráli statesman, with whose ways I was not unacquainted. A common plan they adopt is to state their wishes, however extravagant, at an interview if possible. Rarely can the requests be granted, for they are usually overstated in an amusing way. After this is explained at length, and politely, your visitor retires with gentle melancholy. Next day, or at the earliest opportunity, he will repeat, word for word, his former petition, only to receive an identical answer — not shortened in any way by a feeling of impatience at your having already given it. And so it goes on. I have had an envoy at Gilgit who finally returned to his master at Chitrál with the reply he had been given a month previously, and at least a score of times afterwards. We parted the best of friends. He was a prince, and went away happy in the consciousness of having done all a diplomatist could on his Mehtar's behalf. Any signs of irritation at his pertinacity would have made him unhappy, and hurt in dignity.

Yet in spite of such experiences, Sher Afzul's unvarying letters caused me surprise. So to clear up all conceivable doubt I wrote and asked him if he had certainly received my first communication, dated the 24th February, which invited him in kind and friendly terms to come to me at Chitrál. To avoid the possibility of a mistake, I enclosed a copy of the original letter. As for his allegation about a British officer having been captured at Reshun, I remarked that one headman allowed out of the fort by me had been detained, and therefore no other would be sent. It was suggested that my former messenger might bring me the document. In conclusion, Sher Afzul was warmly urged to save Chitrál the horrors of further war, and enjoined to submit, ask pardon of the Government of India, and throw himself upon its mercy. That Government, he was assured, was merciful and lenient, and would give the fullest consideration to all he had to say. "Be well advised, therefore," ran the last sentence, "and before it is too late, do as I advise you."

Six inches of snow on the ground and a glorious blue sky greeted our eyes next morning. The guards and sentries, particularly those in the covered way, suffered miserably during their long watch, and were wet through; but the besiegers had been quiet, and hardly a shot had been fired at us for twenty-four hours, in spite of there being no light from the moon till two hours after midnight.

About four o'clock in the afternoon a man came down the road from the serai, bearing a white flag. He brought two letters, one from Sher Afzul, and the other, said to be the joint production of all the Chitráli magnates with him. Both documents were of interminable length. The first mentioned contained the curious remark that Sher Afzul had received and understood my first note to him, written on the 24th February, but that he considered such a message on my part was improper.

There was also an enclosure from Lieutenant Edwardes, dated Reshun, the 13th March. For a moment my heart stood still; I could not read. This is the story it told, in a mixture of French and English. Edwardes and his party, consisting of Lieutenant Fowler, twenty of the Bengal sappers and miners, with forty of the Rághunáth Regiment, convoying sixty boxes of ammunition, had been attacked on our side of Reshun on the 7th inst. Compelled to retreat, they defended themselves in a house of that village up to the 13th, when Umra Khán's men, their opponents, proposed a truce, to which Edwardes agreed. Sorties had been necessary to get water, and the severity of the fighting was shown by the casualties—five killed, and thirteen wounded. The letter continued that, just as a parley was agreed upon, a headman named Muhammed Isa, Sher Afzul's foster-brother, arrived with a large company of armed Chitrális, and entered into friendly conversation with Edwardes when the latter went out to meet him. Since Muhammed Isa had come, Edwardes recognised that his opponents were too strong for him.

The contents of the local letters may perhaps be guessed : long recapitulations of what had been already said a dozen times, and professions of a desire for peace. Both wound up with the remark that by sending Edwardes's letter to me my correspondents had given a proof of their sincerity and friendliness. They suggested that my head clerk should be sent to a conference at Sher Afzul's house. I hurriedly sent back two answers, the first to say that a second would quickly follow. In the latter, I declared that I accepted the sending of Edwardes's letter to me as an earnest of the Chitrális' genuine desire to stop further fighting, and expressed myself as willing to discuss the question of terms with them. As a preliminary, I offered a three days' armistice, during which they must not come in front of their sangars, while my men would not leave the precincts of the fort. If this were agreed to, Sher Afzul was to hoist a white flag; we should respond, and my Indian head clerk would go to Sher Afzul as soon as any one came to fetch him. There was still light enough for us to see a white flag run up over my old mission-house. We displayed another. A second letter from Sher Afzul asked for my clerk to be sent to him next morning.

Before my sleepless eyes all night was the certainty that treachery was intended at Reshun. My only hope lay in our contriving some means of getting a letter of warning through to Edwardes; otherwise, I feared we should never see him or Fowler again. Those two young men, both of them admirable examples of the best type of fearless, open-hearted, single-minded soldiers, were new to this kind of warfare, and presumably liable to fall victims of Chitráli wiles. Yet how could they be cautioned? Already, two days, during which Edwardes's letter was detained by Sher Azful, had been lost. I was nearly in despair. The morning was long in coming, and it seemed longer still before my clerk, Amír Ali, was sent for. He had been well primed in his part, and a copy of instructions, to show my conditions for a cessation of hostilities, was given him in case he might forget them from nervousness at his responsibilities. Two objects he was to strive for. Permission for me to send a letter to Edwardes; and a prolongation of the truce. With regard to the first he would require all his tact, because it was certain it would be hard to gain.

I tried to sham as much indifference as I could. Nevertheless, when, in defiance of the white flags, the fort was fired into on two occasions, we took no notice, and let it pass as a mistake. We were playing a game, with the lives of the Reshun party as a prize. There was naturally much excitement in the fort, but that made reticence of great importance. However, I told Campbell, who was torn with disquietude about Fowler and Edwardes, of my views, and said that although I would do nearly anything to save them, yet for us to agree to retire was certain death ; that our leaving the fort would do no good, and once outside we should be certainly butchered.

My first messenger, he who had never returned, now came to take Amír Ali to Sher Afzul. I was closeted with the man for some time, but he was so agitated that he could not, or would not, tell me anything. His wits seemed scared out of him, and his face was drawn as if from paralysis. Perhaps he feared I should detain him, or, more likely, that his treachery was discovered. In any case, I was too anxious to get authentic news of the Reshun party to prolong the interview. My instructions to Amír Ali were four in number. Three were to be strongly fought for, and the other he might give way upon, without referring to me, if hard pressed. He was to say—first, that the truce could not last longer than three days unless a stated amount of flour and two sheep were daily supplied to us. This point was to be urged as an essential condition ; secondly, he was to argue that it was absolutely necessary to open the road to Mastuj for letters, on the ground, for instance, that troops must not press on to our assistance in contravention of the armistice; thirdly, no armed men must approach the walls, nor would any of our party, carrying weapons, be allowed outside the fort ; fourthly, and lastly, a neutral zone was proposed, and its boundaries suggested.

Amír Ali was away a long time. His account of what happened would be tedious to relate in full. He had been conducted to my old house, which Sher Afzul was occupying. In passing through the serai-bazaar he observed that it was strongly fortified and full of Patháns, nearly all of them armed with Martini-Henry rifles. Two princes, escorted by about two hundred Jandolis, received him " in a deprecatory manner." At the gate of the front enclosure he was detained for half-an-hour, while Umra Khán's two relatives were sent for. When they arrived a sort of procession was formed, thirty or forty riflemen going in front, and a similar number following them into the first room. When the durbar room itself was reached it was found packed with people carrying loaded rifles.

After ceremonial greetings my " Salaam " was given to Sher Afzul, and acknowledged. Then there fell a silence. Amír Ali, seeing the prince was a little nervous, spoke first to encourage him, according to his own account. Following this friendly lead, Sher Afzul observed that he had nothing to add to what was contained in his letter to me, whereupon, as is customary all the world over after such a remark, he spoke at great length, recapitulating nearly everything that had happened since the year 1893. He wound up with the declaration that he was still ready to make peace and to be friends ; but on his own terms. It was Nizám, he said, that introduced British influence into the country, but the people were no longer able to bear it. The ancient agreement was that British troops were not to cross the frontier at Somal, a village nearly two hundred miles to the east ; that must now be reverted to.

Then Amír Ali had an innings, and gave my messages. "In an instant," he relates, "the friendly eyes of the audience turned into hatred." Nevertheless, he told his story to the end, in spite of the people not wanting to hear it. All my conditions for an armistice were refused peremptorily. Next, the Shina Chief, Umra Khán's cousin and chief commander, spoke for himself and his brother Khán. For his part, he said he would have no truce. Troops might come from Mastuj if they chose. They could march back if peace were made. Otherwise, they might be useful to me. Neutral zones were all nonsense. On the other hand, the sangars would be approached closer and closer every night. An attack would be instantly ordered, unless Sher Afzul's stipulations were conceded in full. There was but one course open to me; that was to evacuate the fort on the instant and return to Gilgit. If that were done he, the speaker, would be responsible for my safety and that of my troops. Sher Afzul would thereupon be Mehtar, and all the Jandolis could return to their homes. The action of the Government of India in coming to Chitrál meant aggression in Bajour later on, and all Bajouris must fight for the honour of their country.

Once or twice Sher Afzul desired to interrupt the young soldier, but was silenced by a gesture. He meekly confirmed the other, murmuring that the Khán was his mouthpiece. That was the substance of the conference. Amír Ali subsequently drew up a few personal reflections on what he had seen and heard, but he was the slave of his own idioms, as is so frequently the case with Orientals when using our language. This explains a great deal of their irresponsibility and mere wordiness when talking in English. He spoke of machines and wire-pullers, puppets, hungry wolves, of sins being washed away, and tried to think up to mere phrases, which he accepted as his own well-considered opinions. It was obvious, however, that Sher Afzul was anything but a free agent, for he was not even permitted to see my man, except in the presence of the masterful young Kháns.

I wrote back to Sher Afzul that I did not clearly see why he had sent for my clerk; that although he wrote of a desire to make peace, his messages, if correctly delivered, did not sound peaceful, and that he should write in exact terms what his demands were. Supposing I agreed to surrender Chitrál fort, what guarantees would be given that my party would not be attacked afterwards at a disadvantage? What hostages would be offered? And would he, or would he not, let me send a letter to the British officers at Reshun? If he wished to end the truce at dusk, as Amír Ali informed me, he need only pull down his flag and fire a warning gun ; nothing else was necessary. An answer quickly came, written, as usual, very politely. It stated that the whole negotiation would be laid before Umra Khán at Drosh. Until his views were known, there had better be no more fighting. My people must not come out of the fort, nor ought I to permit his men to enter it. He begged me keep my mind at rest. A brief note told him that his suggestions were accepted. There was evidently no hope of getting a letter through to Edwardes, so we had to be content with a few additional days of truce.

Thus ended this long 17th of March, *and our second week of siege.*

CHAPTER XXVI

BAD FAITH AND BAD NEWS

THE armistice was strictly observed by the enemy. We could walk about on the roofs or along the parapets without being shot at, which gave one an odd sense of freedom. There was much activity in the serai-bazaar and at Futteh Ali Sháh's house. It looked as if the latter place was being strongly fortified. As this seemed to be our opponent's way of observing a truce, we set to work likewise, and fitted bullet-proof covers on to the towers, and improvised shelters for the men on the walls with beams brought in from the summer-house corner of the garden, where the little temple and other apartments had been cast down. We also made ramparts of packing-cases and other boxes filled with earth, and with stacks of firewood. Before long, a man came running to say that if Sifat's men did not stop carrying in the timbers they would be fired upon. The possibility of such an objection had been pointed out to me some time before by one of the British officers. I answered the enemy's spokesman that so long as they continued to work at Futteh Ali Sháh's house, so long should we continue to strengthen ourselves also. The man went away and nothing happened.

As will be seen from the illustrations, our fort had four towers, irrespective of the one guarding the covered way. For convenience, we called two of them the

North and East-tower respectively, while the pair
flanking the south wall were known as the Flag and
the Gun - towers.   Why the last - mentioned was so
termed I forget; but probably we merely adhered to
the name given it by the Chitrális.   As a work of
art it was much admired by the country people, who
looked upon it as a memorial to Amán - ul - Mulk's
father, in whose reign it was erected by the Kalash
tribe of slave Káfirs.   But so far from justifying its
picturesque title, the concussion from one round of a
seven-pounder would probably have split the walls,
if it did not bring them down altogether.   It contained even more wood than the others, whose walls
were so largely built up of pine timber.   From the
base to what we may call the first floor it was solid ;
a long inside ladder led thence to a lofty upper
apartment, occupying all the square space between
the walls.   Above that again was a roof partially
enclosed on one side and unscreened on all others.
It was reached awkwardly through a manhole.

Although the Gun-tower was high it was much
lower than the Flag-tower, which was not less than
seventy feet from base to summit.   The only entrance
was up a very long clumsy ladder, whose top rested
against a bracket projecting from the wall just below
a small door.   This ladder being exposed to the full
view of the enemy, the Sikh guards could only be
relieved when it was dark.   Curious to relate, both
the west and the south aspects of the fort were very
badly flanked — the North, the Flag, and the Gun-
towers standing out a very short distance, merely a
foot or so, beyond the walls.   The garden, or south-
east side, was better protected, and could be fairly
well covered by lateral loopholes.   For instance, in the
Gun - tower we cut out a big piece of the northern

wall of the raised lower chamber, and thereby gave sufficient space for two men to fire downwards with a good view of the garden door, which was similarly defended by other smaller openings. The large gap was covered throughout the day by an enormous Morababad tea - tray which we found in the fort. When it was unclosed in the evening the soldiers were strictly cautioned to show no lights.

The top room of the Gun - tower had a little wooden gallery, about the size of a stunted sentry-box, thrust out from its south face, and overlooking the summer-house. With the object of strengthening and improving it, planks were nailed all round, to a height of three feet, and backed by loose boards, thick enough to stop bullets. Looking towards the Flag-tower, a long slit opening was contrived, so that a rifleman, kneeling on the floor, could cover nearly the whole of the south wall. We termed this contrivance our *machicoulis* gallery, only, unfortunately, we forgot the machicolation, through which the foot of the tower could be seen and protected. From the eastern side an unblocked window-frame, extending to the floor, gave a view straight down the garden.

A fruitless labour, begun at this time, was to dig a well in the big yard, just in front of the hospital. Careful cross - examination of several Chitrális led to the conviction that in former days water had been found there. Relays of men were told off to try and find it again. After several days of wearisome toil the task had to be abandoned. We were cheered once by coming upon damp soil, but after that particular layer had been dug through, and hard, dry earth was discovered underneath, we felt it useless to persevere. Perhaps it was better for everyone to know that his life depended entirely upon our holding the waterway.

Before this date, the 18th, our daylight surroundings had been dreary. Except in the far distance, near Sher Afzul's abode, and behind the serai, moving objects were never seen. Most of the enemy's sangars, also, could only be made out when a momentary puff of smoke indicated their position. Therefore, within a radius of 700 yards, there was the quietness of death when there was no rattle of musketry. Often, for hours at a time, no sound would break the heavy stillness, because inside the walls, with the exception of the keen-eyed sentries crouching on the towers, all the garrison were asleep or resting. Sometimes this unnatural silence was so oppressive that an outbreak of rifle-fire came as a relief. Now, during the armistice, cattle and goats were to be seen everywhere grazing placidly. People moved to and fro with the step of everyday life and a low buzz of conversation, even an occasional laugh, was heard in the fort.

About three o'clock in the afternoon, a soldierly-looking man strolled up to the main gate and, seeing a British officer there, saluted in military fashion. This led to conversation. He said he had formerly been a sergeant in the 5th Punjab Infantry, but was now a subadár in Umra Khán's regular troops, as distinguished from his tribal levies. While talking, he "stood at attention," respectfully. Not only was he frank in his comments on passing events, but to cheer us up, no doubt, he lied freely. According to him, Sher Afzul's troops were short of ammunition, and on the point of marching away to Drosh. Of course the clerks went through the farce of bribing him to fetch us food. If you only persevere in a particular line of action, in time you come to believe your own fables, which thereby gain all the force of sincerity, and become convincing.

Our poor soldiers were suffering very much. Bad sanitation, stone dust mixed with the flour, in addition to exposure and snow at night, begat fever and dysentery, while there was no milk to diet the sick, and drugs were scanty—many medical stores having been accidentally left outside by the Indian dispensary doctor on the 3rd March. After dark it began to rain heavily, and kept on all night, drenching the exposed pickets and sentries to the skin. But it seemed powerless to quench the light-heartedness of the enemy, who gathered round blazing fires in the serai. Their drummings, and the cheers with which they encouraged the dancing boys, could be heard long after midnight.

Before seven o'clock on the morning of the 19th the rain stopped, and three hours later a bright sun appeared above the hills. Amidst all the anxieties of our position, one carefully recorded fact on this date was that we had killed our penultimate goose, and that only one other bird intervened between us and a blank dinner-table.

After breakfast, a letter, written by the two Jandol Kháns, was brought to the gate. The gist of it was that I must leave the fort immediately, and march to Peshawer through Jandol and Swát; and that the sincerity of the writers would be shown in the careful and honourable manner they would escort me to Peshawer with all my followers and soldiers. With probably unconscious irony they remarked that the Government of India had long desired that English officers might travel by that road; but hitherto the Jandol people had not looked kindly upon the idea. Now, however, to show the world how strong was the good feeling entertained by the *King* of Chitrál and Umra Khán for my Government, they consented to our going that way. My correspondents were politely solicitous about my health, and then, with an abrupt change of style, the letter ended by saying that if its suggestions were not acceptable, I should say so on the back of the document forthwith, and return it.

I replied that I did not think the present a good opportunity to visit Jandol and Swát, nor, in my opinion, would my going there serve as a cementing bond of friendship between the Jandolis and Government. Answers to my questions were also asked for, especially to that one about sending a note to Edwardes at Reshun. When those were received, it would be possible to resume negotiations. Sher Afzul wrote also, at inordinate length, but with an identical meaning. All the troubles which had arisen were due, he said, to my insensibility to the principles of equity and justice. But in spite of that, he and Umra Khán had decided to escort me to Peshawer with honour. If I were still obdurate, all that need be done was to record that fact on the back of his letter and have done with it. But he was answered politely. I pointed out that the chief points raised by me had not been touched upon, and that such subjects as guarantees, hostages, and my sending letters to Reshun still awaited discussion.

This drew forth a rejoinder reproaching me for my lack of confidence. How could I be so suspicious of my friend as even to think about guarantees! He then naïvely confessed the reason why he had not allowed me to communicate with the British officers at Reshun. According to his account, both he and the two Jandol Kháns sent careful instructions to their troops there how to behave, but, unhappily, the truce had been broken before those instructions arrived. Two British officers and nine Indian soldiers were now on their way to Chitrál—obviously as prisoners, although that rough word was not used. They might be expected about nine o'clock that evening. Another

long letter from the Jandol Kháns simply gave the
same news in precisely similar words, and then urged
me to agree to their proposals for me to retire with
honour from Chitrál. If that were done, a "news-
writer" might be left behind *for the present.*

Concerning the truth of the statements made about
Reshun I had, unhappily, no doubts at all. I was
equally certain that there had been treachery. Even
Sher Afzul and his allies seemed to think it necessary
to write in an apologetic tone. The former went so far
as to confess that he sincerely believed the Government
of India never had any intention of annexing Chitrál,
but only desired the firm friendship of its ruler. All
this made me uneasy, and the small number of Indian
soldiers said to be coming with the two British officers
added to the feeling. The insistence upon our travelling
through Jandol to Peshawer, instead of merely marching
back to Mastuj and Gilgit, was also curious and disturbing. In the meantime, there was nothing for it but
to try, by all possible means, and persuade the enemy
to treat their prisoners well. We must guard our
defences more strictly than ever.

All day long, small groups of Patháns and Chitrális
had been watched coming down the valley. Many
wounded crept along, afoot or riding, and seven or
eight corpses on stretchers were carried past. We
concluded that there must have been sharp fighting at
Reshun. To bring slain warriors so great a distance to
Chitrál for suitable interment, could only mean that the
dead were chiefs or important folk. If this were true
the enemy must have suffered heavily, because, in the
East, the proportion of leaders to ordinary fighters in
the total number of those killed in action is generally
low.

Our Chitrális all agreed that a relief party must be

close at hand, and that their fellow-countrymen had been worsted in a fight. It was also reported to me that messengers during the day, after hinting mysteriously to my head clerk that the two Jandol Kháns were ready to treat with me on their own account, had gone away without further explanation. Lastly, the lady known as the Asmári Queen, little Shuja-ul-Mulk's mother, sent a man to say that the British had beaten the Chitrális on the road from Mastuj, and that I must on no account abandon the fort. But none of these communications brought me any comfort. Word came late at night, that the truce would continue until we fired the first shot. Nevertheless, we watched sharply, and strengthened some of our posts.

Next day, Wednesday the 20th, I wrote to Sher Afzul for the latest news of his captives. One informant declared that Edwardes and Fowler had been separated ; that one of them was to be brought to Chitrál, and the other sent to Mastuj. Long answers came from Sher Afzul, and from the Jandol Kháns, to say that the prisoners were to be brought in during the afternoon, and that riding ponies would be sent down to meet them at the bridge. It was further insinuated that my expressed anxiety about the British officers was merely a pretext for delaying negotiations for a surrender. They reiterated that they would, all of them, collectively, be responsible for my safety on the march to Peshawer, and remarked that further delay in coming to terms would be of no advantage to me. According to them, the breach of the armistice at Reshun was accidental, so to speak, and fresh fighting having broken out no one could stop it. They added that the troops had been censured, and their commander placed under arrest. Once more I was required to agree to their demands forthwith.

That I was to go to Jandol was the main stipulation. Upon that the allies were determined. Consequently, I wrote at length, to argue the question from the point of view of our retiring to Mastuj, and to say that the other plan could not be considered. I said that I accepted their assurances that my officers were safe in their hands, and that they would be well treated. Also, that the attack made upon them during a parley was from a misunderstanding; and that the individual responsible for that attack had been punished. Nevertheless, they must perceive how necessary it was to provide against similar accidents in the future. With me, I explained, there were some fifty men unable to walk, from various reasons. How were they to be carried? Also, we had large quantities of stores of different kinds. How were these to be transported?

What we had to agree upon was really the price to be paid for the release of Edwardes and Fowler. In short, what was the nature of the ransom demanded for those unfortunate young soldiers. I expressed myself as ready to discuss that proposition from the standpoint of our evacuating the fort, and retiring to Mastuj; but before going further, they must tell me what hostages they were prepared to offer for their good faith, and what guarantees that all arrangements for our journey would be properly made.

In the extremely improbable event of Sher Afzul and the Kháns accepting these terms, as the basis of further negotiations, it was decided that the hostages to be finally demanded should be no other than themselves! A reply came that the captured officers would only be handed over to me at Chitrál, if I gave my word that I would surrender the fort; I had but to say that, and Edwardes and Fowler would at once be permitted to write to us.

Soon after three o'clock in the afternoon, immediately behind a melancholy little procession of corpses, a close crowd, of about a hundred persons, was seen coming up from the bridge, with a couple of riderless ponies following. At the same instant, armed men flocked into the sangars on the west, which lay between us and the roadway, to prevent any rescue party issuing from the fort. This showed that our opponents relied upon our respecting a flag of truce very little more than we trusted them. Every Britisher in the fort, except, of course, poor Campbell, was on the parapet, straining his eyes, through field-glasses, to see if Edwardes and Fowler were in the throng. They were not discerned, and it was agreed (with myself as the sole dissentient) that they were not there; but optimism is a privilege of youth, and it is easier to convince yourself of what you desire even against the strongest evidence, than any one would believe who has not experimented on the subject. Hence, the manning of the sangars was looked upon as an artful subterfuge of the enemy, and the whole performance as an elaborate stratagem.

In the evening Amír Ali went to see the prisoners, escorted by our deserter friend, formerly of the 5th Punjab Infantry. He took with him large presents of money for both the Kháns; and tobacco and pipes, as well as other small articles, for our friends, which he was allowed to hand over to them in the presence of their custodians. Some conversation was also permitted in the Hindustani language, from which we learned that the poor fellows were well in health. Under the influence of the bribes the two Kháns grew friendly, and sent me a request for a couple of watches, revolvers, and cartridges. Several of their followers also eagerly assured Amír Ali of their wish to serve us, only they were not allowed to approach the fort. This, of course, meant that they, too, desired presents.

The Kháns again promised that our friends should not be injured, but be made as comfortable as possible. We found that they had been stripped of everything except the garments they wore ; but we were allowed to send them underclothing, tea, sugar, and plates, although uncertain of their receiving those articles. Of an escape there seemed but little chance, for Patháns were in the British officers' room all night. My only hope, and that a poor one, lay in working upon the cupidity of the Kháns.

The fort no doubt looked strange to Edwardes and Fowler, as they were marched up from the river. Perhaps, through the thickly-planted but bare and wintry trees, they had glimpses of the enemy's works close up to the main gate enclosure. But the press of their escort, more probably, allowed them only to see our ruined precincts, the loopholed walls and the white flag waving from the highest tower. All the walls must have had a curiously dishevelled outline, for the back cover, intended to protect the soldiers on the banquette, consisted chiefly of long planks, set up on end, without any uniformity of height or regularity in grouping. In some places they were clustered together, while at others, less important, they were sparsely distributed.

The low parapets of the towers had been raised by superimposed boxes full of earth, propped up by boards, while some of the towers were capped with a very rough bullet-proof head-cover. Probably, in such circumstances, men note appearances unconsciously, and the officers, with the possibility of a violent death never far from their minds, thought more of their friends inside the walls—eager, though powerless, to help them—than of the extraordinary look of our defences.

Correspondence of the usual kind was resumed on the 21st. Amír Ali told me, that the night before, the Kháns had said that we had no alternative but to do as they wished. We were now ordered to desist from carrying in wood from outside, although the hostile sangars were being strengthened industriously ; but it was necessary to submit, for the enemy had the whip-hand of me in all minor matters now. Amír Ali was again allowed to go and see Edwardes and Fowler, whom he found seated in durbar, with Sher Afzul, the young Kháns, and many other notables. It was repeated that I must go to Jandol. My agent answered, gently, that it could not be done. Much discussion followed. According to my clerk, the cogency of his arguments was admitted by Sher Afzul, who, nevertheless, insisted upon his own conditions being accepted.

Edwardes wrote to say he wanted to see Gurdon, and that his captors had agreed to his doing so. This was mentioned to Amír Ali by the Kháns, who were told that I would allow Gurdon to meet one, or both, of the officers at a particular place not far from the fort. This concession was scouted.

I also sent out a Chitráli headman, an ancient warrior with a slashed visage, to see what he could effect. This man was, undoubtedly, faithful to me, because Sher Afzul was known to owe him a grudge, and would certainly kill him at the first opportunity. He went to see the two, and found them firm about my surrendering. Amongst others, he saw a certain man named Gulwali, whose business seemed to be to watch those nobles on Umra Khán's behalf. This individual sent me word, confidentially, that his master was all for peace, and that it was the young chiefs who were the instigators of all the evils we suffered. Umra Khán, he said, was now only anxious to arrange matters so that the faults he had committed might be forgiven, but the other two played for their own hand—merely to get money.

The doorway leading into the stable enclosure was protected during the day, at Sifat's instance, by a semi-circular outside wall, properly loopholed—a moderately successful work. To build it was, however, difficult, on account of the ground being saturated with rain-water and sewage which we could not drain away.

My discomfort and weakness attained their worst on this day. Both were extreme, but henceforward I began to mend rapidly.

CHAPTER XXVII

OUR LOWEST POINT—AND A FLAG

NEXT morning, Friday, our deserter acquaintance brought me a note from the Khán of Shina, asking me, formally, to permit a conference between one of my officers and Edwardes and Fowler. He solemnly declared that he would be personally responsible for the safety of anyone I sent, and that, consequently, there need be no cause for anxiety on that score. I answered the ex-sergeant from the parapet that I was willing to send an officer to a particular pollarded tree, which I indicated, but no farther. The man answered that his master would only allow the interview to take place at the Musjid in the bazaar. He was then told that my answer was final.

Whitchurch got a short note soon afterwards from Fowler, which told us that, out of their whole party, only twelve were alive. We learned, for the first time, some details of what took place at Reshun during the parleyings there. The story has already been told ; it is only alluded to here because it confirmed, if confirmation was necessary, the suspicion that there had been perfidy. Our unhappy friends, while watching a game of polo, at the invitation of the rascally Muhammed Isa, were seized, thrown down, and bound.

Umra's Diwán came to pay me a visit during the afternoon. Gurdon and I saw him together. He gravely advised me, as a friend, to give up the fort, and not die of starvation. This remark pleased me, as the Chitráli I sent to the Kháns, the day before, foolishly bragged that we had food enough to last for months. Happily, our besiegers, reflecting upon the characteristics of their race, believed the exact opposite of his assertion. A long talk ended in the Diwán Sahib going away unsuccessful, but cheery.

In the fort we were far from happy. Not only had the enemy captured a large number of rifles at Reshun, but also the whole of the ammunition intended for the levies ordered up from Gilgit. Worst of all, it was known that Fowler had a large quantity of gun-cotton with him, and that his surviving Sepoys, all Muhammedans, knew how to use it. These facts spread a certain consternation through the fort for a few days — more, indeed, than I was aware of, until after it had subsided.

Now, my head clerk went on a secret errand to the Kháns. He took with him revolvers and watches for their acceptance, and did his best to stimulate their covetousness, but to little purpose. Loyal he certainly was, and not without ability, but it is no disparagement of him if I record my belief that my old friend and clerk, Abdul Hakím, would probably have been more successful. He was more experienced, had greater force of will, and more power of concentrating his mind on a particular object. Amír Ali whispered to the Kháns that, if they would hand over Edwardes and Fowler to me, or get them into the fort in any way they pleased, they should receive a large specified reward. The bribe was to be paid in uncoined gold, lent to me by the little Mehtar. Consequently, it could be paid without anyone's knowledge.

I also sent them a solemn promise that, if they would do as I asked, the service should never be forgotten, and they might rely upon me as a friend ever afterwards. It seemed that, on hearing my message, they talked together in undertones for some time, and then told Amír Ali that, willing as they were to oblige me in this matter, if they could do so with any hope of success, my proposal was impracticable. They were watched, they said, by Sher Afzul's men. Moreover, the facts must eventually leak out, and bring them to shame before the whole Musalmán world; while Umra Khán would be furious. Amír Ali pressed them, as far as he dared, but unsuccessfully.

He told me afterwards that the chiefs were not really afraid of the Chitrális, nor were they influenced by anything approaching to shame, but that Umra Khán had spies everywhere, and that it was Gulwali, the man already mentioned, and others of the same class, that they feared. After the conference had lasted a considerable time, Sher Afzul got news of it, whereupon he at once hurried thither with all his headmen.

Then followed a long talk, in which Amír Ali played a spirited part. We have his own word for it. He argued, unanswerably, in reply to many attempts to seduce him from his allegiance, that, according to the principles of Islám, Musalmáns must pray for and serve their ruling king without any regard to the religion professed by that king; therefore, the Muhammedans in the fort were acting in obedience to the teaching of their Koran, and were ready, all of them, to sacrifice themselves and die for their king and superior officer. He was then laughingly asked how reinforcements could cross the Shandúr at that time of the year. "The Pass," answered the alert Amír Ali, "will be worked into a plain by the thousands of men tramping over it from Gilgit."

S

After seeing Edwardes and Fowler, and listening to their unhappy tale, he returned, bringing with him the Diwán Sahib, who asked to see me, so that he might be given a final definite answer to take to Umra Khán. I excused myself, however, because it was so late, and bade him come back in the morning. We did not trust our opponents enough to give anyone an excuse for approaching the walls after dark.

Nevertheless, Gulwali was allowed to see Wafadár, and the individual with the scarred face. There was a great parade of secrecy, and Amír Ali was not permitted to be present. Afterwards, they told me that Gulwali asseverated that Umra Khán was extremely well disposed towards the Government of India, and then added, as his own private conviction, that the two Kháns in Chitrál were "a prey to avarice." He also expressed a wish to see me, secretly, at night, and offered to take a letter either to Umra Khán or to Peshawer. There was a suspicion, not to say a hope, in my mind that Gulwali was himself a "prey to avarice," and I determined to test this at once.

Amír Ali told me that he had seen, with Sher Afzul, my little friend, Muhammed Wali, who was, he thought, friendly to me at heart, and therefore all the more obliged to pose as an irreconcilable. On the last occasion that my clerk went out he took a Gilgiti servant with him, who contrived to get hold of certain news which was believed in the bazaar. It was that regular troops, as well as Hunza, Nagar, and Gilgit levies, had reached Mastuj.

Saturday, the 23rd March, brought back the crafty Diwán for another long conversation with Gurdon and me. He wanted a definite answer, he said, about my going to Jandol, and nothing more. But it was pointed out that he had already received it. Forthwith, he

proceeded to argue the whole question yet once more.
Then he touched upon the importance, the necessity, of
my sending an officer to talk to Fowler and Edwardes.
I gave my former reply, but the Diwán Sahib insisted that neither one nor both of the officers could
be sent to the place fixed upon by me. Whereupon
I expressed my sorrow. The envoy rejoined by playing his highest trump. Looking me straight in the
face he asked, "Supposing Umra Khán's conditions
were not agreed to, what is to prevent us from taking
the two British officers down to the river and killing
them?" I replied gravely, "What prevents me, Diwán
Sahib, from ordering you now into the courtyard to
be shot?" A shade slowly passed over his face and
left it grey and relaxed. Probably the Diwán Sahib
had never been so taken aback in his life. I improved the occasion and sermonised a little, when he
plucked up again, but without his former assurance.

He professed to know nothing of the circumstances
attending the capture of the Reshun detachment, so that
most of my remarks about the shamefulness of treachery
fell rather flat. Reverting to his first proposal, he confessed that Umra Khán knew that he had committed
himself, and now wanted to make amends by acting
as my protector, and by escorting me honourably to
Peshawer. He added that all the tribes were up from
Chilás to Bajour; even Hunza, Nagar, Gilgit, and
Khushwaktia had risen. Naturally there was no reply
to any of these statements save a gesture of composure. Well, would I give him a letter to Umra
Khán? "Certainly I will." "When is the truce to
end?" "At the pleasure of the Kháns."

Finally, he declared we need be in no anxiety about
our friends; that he, personally, would watch over them
and never let them out of his sight until they were

safe with Umra Khán. This was an indirect intimation that he wanted a *pourboire*. We were obliged to conciliate this man in spite of his irritating rudeness, for he obviously had the power to worry or help Edwardes and Fowler. So we gave him money and soft speeches instead of the harsh reprimand he deserved. My letter, which he carried to Umra Khán, after mentioning the capture of two of my officers, went on to say that if they were taken in fair warfare I had nothing to complain about, but if they were seized by perfidy then "you ought to send them back to me at once with a letter of apology." By so doing, he was told, he would show himself a man of honour and a princely character. He was furthermore exhorted to send back to me all his prisoners, to withdraw his forces from Chitrál, and trust to the leniency of the Government of India.

At dusk Sher Afzul hauled down his flag of truce, so we had to do the same with ours. I hoped to have prolonged the armistice for another day or two, but had no plausible excuse. However, there had been a formal cessation of hostilities for six whole days, and no firing of any kind since the night of the 15th, with the exception of the two shots on the 17th, while the white flags were flying.

So there was to be no more free and easy strolling about the fort, except at night. Even during the truce, Wafadár, knowing his fellow-countrymen's natural instincts, was always begging us not to expose ourselves on the west wall. A European head within thirty yards of him would, I suppose, have been a heart-burning temptation to any Chitráli or Pathán with a rifle in his hands.

It had been settled that the man, Gulwali, was to be brought into the fort after dark to see me secretly.

Gurdon had a faithful Chitráli servant, who was sent out to fetch him in from a pre-arranged place. When he got there he found himself in an ambush, and men sprang forth to seize him, but he kept his wits, tearing himself away from his would-be captors, at the same time calling out loudly to the soldiers on the Gun-tower to fire. There was a little shooting, but all soon quietened down, although the Kashmír riflemen on the garden parapet kept sending reports that large numbers of the enemy were massing to the south-east.

For two nights in succession it had rained hard. The tops of the walls had to be covered with tar-paulins to prevent their melting away, because the parapets had little or no wood in their construction, and consisted merely of stones and mud mortar.

This night (the 23rd) I tried, with only moderate success, to illuminate the west wall by means of a large bonfire. During the night Sifat's enclosure was left un-guarded. It was imperfectly loopholed on each side of its huge gate on the west, and when we retired from it at dark, the one or two loopholes there were could be used by the enemy from the opposite side. A great fire of logs was lit in the middle of the quad-rangle, between the fort main-door and the enclosure gate just referred to. Our strong fort entrance was securely barricaded every night with stones and timber ; but it had a square manhole, about four feet above the ground, which would give exit to any one tending the fire. But, as may be supposed, nobody was anxious for the job, therefore, long before morning it faded down. No fire, however big, could be expected to last till daylight without being properly stoked.

Early on the 24th the old familiar sniping into the fort from Danín began again. The rain poured down in a ceaseless torrent, carrying away, at length, a good large mass of the parapet wall on the west. Every one was wet through and miserable, while the sentries and the water-guards were in a deplorable condition. A little rum was given to those who liked it, and tea to the rest, as they came off duty. During the morning some one imagined that he heard the sound of a gun booming in the distance, but it was not repeated, and the excitement caused by the statement soon died away again.

Harley's orderly, one of the 14th Sikhs, got a bullet through his turban; his scalp also was slightly cut. As soon as his head was dressed in the hospital he resumed his work; but instead of being grateful for a lucky escape, the man went about muttering extreme annoyance at the damage done to his head-dress. He was amusingly inconsolable about it.

The enemy were persistent, if not particularly energetic, and we had no communication from Sher Afzul all day, a noteworthy circumstance. Our friendly Chitrális were downcast. In their eyes I had behaved wrongly in declining to accept the terms offered me. Even my friend Wafadár waxed gently reproachful, although he put his complaint in the form of an historical reminiscence. In that country, he remarked, in a dreamy manner, as though addressing nobody in particular, whenever a small garrison found itself helpless, and beleaguered by a large force, it was always the custom for it to capitulate, when it invariably received good treatment. Such observations indicated that Wafadár had not been uninfluenced by the crafty Gulwali. Yet I did not distrust him. He was very impressionable, but not disloyal. But if he spoke the feelings of the most trustworthy of the boy-Mehtar's followers, the sentiments of the rest could be easily guessed; a sleepless eye must be kept upon them.

Rain continued to fall heavily all the day, and we were surprised as well as delighted at the comparatively little damage it did to the walls. For seventy-two hours there had been no mitigation of the downpour. The men could hardly get dry in the daytime before being drenched again in the evening, when they had to stay near their alarm posts. All night long they were sickening with fever and dysentery, for the cold wind, blowing on their saturated clothes, chilled them blue. As the officer of the watch went his rounds every half-hour, he was, for all practical purposes, continually in the open. His plight was as bad as the men's.

Our third week of siege finished as miserably as the enemy outside could have desired.

Early next morning (the 25th), the clouds seemed breaking, as I viewed them from the top of the short flight of stairs which led from my room to the continuous roofs. A man accustomed to make the best of circumstances often finds some compensation for the most discouraging events. Hence the comforting reflection came to me that whatever harm the continuous rain was causing us, it secured us against an outbreak of fire, a contingency which we always had in mind. Bringing my eyes and thoughts from the clouds I noticed, at my feet, what looked like a very small flag stuck into the mud of the roof. Two or three other little banners also displayed themselves. In answer to my questions, a man shouted back from the Gun-tower that they were put there to stop the rain; and certainly the sky was fast clearing up.

On further inquiry, I learnt that Shuja-ul-Mulk observing the great discomfort we were in from the rain, had asked Mián Ráhat Sháh, our shifty fellow-subject from Peshawar, to stop it as a favour to him.

The method used by the Mián, a man none the less venerated because he was a notorious rascal, was to write verses from the Koran on slips of paper, and then fix them in the cleft end of suitable sticks. Possibly the wily fellow perceived that the atmosphere was getting lighter. However that may be, the sky quickly cleared, the sun burst forth, and the earth began rapidly to dry. The Musalmáns in the fort referred to the incident with gestures of smiling self-depreciation, as if fearful of appearing vain-glorious, but not without a glance of mild and half-contemptuous triumph, which plainly said, " What can your religion show to rival this ? " I have frequently seen bad weather change, after peculiar ceremonials, on the Indian frontier, and if I could forget the times of failure also, my human tendency to vague wonderment would have been greatly strengthened. Failures, nevertheless, in my experience, are much less frequent than successes, a fact probably attributable to the weather-wisdom of my cloud-compelling friends. There was a good deal of shooting the whole of this day, and a little desultory firing kept on until half-past nine. Afterwards there was quiet.

Tuesday, March 26th, marked the final appearance of the seven-pounder, which has been already related. A Sikh was killed in one of the towers from a bullet which entered at a loophole. The enemy did not like the gun being used, and opened a furious fire upon the fort. At night, as was our arrangement for dead Hindus, after the proper rites had been observed, the corpse was carried down to the waterway and thrust out into the river with some unavoidable commotion, which attracted notice, and started a fusilade.

Campbell had, and doubtless still has, a remarkable liking for Easterns, and in return possesses a power of attraction for them. His servants and orderlies were devoted to him. Uncommon linguistic gifts increased his influence, and he was constantly having Oriental visitors in his sick-room. In this way, he used to hear the opinions current in the fort, and, without perhaps being conscious of the fact, he was in himself a useful intelligence department. Of course, at times they told him the wildest stories, probably with the amiable intention of cheering his spirits. His orderly at that time, an exceptionally handsome Muhammedan cavalry soldier from his own regiment, the Central Indian Horse, used to report to his master the common talk of the garrison. This man warned Campbell that a great attack might be now expected, as it was the end of the annual fast, when Musalmáns are exceptionally fanatical. The predicted danger was a straight, determined charge across the streak of white sand, from the big sangar up-stream on the river's edge, delivered suddenly in broad daylight against the covered way. Campbell passed on this warning to me, and from that time forward we had a picket in the water-passage all day, as well as by night.

Long after dark there was intense excitement for a while. It was reported that a man outside, after shouting for one of our local servants by name, appealed to the guards not to shoot, because he had a letter for me. Gurdon hurried to the parapet with the Chitráli asked for, but they could get no answer to their call. The sentries explained that the first man had been joined by another, and that both had then gone away together. We were, consequently, left in doubt whether it was really a messenger for us who had approached the Guntower, or whether it was some "devilry" of the enemy. The man never came back. The enemy lit a blazing fire inside their sangar in the middle of the garden. We volleyed at it once or twice, but without perceptible effect.

The next day (the 27th), at noon, there was jubilation over a story that one of the Sikhs had killed
a man, whose body, in testimony thereof, lay exposed
some seven hundred yards distant.   However, there
was some uncertainty about the object pointed out,
and as no one ran forward to carry it away, it probably was not a corpse.   But the little incident
indicates the difficulty we found in retaliating on the
Sher Afzulites.   Since the 3rd of March we had thus
far suffered nineteen casualties ; but we were not
absolutely certain of having hit one of the enemy in
return.   It is very hard, even for a good Sikh, to
shoot a running man at a range of 800 or 1000 yards.
The only reasonable chance is to volley at him, but
our ammunition required to be strictly conserved.
Moreover, even at those distances we never saw any
one, except for a very short time, as figures occasionally ran from cover to cover or darted through
the trees on the west of the bazaar.

As this was the last day of the Muhammedan
Fast we conjectured that a desperate attack might
be made on the eve of the famous festival, which
would begin with the first sight of the new moon ;
but there was no such attack.   Indeed, the care of
themselves that the Pathán part of the enemy showed,
and their want of enterprise, always surprised me,
until I learned long afterwards of the deadly nature
of the fighting at Reshun, not only before, but after
the two British officers had been decoyed on to the
polo-ground and seized.   The story goes, that the
final rush after that catastrophe was so valiantly met
by Dhurm Singh, the brave Gurkha subadár, and his
men, that the Pathán losses were terrible, and not fully
realised until the dead came to be buried.   Umra Khán,
it is said, was so angered and troubled when he heard

the truth, that he gave emphatic orders for no more direct assaults on our troops, when entrenched, ever to be made. If this is true, the devoted little band that marched to our assistance with such amazing courage, did greatly relieve us from our enemies even at the very moment it was overwhelmed and destroyed.

The night passed off with no excitement, except between two and three in the morning, when the Kashmír Rifles burnt a good many cartridges. It was explained that they heard suspicious noises at the foot of the wall.

Thursday, the 28th, was the great Muhammedan Festival of the *Eed*. We supposed that the comparative lassitude of our besiegers might, perhaps, be due to their obligation to fast daily till sundown; and that now the trying month was ended we might expect them to show more resolution. In the afternoon, one of the Chitrális in the fort gave way to passionate sorrow. The poor fellow's younger brother had called from outside that their father had been killed by us in a sangar at Danín.

Just before sunset, letters were brought to the gate under a "cease-fire." They were from Drosh, one from Edwardes, and one from Umra Khán. A short enclosed note from Fowler begged Campbell, if ever he got the chance, to take care of the pony mare stolen from the writer at Reshun. Edwardes made us melancholy with the details of the tragedy at Reshun. Umra Khán wrote that he had received my letter, and appreciated its remarks. "Having sent for the Englishmen," he continued, "I told them they were at liberty to choose one of the three following proposals:—

"(1) if they wished to go to the colonel at Chitrál I would send them there;

"(2) if they wanted to go to Jandol I would take
them to Jandol; and

"(3) if they liked to remain at Drosh they could
do so.

"Both the Englishmen said that they would go to
the colonel at Chitrál, if their Sepoys were also released
with them; but, otherwise, without the Sepoys, they
would not go to Chitrál. I told them that their Sepoys
would not in any case be allowed to go with them.
For this reason they have remained. I told them to
write to you whatever they wanted to write, either in
English or in Persian, as they liked. They said 'Very
well.' God willing, both letters will reach you and
make known all particulars. Further, rest assured as
regards me, and always let me know about yourself.
I have detained the Sepoys because they are Musalmáns, all Muhammedans being brethren."

Edwardes confirmed what Umra Khán had written
about his offers to them. It is generally believed
these were made by Umra Khán in a hilarious mood,
and they were undoubtedly received by most of his
hearers as an excellent joke. Supposing the British
officers had elected to return to Chitrál, it is certain
that they would still have been detained, with or
without plausible excuse, for Umra Khán's chief hope
at this time, lay in the high value of his hostages.

This was a remarkable day in the annals of the siege.
I had often lamented not having with me my British
Agent's flag, which had been left behind at Gilgit.
Possibly I was getting superstitious on the subject, and
imagined that its absence brought us ill-luck. It seemed
almost improper, not to say illegal, to fight without
the Union Jack floating over our heads. Also, many
people were getting downhearted, for our prospects
were undeniably a little cloudy. So we went into

committee on the subject, and decided we must have a flag. Harley, of course, at once produced a Sikh soldier who was a good needleman; he had men equal to every emergency. Shuja-ul-Mulk gave me some cheap, red-dyed cloth; a blue turban being also contributed, and some white cotton material. Whitchurch's share was important. He possessed an empty tin of navy-cut tobacco with a picture of a Jack upon it, which we used as a pattern. The others gave advice. With scissors, needle, and thread the Sikh set to work. The width of the stripes and their other proportions were earnestly debated; the pole, and everything connected with it, were also anxiously discussed. When the flag was finished, a day later, and brought for final inspection, we found it admirable in every way, except that its contriver had sought to improve upon our national ensign by sewing in the middle a crescent and crossed swords cut out of white stuff. He was a little upset by our want of appreciation, and went away slowly to remove his own particular creations.

The flag was carefully erected on the top of the lofty tower to the south-west, at night, for it was a long operation, and we did not want anyone hit, as that might look like a bad omen. At early dawn, and every morning after, when one capped to the fluttering rag, a smile of confidence, one might almost say the smile of adoration for a fetish, accompanied the action.

During a siege, as well as in all other occasions of a man's life, there is plenty of room for superstition. We, for instance, will always believe that this flag turned the scale of our fortunes from the moment it was run up. In truth it helped us greatly. It cheered our hearts and stiffened our backs. Critical eyes have since discovered that it was made incorrectly, that certain narrow white stripes were all of the same width, so that it could never have been flown upside down as a signal of distress. Happier are we that such a contingency was never provided for. Sentiment still hangs about this improvised Union Jack. It is one of my dearest possessions.

CHAPTER XXVIII

REACTION

THE daily detail of work in the way of strengthening old defences, inventing new ones, or in devising screens or fresh places for bringing a flanking fire upon important points, would be tedious to record ; but every night all spare hands were thus employed in carrying out plans which had been devised during the day.

A committee was convened, with Townshend as president, and Gurdon and Harley as the two other members, to recommend Whitchurch for the Victoria Cross, in compliance with the official regulations on the subject. Upon the proceedings being handed to me, I wrote a forwarding note to go with them, in which I fulfilled, to the extent of my power, the solemn promises I had made to the dying Baird. It was well to have this record completed properly, and betimes, for no one could say what might happen within the next few weeks, who might be killed or who left.

On the 29th March I sent a note answering Umra Khán briefly ; a mere polite acknowledgment of his letter. Campbell also wrote to Fowler, with the object of cheering him and Edwardes. The Jandol Kháns sent me word that Umra Khán had already left Drosh for Bajour, so that if I wanted to make peace (their term for a surrender) I must give fifteen days' notice beforehand, to allow time for them to communicate with their chief. He himself had bade me be of good cheer, and started off with the encouraging remark that, by his orders the fort was not to be "rushed." Umra Khán was undoubtedly a person possessed of some humour of a peculiar kind.

A man who came for my letter produced a shoulder of mutton and some country tobacco; a bit of the meat, to make quite sure, was offered to a dog, who enjoyed it, and so removed our doubts. The joint was then devoted to the sick people in hospital.

We were closely beleaguered. A double cordon stretched round the fort tightly. On the night of the 28th a very good fellow, Mír Hamza, who deserves to be recorded—even if my collection of uncomfortable names in this book is already large, —tried to pass through the enemy's lines with a note, but only a few yards from the walls he was challenged, and obliged to race back. This man, years before, is said to have saved Colonel John Biddulph, an admirable author and a renowned frontier officer, from capture by the "Wrestler" (referred to on page 25).

Any attempt upon us would have been out of the question on this date, so light was the sky with its young crescent moon. To the north, that wonderful mass of snow mountain looked as lovely and as unsympathetic as ever. Its beauty always made one melancholy, nor could it be looked upon without a long sigh and sad thoughts of those far away at home, who were, we knew, suffering much more for us than we suffered ourselves. We could only repay their anxious thoughts with others as tender. If we could but have sent them a single line of love, a weight would have been lifted from our hearts.

We achieved a notable triumph this same evening. It has been already told how we sought to illuminate the

walls at night, and so keep the besiegers off them, by
fire-balls during demonstrations, and by log fires in
front of the main gate. Such experiments were successful to a limited extent only. Wafadár now explained
to me a local method, with the same end in view,
which sounded more promising. He showed how little
platforms could be thrust out through horizontal slits
cut in the parapet walls, and heaps of pine chips be
kindled and kept alight upon them. One man would
have to be employed, continuously, for each of these
cressets, to feed the flames, but nothing except his hand
and wrist need ever be exposed, and then only for
short periods at irregular intervals. We determined
to try this plan experimentally on the west and the
river sides, therefore little gangs of Chitrális were employed to construct the platforms and fix them properly. The result was good, and would be still more
hopeful when certain minor faults had been rectified.
Great care was required in their manipulations, so that
the fort might not be set on fire. When the breeze was
even moderate, these illuminators could not be used
upon the windy side. At other times, all that was
necessary was to put one trustworthy sentry in charge
of the Chitráli who added the fuel, and to keep alongside
of each platform a large skinful of water.

The shock caused by the Reshun disaster had
affected us all greatly, nor was it lessened by vague
rumours of yet another catastrophe to a second force
marching from Mastuj in a devoted attempt to rescue
Edwardes. For obvious reasons, discussion on the subject was discouraged; but, for several days after the
prisoners had been brought to Chitrál, a sadder-faced
company than we in the fort could scarcely have been
found. And still, any reference to Edwardes or Fowler
gave one a cold feeling at the heart; their fate was

T

so doubtful. Terrible stories of the cruelties practised
by Patháns on helpless captives rose to the mind, and
there we were, impotent, and shut up like whipped
children, within our four walls! We could only fix
our jaws and grip our hands in useless anger. That
our poor friends would in the end escape murder hardly
engaged our thoughts, whatever our time-serving lips
might say. I worried my nights with doubts if enough
had been done to save them. My cooler judgment
said yes. My tired thoughts continually touched the
question, to glance off, and then return again and again
with exhausting persistence. But mental time moves
with the speed of a hurricane, and in particular circumstances, ordinary conceptions of days and periods
have no meaning. Already the events of scarcely more
than a week past seemed ancient history, so far distant
that half-forgetfulness had begun to play its consoling
part. The more acutely one feels the sooner comes
relief, no matter how deep are the sore places which
remain.

Now reaction had begun, and was nearly equal to
the former heavy depression of the garrison. The
"boys," as Campbell termed them, were in high spirits.
Old tins fixed to the tails of stray dogs made them
charge the bazaar madly, and the enemy, gaping with
surprise, was more convinced than ever that no Britishers
are quite sane. Then after a quiet night a glorious
spring morning ushered in Saturday, the 30th March,
and turned all youthful fancies to thoughts of gaiety.
Two dummies, atrocious caricatures of a helmeted
British officer and his turbaned orderly, were made,
and set up the following day on the top of the
inner dividing wall of the fort. At a few hundred
yards anything passes for a man. I have mistaken
artfully - disposed upright stones on a housetop for

night-guards, and small groups of wooden statues for possible foes, so it was no wonder that the besiegers were fooled. They started a furious musketry fire, and it was long before they guessed that there was something more than human in the imperturbability of the effigies. It was interesting to note, when the figures were brought down in the evening, for after being displayed they could not be withdrawn in daylight, that they remained untouched. All the bullets fell low, while the woodwork of the window of the durbar hall underneath was peppered all over. Probably the vigorous young foliage on the trees hid the straw men from the middle distance sangars, while many of the others were so close that the fort walls interfered with their view. Consequently, most of the aiming was done at over-long ranges.

Upon this Saturday we had a stock-taking, and reviewed our position. At the then rate of expenditure, our rations, such as they were, would last up to the 11th of June—a comfortable reflection. We numbered altogether 543 mouths, of whom 403 were soldiers; but only 342 of the latter were riflemen actually on duty, the remainder being in hospital. The guard and sentry work was very heavy. It may be interesting to show how the men were distributed at this time. At the main west gate were ten soldiers, and at the garden entrance six. Each of the four parapets had ten men told off for it, and each of the four towers absorbed another six. There were ten soldiers employed to look after the Chitrális. Campbell's covered way had a picket of twenty, the water-tower twenty-five, and the stables a similar number, while the doorway leading out into the stables was guarded by ten Sikhs. After we had gone over the list many times in consultation, it was found impossible to reduce this total. The only other guards were six men over the Rághunáth Snider ammunition ; that of the Sikhs (Martini cartridges) was kept at the main gate. One hundred and sixty-seven fighting men remained for other possible work, sorties, reinforcements, and so forth. On the whole, we had no just cause to complain, and, provided that the Kashmír Rifles had "come again," we should take a great deal of beating.

Discipline was carefully maintained. Bugle calls were given as regularly as in a cantonment. At first, the opposition bugler used often to blow at the same time, but not of late. Possibly, we thought, he had gone up the valley, Mastuj way, with the Chitráli contingents, which were seen to be constantly moving in that direction. These contingents travelled along the ridges to the west on the sky-line just out of range, a sensible precaution, but none the less irritating on that account.

All the Sikhs were wonderfully cheery and eager. Excitement delights them ; thoughts of bloodshed brighten their handsome faces with pleasant smiles. Commanding them, under Harley, was their own subadár, a splendid old fellow who had grown grey in the service of the Queen. Strange as it may sound to Western ears, he was everlastingly haranguing his company. His voice was strident, and lacerated one's nerves with its monotonous clamour, but no one would have dreamed of asking him to modulate it. Many Easterns are like some Anglo-Saxon women, and have to talk to help them to think. This old Sikh officer was as strict as he was brave. I never approached the main gate, which might be looked upon as the headquarters of Harley's men, although they were also at the water door, on watch over the Chitrális, on the

top of the towers, and at every other important place,
without the guard tumbling out to present arms, while
the bugler sounded a point of war. The old subadár
would have been disconsolate at any remission of military courtesy, although subsequently he was induced
to relax it to some extent. At the beginning of the
siege, I was generally known as the "Colonel," an
honorary rank bestowed upon me for convenience,
the word "British Agent" being troublesome for
Orientals to pronounce; but the Sikhs had now
given me the brevet of "General," which stuck to
me long afterwards, and, like my former descrip-
tion, was not a little confusing to people who did not
know me well, but had always heard that I was a
civilian.

Perhaps the most pleasant thing about the Sikhs,
was the kind, gay, friendly looks they gave one, as if
there were some simple old joke always on hand. Men
who could so keep up their spirits after the hard work,
bad food, and continual exposure they had experienced,
must be practically invincible.

They were a great contrast to the sad, heavy faces
of most of the Rághunáths, whether Gurkhas or Dogras.
Yet it must in fairness be said that these men knew
little or no Hindustani, the speech used by the British
officers; and that to draw forth the splendid soldierly
qualities of Gurkhas, particular officers are required,
who are accustomed to them, and able to gain their
liking in intimate converse. With one additional
officer, for instance, my former companion and assistant, C. G. Bruce of the 5th Gurkhas, these men would
ever have gone about with the national grin, a thing
which darkness scarcely hides. But we had only three
British officers altogether for regimental duties, and
they were overworked, so that the Kashmír soldiers

had to be left greatly to their own leaders—brave but ill-instructed men.

Sunday, the 31st of March, was the last day of our fourth week of siege.

Our Chitráli friends stated their conviction that the morning would reveal new sangars close up to us on the west. They were right in supposing that we should have evidence of the enemy's activity, but they did not guess the exact form it would take. At the north corner the Sikhs, hearing a rattle of stones during the night, fired a few shots. Daylight showed that some eight or nine yards of rough wall had been erected, sloping from the enemy's up-stream sangar towards the water's edge. The firing from the North-tower had, seemingly, stopped the building of a screened way, more or less parallel to our own, on the farther side of the sand-spit. Again, on the opposite side of the river, a brand new approach displayed itself exactly opposite to the end of Campbell's covered passage. It could not do very much harm, however, for the addition of a few timbers, thoughtfully arranged, parried it sufficiently. Probably it was designed chiefly to guard against men being sent out of the fort at night to swim down the river. One peculiarity of all the sangars, except that facing our west front, was that no loopholes could be discerned, even with the best field-glasses. They were so cleverly contrived that one never knew the result of a shot, or where to shoot; consequently, as our cartridges were precious, we rarely fired at them at all.

At half-past four in the afternoon there was another parley. We ceased firing, but the sangar across the river probably could not see the white flags displayed, for it kept rattling away at us, but did no harm. The envoy was the ancient woman, who came to say, by

word of mouth, that Sher Afzul was prepared to give
me a safe conduct to Mastuj, and also to mend the
roads. He would, in addition, have all our stores and
baggage carried by villagers. In short, he proposed
that we should evacuate the fort with all the honours
of war; but this was to be my very last chance.
Supposing I refused to listen to him he would not
attempt to negotiate with me again.

One encouraging remark the old woman made was
that no troops were advancing from Gilgit. As this
was gratuitous—and bearing in mind that Chitrális
stick to the truth so tenaciously, as somebody has remarked, that it is impossible to get it from them—
it looked as if a relieving force were approaching.
The woman also handed in a letter, neither signed
nor sealed—but said to be written at the dictation,
and on behalf of all the notables of Chitrál—which
calmly stated that I, personally, had told them at
Gáirat they were at liberty to choose anyone they
pleased as Mehtar. Although it seemed almost unnecessary to answer so absurd a statement, I contra-
dicted it dispassionately in a signed document, for
perhaps some person was disseminating falsehoods
which my silence might be held to substantiate.
On the other hand, it was equally probable that my
answer would be read out as an admission of that
or any other untruth.

The Chitrális in the fort were allowed to talk freely
with Sher Afzul's messenger, but some of my people
were present to hear what they said. The rest of her
news proved of small importance. In reply to Sher
Afzul's verbal message, she was told to say that he
had better send a letter. She had only been gone a
very few minutes, when men hurried up to the gate
with a polite invitation for Amír Ali to go and play

polo with Sher Afzul! We had anticipated a very different reason for their hurry ; and if our besiegers were humorists, which doubtless they were not, they certainly "sold me" this time, as the slang phrase runs. With equal politeness, they were assured by my clerk that stress of business alone prevented his going back with them.

We had in the fort a man who had given us valuable help all through, but particularly before the siege began. He was a person of high rank, and, happily for us, he knew that the triumph of Sher Afzul would be synchronous with his own death, for there was hatred between them. On this account, chiefly, our friend Futteh Ali Sháh, whose house, already referred to, was directly opposite, at seven hundred yards interval, our south wall, had done all in his power to help Gurdon to collect the supplies which alone enabled us to maintain our position. He was as faithful as Wafadár, and for identical reasons. On the 1st of April he told me that two little companies of men we had observed travelling down the valley, were very likely returning from Mastuj, and that, in his opinion, a Gilgit force must certainly have arrived there. Should that be true, he thought Sher Afzul would probably make a grand attempt to get hold of the fort by stratagem within the next four or five days. While it was yet dark, soon after three in the morning, two Jandolis near the Gun-tower shouted that they had brought a letter for me, from the Commissioner of Peshawer, and wished to deliver it personally. The British officer on watch shouted back, using Wafadár as his mouthpiece, that they should place the letter on a stone and themselves retire, or else bring it in the daytime.

Small numbers of the enemy were then observed to

be collecting round the *soi-disant* messengers, whereupon
the guard was ordered to fire. This little incident
subsequently diverted our thoughts, for, of course, the
men might have been well paid to get a letter through,
which could not be done secretly except in the way they
adopted. On the other hand, it might have been merely
a rascally attempt to get sufficiently near the walls to
light a fire under the tower, the adventurers themselves being secure from harm after the "cease-fire"
had sounded. We could not remember how the wind
blew that night, whether on the south wall, so as to
help an incendiary, or in another direction. However,
what is quite certain is, that Gurdon was right to run
no risk, and therefore to give the order to fire.

One of the agreeable observations of the ancient
dame, on the previous evening, was that the Sher
Afzulites were busily engaged in making scaling ladders
for a determined attack. The Chitrális in the fort also
told Campbell that they thought hostile marksmen
might build themselves bullet-proof nests of fascines or
faggots in the surrounding trees, and harass us greatly.
To be ready for a scaling party, which by common
consent was to attack the south wall especially, for that
was admittedly our weakest flank, Wafadár and I got
out some long spears from a storeroom, and placed
them conveniently for my scratch picket to use through
certain long, slit loopholes below the banquette on the
south. As for the men climbing into the trees, there
was never much anxiety on that point. The Kashmír
Rifles riddled the upper branches habitually, and very
likely, from their inferior shooting were, in that way, a
real protection to us.

Everybody asked after the siege why we had not
cut down those trees. Nobody reflected on the time
necessary for such an operation, even if we had possessed

good axes and skilled woodsmen. As a matter of fact, we went in with bare poles all round us, and in a hurry; we came out with the trees in full foliage. There is no doubt that, in this particular instance, the dense foliage on all sides did little harm; for, if it allowed the enemy to get fairly near, it also gave us a valuable screen. If our opponents had been determined enough to climb into the fort along the two or three overhanging boughs, or to assail us from the upper branches, they would certainly have been able to capture or demolish the Gun-tower, more easily, by rushing in and starting a dozen simultaneous fires against the walls, selecting a time when a favourable wind was blowing. After that there would have been stubborn fighting, no doubt, but we should have been still far from hopeless, while the enemy must have perished in hundreds. Reshun had taught the Chitrális and their Pathán allies the price they must pay for a masterful attempt to capture the fort.

All Sifat's men in any way fit for such work were now (April 1st) enrolled as levies and armed with Snider rifles, as well as with Eastern swords. Everybody knew, without being told, that the siege was entering upon a last and more desperate phase. We had been shut up for a whole month, and the long arm of the Government of India must be stretching itself forth to rescue us, whilst the besiegers could not but be aware of that fact, and must feel that they had little time to lose.

I thought at the time, and I have always thought since, that the hoisting of the Union Jack was the turning of our luck. I know, at any rate, that coincident with that event there was a wonderful return of cheerfulness, confidence, and determination to be seen on most faces. Trials and keen anxiety were in store for us all; but the unhappy week of the truce was gone for ever. It was then we reached our lowest point. The daily routine of work went on now more pleasantly, because we were all happier.

Superstition, the belief in luck, and similar fancies are far beyond the control of reason. Many times I laughed at myself for yielding to such influences, but yielded nevertheless. For instance, I used at odd times to play a "Patience" game; but whenever the cards came out properly there was invariably a noisy demonstration by the enemy, with its usual concomitant of excitement and disturbance. It almost seemed that one must deliberately play to lose, or else bring on a hostile attack! Fantastic ideas of this kind have a real meaning for many men, and for all lovers of games of chance. But I care nothing for gambling, so with me it must have been genuine inherited superstition. "Patience" was abandoned for good. Then, towards the end of the siege, when I used to pass the greater part of my night, if there was quiet, in the mess-verandah, sitting over a small charcoal fire, one of the young Chitrális in the fort often brought his long-stringed guitar and sang to its music, either alone, or with Wafadár and another in a trio. Gradually I became convinced that their music, though, of course inaudible to the enemy, was inevitably followed by an outburst of firing and by an alarm. It was useless to scorn one's self as a fool and to persevere. The rule held good many times, and it had not one exception. Finally, fancy conquered common-sense, and the musicians were asked to come no more.

Sifat's men were busy all the night of the 1st April in digging a trench leading to the waterway, and parallel to the river wall of the stables. It was to form a sunken road for the better protection of the water-carriers labouring under their heavy burdens from the river. On the outer edge a line of heavy beams was stuck on end to shelter, as well as to conceal, those using the ditch-like path. I saw the work after it was finished, and, though roughly done, it was effective. But immediately afterwards there came a steady downpour of rain, and by the morning all the beams were lying on the ground, and the sunken way itself was full of water. A fatigue party of Sikhs told off to repair the damage had poor success. So Sifat tried his hand once again, and on the following Thursday (the 4th) solved the difficulty, the rain stopping at the same time.

CHAPTER XXIX

SHORT RATIONS

SHER AFZUL recommenced negotiations on the 2nd, 3rd, and all the 4th April, in the usual way, by letters, in which he represented himself as an injured innocent and me as an aggressive person, followed by demands that I should come out of the fort; and all the time his envoys simply cooed with his protestations of friendliness and loyalty towards the Government of India, as well as of his wish for peace. According to the messengers, Sher Afzul was languishing for my personal friendship, and was merely the ally of Umra Khán, because he could get no encouragement to desert him and throw in his lot with me. Consequently, they said, he was at a loss to know what to do. I replied advising him to submit, and, perhaps somewhat disingenuously, asked him not to hurry a decision, but to take at least a fortnight to think it over.

We now got hints for the first time of the shocking massacre of Sikhs at Kalak.

Another letter Sher Afzul sent, really gave the lie to every statement I had made, and was more like a document drawn up in defence of a prisoner in desperate case than an ordinary argument about a parley. All the same, the men who came with it were as oily-tongued as ever. They even brought a goat and some tobacco for my clerks. With great earnestness they asseverated that Sher Afzul was most anxious for

301

peace—a statement I was also beginning to believe. He was evidently much disturbed at some event unknown to us.

With me was one of Sher Afzul's half-brothers, an ancient friend who, in Chitrál fashion, used to seek every opportunity to caress my hand, and gaze affectionately into my eyes. Of late, this prince had grown less demonstrative, and more and more thoughtful. Sher Afzul now asked for him to be sent out as peacemaker and go-between. He further observed that this mutual friend could go with me as a hostage if I agreed to march back to Mastuj. It is a remark of this kind, that I should give up to Sher Afzul a man to be afterwards sent to me as a hostage, which shows there is some subtle line of thought in the Chitráli mind not easy of grasp even by an European who has studied the people earnestly. I declined to part with my long-time friend, a compliment which that friend tried hard to be grateful for, but he only succeeded in contorting features, already dark with chagrin, into the phantom of a smile. The poor old fellow had a son known to me ever since he was a little boy. To cajole me into letting the father go Sher Afzul sent this youth to the fort, but I was just as determined to keep my few magnates together as Sher Afzul was anxious to show that he had all the people of rank in the country with him.

Probably to insinuate the futility of further resistance, this boy brought me a letter said to have been received by Sher Afzul from a man I had never heard of, a resident of Jandol. It affirmed that everything was quiet in Jandol, and that Sher Afzul might therefore attack us without fear; also, that all the Musalmán tribes and clans were united in his support. This made me wonder if a relieving force could possibly be starting from Peshawer.

One of the humours of this period was when Sher Afzul's emissary gravely produced a tiny Quackenbush cartridge, and said how gratified his master would be if I would kindly fit a rifle to it. My answer was not worthy of the occasion. It was that I should be charmed to let him have the little rifle in exchange for ten goats or sheep. No doubt he blushed for me and my sordid commercial spirit. We had, it is true, one of these toy guns, but Campbell had been brought out of his bed and propped up in a chair in the mess-verandah, where he divided his time between reading books, and missing sparrows for dinner. But, nevertheless, one did not know that the Quackenbush might not get us something some day.

Sher Afzul protested that he intended to drive into the fort the families of all the Chitrális who were with me. This was, perhaps, because of a message I had sent him, that in future, an armistice must be paid for at the daily rate of six goats and four hundred and eighty pounds of flour. He solemnly vowed that he would give me back Edwardes and Fowler at the village of Danín after I had marched out—an idle promise, for those officers were then far away in Bajour.

His last "bluff" was that he was not only prepared to think over my observations for a fortnight, as had been suggested, but that I ought to think over his offers for at least three weeks before coming to a decision. Only, he added, the siege would be pressed all the same. He did not wish to inconvenience me, but if I liked quarrels and trouble there was no help for it. That was the last letter but one Sher Afzul ever sent me; and the last was written in very different circumstances, and in a very different tone, some weeks later.

There had been very little firing at night or shouting for some days, but on Friday morning, the 5th, between one and six o'clock, there was a good deal of noise and much letting off of guns round us, while the enemy's bugler re-appeared and blew the "assembly," "fire," and several other calls. Two new sangars were discovered soon afterwards, and rumours spread that approaches were to be made behind the great plane trees, close to the walls, and also that we were to be mined.

Another form of assault, now started in an organised way, was that of abusing us, whereat, it must be confessed, the Patháns showed proficiency. The summerhouse corner was not twenty-five yards from the Guntower, and as the wall there was high, and gave perfect shelter, anyone could come near enough to make every word distinct. Near the East-tower, also, the enemy could approach, with safety, almost as close. But only a few people in the fort understood what was shouted. One of these was a Gilgit man, of some position, who had been under a cloud since the 3rd of March, when he behaved indifferently. He now saw a chance of displaying certain hitherto hidden talents, and, from the top of a tower, eloquently answered back the vile things, whatever they were, which were shouted from outside. All this, doubtless, sounds archaic, but the siege throughout was anachronistic.

At nine o'clock there was an explosion, as if a big gun were being fired from across the river. No one could guess its meaning, but in the end we decided it must be a device to persuade us that the enemy possessed cannon. This may seem strange to Western ears; but I have been regularly bombarded morning after morning, on the Gilgit frontier, in this harmless way. Campbell's orderly was confident that a relieving force, with mountain artillery, was engaging our besiegers.

The previous evening the son of the old prince again

came to the gate, but, as it was late, he was asked to
return in the morning. He arrived, after mid-day, with
long verbal communications from Sher Afzul, as well as
strict injunctions to bring back his father. To move
my hard heart he faltered, with wistful pathos, that if he
were seen returning by himself he would be fired upon.
He was sent away alone, and told to say that I would
receive no more messages through old women or little
boys.

A noisy night followed, in spite of its being beautifully clear and not very dark. Soon after nine there
was an interchange of shots followed by incessant yells
and war cries from the end garden wall. Then the
enemy made a series of pretended rushes which ended
in nothing. Pipes were sounded, to be presently
drowned in choruses of insult, and the racket outside
was surprising. To it we contributed, at intervals, by
steady volleys. After eleven o'clock the outcry lessened,
but the shooting was kept up till daylight. Every
one looked about sharply to find what new thing had
happened. It was sufficiently bad ; no less than three
new works were seen. A large sangar faced us not
thirty yards from our west wall. It looked as complete
and well-built as it was big. For such a structure to
be erected between darkness and dawn one had to
go to the " Arabian Nights " for a precedent. Then
there was a second, half-finished, in the middle of the
garden, and a something that looked as if a covered
road were being made from the enemy's river bank
up-stream sangar to the out-of-doors durbar place, which
we termed the " chabutra," just outside of Sifat's enclosure, and close to, but to the north of, the great
mushroom approach which had sprung up so porten-
tously in a single night. After six o'clock the enemy's
fire slackened. We had to work hard all that day.

U

Townshend used to come to my room every morning at eight, read his diary and copy it out for me ; then we discussed together the work to be attempted within the next twenty-four hours, our decisions being duly recorded in his note-book. For this day we designed much additional loopholing, while, after dark, we intended to build a strong barrier wall, properly perforated for rifle fire, at the west end of the stables enclosure, flanking this new erection from a small square building, now turned into a blockhouse, which stood at the top of Campbell's waterway. In addition, there was a great deal of defensive work to be done in the East-tower, especially in that portion of it commanding the eastern extremity of the stable outpost. That important position was, indeed, made very strong, well able to protect the water passage on both its flanks, while, in proportion to our total garrison, the interior of the covered way and the tower over it were most liberally supplied with soldiers. We likewise took Sifat's enclosure in hand, which the big new sangar so closely menaced. During the afternoon, many fresh loopholes were made in its west wall, which twelve Sikhs were to maintain during the night, and also on the side facing the river, where a detachment of our newly-enrolled levies, with a couple of Gilgit Rajahs, stationed themselves at sundown to watch sharply against a sudden charge of the enemy across the sand at the water's level. Certainly, these elaborate arrangements once complete, it would be bad luck if we were to lose our waterway and have to retake it. But, practically, that part of our defences was now impregnable.

The enemy worked busily all day at the summer-house post, but no amount of watching from the Gun-tower could detect his object. He was also fussing a good deal at his latest new approach, and one bundle of faggots actually lay upon the chabutra, protruding beyond the edge which overlooked the steep path leading up from the river bank sangar. We decided to go out at nightfall on the chabutra and try to find out what was being done there, and then, if it were practicable, to build out a small sangar to flank the west wall of Sifat's enclosure, and prevent a work being constructed upon the chabutra itself. Of course, the great sangar, the astonishing growth of a few hours, as it appeared to us, was of enormous interest. It was exciting to be so close to the enemy, for not more than twenty yards now intervened between our respective loopholes. Townshend and I were in Sifat's enclosure the greater part of the afternoon, discussing matters and directing the workers. Near the south-west corner, the old gun port had been hastily filled in, and we were nearly caught napping, while standing there, for a bullet came through one of the interstices of the stones, and smashed itself into fragments close by my leg ; a happy let-off, to use a common expression.

A little later I borrowed a rook rifle and had a kind of duel with one of the enemy. Cautiously peering through the edge of a loophole, to watch a similar aperture of the enemy's sangar, at length too much of my face was exposed, and a bullet struck the wall noisily outside. It was a shockingly bad shot, but probably the man who fired felt as excited as myself— not the best state of mind and body for drawing a fine sight on a very near object. There was a pause, and again I approached the hole, at the same instant that the enemy's loophole showed a kind of pinkish tinge, instead of being black, which showed that it had a man's face for a background. We both started away, and I suppose he, like myself, was standing well back, looking down the barrel of his rifle. Then I shifted quietly to a loophole farther north and watched carefully. After a considerable time, the enemy's loophole turned pink once again. Probably he had decided that his *vis-à-vis's* loophole must really be empty, and he wanted to see where else he could shoot. My finger began to press the trigger as slowly and steadily as my eagerness would allow. Off went the rifle, after a couple of seconds or so, which seemed like hours, and the particular loophole I had been watching remained vacant for the rest of the afternoon. Whether the man was hit, or only scared, it is impossible to say. Shooting at close quarters, with accurate rifles, is, however, a very different thing from the long-range firing I had been in the habit of indulging in occasionally from the Gun-tower, at running men, eight hundred yards distant. But that was more for range-finding, and to help to instruct some of the more remarkably ignorant of the Rághunáth riflemen, than with any idea of hitting a particular individual.

The evening closed in, and we sat down to our frugal dinner of inferior horse-meat and spoiled rice, preceded however by the pea-soup, which we should have been more grateful for, if it had not grown distasteful from monotony. A horse was first killed for food on the 22nd of March, after much discussion. Gurdon would not soften to the idea, while Whitchurch, with intense disgust on every feature, lapsed into speech to observe that he would as soon eat dog. Upon that date I was the wretchedest invalid imaginable, and the cook's first experiment was to try and make soup for me. He prepared something or other which was brought in a bowl. One sniff of that dreadful fluid sufficed. How it had been concocted was unknown, and never inquired into, but its odour was appalling. Perhaps, after all, Whitchurch and Gurdon were right, and there was something about our horses, or their feeding, that made them uneatable. Nevertheless, we persevered, and ordered a beef-steak, which proved excellent from the point of view of hungry men closely besieged.

Following that success, we had horse-beef every day, and its former opponents waxed loud in its praises. Whitchurch regulated the killings. No man knew whose pony he was eating. Campbell, who has a great tenderness for horses and dogs, was moralising once on this subject. He observed that it was all sentiment, and that a little black pony he was very fond of would of course have to be killed, although he himself would eat none of it. That particular animal had been consumed several days earlier, and he had partaken of it with the rest. One of my ponies, which really belonged to Lieutenant Dew of the Guides, who had lent it to me, was very sick with fever; the other had been driven out of the fort. The poor dying brute was begged by some of the Musalmáns and slaughtered for their use. We were really very fortunate about our messing. The fort contained a large stock of salt, which enabled us to pickle our beef and so have no waste. Nothing could induce the Hindus to touch the meat, so they lived entirely on the gritty flour, and crowded into the hospital. Whitchurch at this time (6th April) had more than seventy patients to look after.

Perhaps our table talk is worthy of record. It was remarkable for its limitations, and for the gusto with which its favourite topic was discussed. Whitchurch was gratuitously supposed to have matrimonial leanings, and no meal passed without a reference to that. He was a capital person to chaff, for he was intensely good-natured, somewhat shy, and

never retaliated. But the solid talk for ever
converged round a subject of never-dying interest, and
always began after the first pangs of hunger had been
assuaged effectually, if not altogether satisfactorily.
Someone would say, "What excellent dinners they
give you at the Savoy!" Then everybody brightened
up, and ate Savoy dinners or suppers over again in
imagination, and gloatingly. This theme never staled.
It came daily as the savoury at our evensong banquets.
Probably it was natural, for the nutritious but uninter-
esting pea-soup, the more than half-starved horse-flesh,
and the damaged rice, day after day and meal after
meal, required an imaginative condiment of some kind.

We had, in the commissariat stores, a small quantity
of rum of a peculiarly coarse flavour and odour. By a
careful calculation, it was computed that each British
officer might have a pint bottle of this deleterious spirit
every twelve days without the Sikhs and Gurkhas being
deprived of their share. Of course, Muhammedans will
not use alcohol in any shape, and the Dogras also
refused to partake of it. They were given a little tea
in compensation. About the rum ration, a comical
incident occurred. One day an officer came to me
with a perplexed and somewhat injured look on his
face, and a small volume in his hand, which, he explained, was Wolseley's soldiers' pocket-book, or some
such work. He proceeded to state his case, which
was that Wolseley had distinctly laid down the exact
amount of an officer's tot of rum. "Why, then," said
he, "am I only to have a pint bottle every twelve days
instead of the authorised quantity?" It was gently
explained to him that Wolseley had seemingly not
legislated for the contingency of there not being
enough rum to distribute on his liberal scale—a serious
omission.

There was one mystery in connection with our kitchen which was never explained. We had no butter, fat, or any other form of grease. How, then, did the Indian servants contrive to fry us gutta-percha beef-steaks, and similar delicacies?

CHAPTER XXX

THE FIRING OF THE GUN-TOWER

ON this particular night, the 6th April, we were peculiarly on the alert, for, just before dark, some forty or fifty men had been seen moving from the bazaar towards the river, where there was a hidden path under the bank, which led to the loopholed end of the garden. It was by that road that Whitchurch had brought in Baird on the night of the 3rd of March; probably more of the enemy were to follow. Campbell's opinion, from what his visitors told him, was that we should have a lively night, and that probably an energetic attempt would be made by the enemy to carry the stable picket. All our thoughts were therefore turned upon that part of our defences, but, knowing what we had done to protect the river flank, the waterway and its approaches, we waited with confidence whatever might happen.

About ten o'clock, the night being quiet, I essayed to see with my own eyes what was going on near the chabutra, and to find out if we could, with advantage, push out a work on to that structure. Wafadár and Sifat were with me to advise and discuss, and we began, as silently as possible, to dig a hole through the enclosure wall. The work was more difficult than was anticipated, and over two hours had passed before there was a sufficiently large aperture for a man to crawl through. We then slowly passed out beams and boxes full of earth, and soon had a more or less effective little sangar, except that its walls were so low that it could only be used in a crouching attitude. From it, we commanded the whole of the west wall of the enclosure, admirably.

On the parapet behind us were the Sikhs, with the old subadár overlooking them personally, and watching what we were doing. He had been carefully warned that one or more of us might crawl out on to the chabutra, and that he must not fire. Although, as I have said, we worked as quietly as we could, a certain amount of noise was unavoidable. Yet, wonderful to relate, or wonderful as it seemed at the time, the big sangar took no notice, and remained as silent as if deserted. I imagine that all my palpitations were superfluous. Between our little party, working on its stomach, so to speak, and the hostile sangar, was the great trunk of a mighty chenar tree : and we tried never to have any of the enemy's loopholes in view, which meant that we were in good cover, the tree intervening. Every now and then, however, a loophole would show, and one naturally expected that the sight would be followed by a flash and the whizz of a bullet, an uncomfortable thought when the range, thirty yards at the outside, was remembered. But the sangar kept quiescent, until its very silence seemed uncanny and disquieting. With my heart in my mouth, I ran forward and crouched behind the great tree-trunk in the middle of the chabutra. There was only time for me to note that the bundle of fascines was solitary, with no wall behind it, when a hubbub arose on the Sikhs' parapet. Words of warning were hissed over the wall, which brought me back as quickly as possible to my mouse-hole, keeping the tree-trunk between me and that argus-eyed sangar as far as I could. An eager messenger from the old subadár was waiting to whisper that the enemy had been seen on our side of the tree-trunk, and the Sikhs were about to shoot. Obviously, I was that enemy; I thanked my stars that the splendid, thick-headed, old gentleman had sent his caution before he fired. However, it was now past two o'clock, and we had seen all there was to be seen; so I went away to lie down, leaving a note for Townshend, who was in bed, to say what had been done.

It seemed to me that I had hardly laid my head upon the pillow, although, in reality, two or three hours must have passed away, when there was a heavy rattle of musketry from the North-tower. The Sikhs were volleying in reply to a sharp discharge of rifles, accompanied by shouting, from the west, beyond Sifat's enclosure. Then a Sikh was brought in from the outwork, through the manhole in the fort gate. He had been hit in the leg, at the very spot where I had so nearly escaped in the afternoon. In the dark, the poor fellow had not perceived how roughly the old gun-port had been blocked up. There was an uproar on the west front when I, with my party, got to the inner end of the main-gate passage, where the inlying picket, with Townshend and Whitchurch, was collected. We had first made a rapid tour of the south wall, where everything seemed quiet, but here, on the west side, there was an ear-splitting noise. Whitchurch, silent as usual, had a double-barrelled rifle in his hand, and his long Chitráli brown robe pulled up through his belt in a business-like way. Why, I wonder, does a silent, motionless man, in the midst of excitement, give the impression of large reserves of strength! Gurdon and Harley were on the parapets at their proper places, the former to the south, and the latter on the river flank. Townshend and I discussed the situation exhaustively. We decided that it was a real attack, but which side

was actually menaced? Was it the waterway? It
could hardly be the North-tower. Probably, arguing
by past experience, it was coming from the garden
side.

Suddenly a glaring light showed from the south-
east corner of the fort. Upon this night the machicoulis
fires were not to be lighted without order, the wind
blowing rather strongly from the south. "Hullo," was
the remark, "Gurdon has had to light up after all."
At that instant a man came running across the big
yard with a message from Gurdon that the enemy had
fired the Gun-tower. It was an awful moment, no
doubt, but all my thoughts turned into energetic
anger, which expressed itself partly, I fear, in exple-
tives. Curiously enough, it was not alarm at the
terrible danger, but anger, I may say fury, against the
enemy which filled my mind. Running, and shouting
as I ran, officers' servants, native grooms, coolies, every
unarmed man except the Chitrális who were safe in
their rooms, was quickly collected in the lower storey
of the Gun-tower and on the promenade roof which
led into it. Marvellously quickly each fell into his
place, as though he had been carefully drilled for such
an emergency. Lines of men were organised, or, perhaps one should say, organised themselves; and either
passed buckets, pails, or pots of water from hand to
hand, or carried up earth in their coats, Wafadár being
particularly insistent on our trying to smother the
flames with earth. As there was no aperture on the
summer-house side in the lower room, we had to
struggle with the fire from the apartment above, where
was the machicoulis gallery — but, alas! without the
machicolation in its floor! There was a still rougher
arrangement at the other window or door-frame which
looked straight down the garden, where the outside

screens were fixed upon one enormous beam, which had been laboriously taken upstairs. One end of this beam projected some feet through the window, and upon it a rough three-sided barricade, waist high, had been contrived.

It was the south-east corner of the Gun-tower which had been attacked, and already there was a great fire blazing noisily on each of its sides. That facing the summer-house was much the larger, and was burning as merrily as if it had been carefully stoked for hours. The fire on the other side of the apex was comparatively insignificant, and a fine old tracker, Sultán Sháh a servant of Campbell's, sat out on the beam, and was so industrious in casting water and soil upon the flames that he could not be supplied fast enough with those extinguishers ; and during all the noise and clatter his voice was heard calling for more, until it was silenced, poor old fellow, by a couple of bullets, one into the hip and the other through his arm. But he had effected wonders before he was hit, and his fire was almost out. On the summer-house side, however, the flames seemed to thrive on the water, mould, and stones hurled upon them from the gallery, and roared like a furnace. It was very hard to get at them. The only way was to throw the water over the three-foot-high side walls of the machicoulis gallery, which meant danger to the man at work, for, however careful he was, it was impossible for his arm and hand not to be seen by an enemy only twenty-five yards distant.

The noise was astonishing. The fierce, but intermittent rushing sound of the flames below, the smashing or splintering of the boards of the machicoulis gallery as they were volleyed into at such a short range, and the yells and triumphant shouts of the enemy, combined with the high-pitched vociferous prayers of the priests, all

contributed to form a bewildering clamour. Every now
and then a higher leap of the eager flames poured a
glare of light into the tower — a light which seemed
strong, yet left the faces of the workers in shadow.
They hurried about breathlessly, and were merely black
figures flashed upon a ground of rosy light one second,
and the next were hidden in the darkness. The loose
boards, used as backing for the sides of the gallery,
jumped up and down or were thrown bodily over by
the impact of the volleys ; so that the little Gurkha,
squatted on the floor, had to keep hastily replacing his
own defences, in the intervals of ladling quenching
materials on to the fire. Bullets crashed into the great
timbers supporting the roof. The wonderful sight was
to see the gangs work silently, for none but Sultán
Sháh could make himself heard in the din, and Wafadár
had to scream right into my ear before I could even
half-understand him. But with unflagging vigour they
strained and laboured. They felt how critical was the
danger. For a long time all our exertions seemed
useless—one instant the fire would seem crushed and
overwhelmed, only to rise madder than ever the next,
as if it redoubled its fury in response to the yells
of our wild foemen.

After Sultán Sháh was so badly hurt, we pulled him
inside and carried him to a corner, but his post was
left unfilled. I had, at this time, to send down to
Townshend for more men. He, of course, was still
with the inlying picket, for no one knew where else
a determined attack might not be attempted. In
response, Whitchurch brought up six Sikhs—it was
fighting men that were wanted—and went back to
encourage the water-carriers to still further efforts.
Then the brave little Gurkha in the gallery, which
could only hold one man at a time, was doubly

wounded, through its wooden walls. We dragged him in, but who was to take his place? Looking closely into men's faces, I recognised the Gurkha subadár, Badri Nár Singh, who had fought so well with Gurdon, and afterwards stuck so nobly to Whitchurch on the 3rd March. I put my hand on his shoulder. He understood, and changed countenance, for he was not a bullock, but that bravest type of soldier whose imagination reveals all the dangers of a situation, which yet have no power to shake his nerve. Creeping out on to the gallery, he quickly replaced the boards, which were leaping about as if alive. With quiet courage he kept there at work until we all went down to the room below. Happily, he was not hit, and his bravery did not go unrewarded.

One of the most uncomfortable ordeals imaginable, was to pop one's head over the side of the gallery to examine the fire. It was the signal for a still hotter outburst of shooting, accompanied by a fury of yells and abuse. Extreme fatigue is an anodyne to nervousness. I was soon utterly tired, and all excitement died out. At length we began to win. We redoubled our exertions; the enemy his execrations. Gurdon had been busy on his parapet, trying to keep down the enemy's fire by volleys; but our assailants were well protected behind a wall, and Gurdon's men could only, at the most, have hit the loopholes slantingly. He himself had frequently run in to help me, and he now came in again with a message from Townshend to ask if I thought it advisable for a sortie to be sent out. It was then nearly broad daylight. The enemy were in great force, and on the watch for such a move. For the last time, one had to look over the machicoulis gallery, when it was found that the original fire was practically dead, but that the tower wall itself was blazing. Consequently, a sortie would be useless, for there was nothing but red ashes at the foot of the tower, while the jerky sheets of flame were clinging high out of reach. So I answered no; and shortly afterwards we all moved to the room beneath.

If it had been dangerous above, it was no less dangerous below. There was no opening of any kind in the burning south wall; consequently, holes had to knocked through hastily, to get at the lighted timbers. In a previous chapter, the construction of the tower walls was described, and it was explained that they were, in short, two huge wooden crates, separated by about a foot of stones embedded in mud mortar. It was also explained that the Gun-tower contained more timber than any other.

There was still another danger, namely, the risk of the fire outside, and us within, weakening the structure, and deranging its somewhat delicate balance, and so causing it to collapse. Wafadár, always cool and helpful, was our consulting engineer. He quickly, yet with confidence, marked certain spots where the walls could be safely perforated. The first hole, about a foot square, and breast high, immediately became a mark for the enemy, a mark which, unfortunately, none could miss at the short range. Luckily, nearly all the bullets whisked through, slanting upwards, and caused little harm, if much noise. The yelling folk outside at times cheered, as if about to charge, but, nevertheless, kept under cover closely.

The post of honour was at the opening first made. A tall Sikh, delighted with encomiums on his bravery, although, no doubt, he would have worked just as well without them, ladled water through it manfully, smiling agreeably, in spite of the bullets. Only his right arm and hand were necessarily exposed, but he was certain to be hit sooner or later. There was little confusion, and everybody worked well. We were all hopeful now. Near the floor, at the south-east corner, the wall was very hot, so a Hunza servant of Gurdon's, a man named Rajab, with others, broke into the masonry, to discover that the fire had penetrated between the inner and outer wooden frames. Rajab, stripped to a pair of cotton trousers, sawed away at the timbers to make a hole large enough to pour in water.

All this time I had been wearing a fur greatcoat over a sleeping suit. Now, the temperature compelled me to pull off the outer garment; while doing so, a bullet struck a wooden pillar at my back with the force of a cannon ball. It must have come from a long range, and not from below. Sifat drew a quick breath at the narrow shave, when an absurd story of Marryat's came to my mind—at that unlikely time and place—about a mariner, who declared he always kept his head in the first hole made through his ship's side in a sea-fight, and was then safe, for no shot ever followed another exactly. This could not be translated to Sifat's understanding; but I smiled at the recollection, and also because we were confident that the enemy had been frustrated. Bullets kept rushing through the hole where the Sikh was, to strike the ceiling and bring down showers of fragments. While bending towards Rajab, to explain what he should do, something struck me so heavily on the left shoulder, that I stumbled and fell. It never occurred to me that I was hit; but it seemed as if something heavy, dislodged from the ceiling, had fallen upon me. Sifat's face, however, before he spoke, told me it was a wound.

Like a flash, the horrible shoulder injuries I had seen Whitchurch dressing in the hospital, during my daily visits there, came to my mind, and I scuttled across

the roof, followed by Sifat, to the top of the little
stair that led to my room. Dragging off the coat
part of my sleeping clothes, I began, in front of a
tiny looking-glass, to feel about the bony projections
of my shoulder, dreading to find one of them give
way beneath my finger. But nothing of the sort
occurred, and my left arm moved in its socket easily.
So when Whitchurch came to me, running, and a kind
of faintness brought me once more to the ground, I was
actually exulting. The wound was large and deep, and
had carried away a good deal of the shoulder ; but it
luckily avoided the bones. Perhaps a Snider bullet
never made more fuss with less result. I was carefully
bound up, and put to bed, and began to suffer a reaction
from the excitements and exertions of the past twenty-
four hours, which were, perhaps, as full of incident as
any I remember.

Reports were brought to me, continually, about the
progress of the fire. Everything was well, but Nature
herself seemed to be warring against us, or, at least, not
baulking our enemies ; for every time the flames were
dying away a blast of south wind would revivify them.
At length, about half-past nine, Townshend came to say
that the fire was practically out. It smouldered on for
some time longer. Rajab was badly hit, so was the
brave Sikh, and three or four others. The hole through
which my bullet came was filled up thoroughly, it was
supposed. But there was one crevice left ; and, just
as all was over, and the tired workers were about to
withdraw, a fateful shot came hustling through, and
penetrated the soldierly breast of the Central Indian
trooper, Campbell's orderly. Poor fellow, there was
little or no chance for him, Whitchurch told me. In
quiet courage and faithfulness, this man was an admirable representative of one of those Punjáb tribes of

X

Muhammedans who preserve the martial instincts and gallant appearance of their Rájput ancestors, defeated and forced into Islám long ages ago.

That the sentries in the Gun-tower—men of the Kashmír Rifles—had not been vigilant was clear, and during the day better arrangements for watching were made. Sikhs were put on all the towers, as well as some of Sifat's men. Both were keen as hawks, but the latter were also possessed of local knowledge, and a better appreciation of local sounds. The machicoulis gallery was re-modelled and made strong. A small square window on the east face of the Flag-tower gave a clear view of the ashes of the fire, but it had not been utilised hitherto, because there was a risk of shots from it going dangerously near the soldiers on the south parapet. But, to-day, a careful marksman was sent there. In addition, thoughtful plans were made by the fort Commandant, to provide against incendiary attacks in the future. Whitchurch was to control them, with Sifat as his lieutenant. Heaps of earth and water were collected on all towers, and large stones were carried up also, to disperse and crush out incipient fires by sheer weight. Numerous miniature tanks were devised by letting waterproof sheets into holes in the ground. By the time these precautionary measures were finished, or nearly finished, darkness came round again, and we waited anxiously for the next hostile move.

In every camp, in war time, there are curious rumours, called "shaves," which originate no one knows how, and are disseminated with equal mystery. They are sometimes fantastic, but often curiously accurate, and they, not infrequently, give valuable hints to those at the head of affairs. Upon this day everyone had heard—from nobody in particular—that the Chitrális, about midnight, would swim the river and

distract the attention of our water pickets, preparatory
to large numbers of men hurling themselves boldly
upon both flanks of the covered way. Just after dark,
when the hurrying officers had scarcely finished inspecting the watch and ward for the night, Townshend
came to me with surprise and perplexity on his face, to
say that, in spite of all that had been done, some live
embers of charcoal had again been thrown at the very
foot of the Gun-tower, although a bundle of dry twigs,
which they were to kindle, was dropped a yard or two
away. Yet, all the time, dozens of eyes had, one would
suppose, been fixed upon that spot, and nobody had
been observed to approach the wall. My informant
declared it was like witchcraft. However, the incident
prevented any further slackness. Ever afterwards, a
trustworthy Sikh was to be found lying prone, watching
through the opening in the floor of the machicoulis
gallery.

It was more than surmised that our times of
changing guards had been studied by the besiegers,
who seized a moment when the soldiers were shifting
places, to throw down the charcoal, although the
thrower's nerve failed him at the last; hence, the
faggots were not properly placed. This led to an
alteration of the time for relieving sentries. Strange
to say, we expended few cartridges during the previous
night, not more than three hundred rounds altogether.
As usual, stories were told by the Sepoys of the
wonders they had done in the way of killing. It was
asserted that a dozen corpses were left on the ground
by the enemy, but Townshend, who had seen service,
was sceptical; his doubts were justified, for we subsequently learned that only two or three men were hit
throughout the day, all of them on the west side of the
fort.

So ended our fifth week of siege.

The night which followed was one of the unhappiest I remember. It was not so much the pain of the wound, or the dreadful inconvenience it caused, by compelling a constrained attitude, as the aching depression which crushed me down. There was a little desultory firing from time to time, hardly enough, one might almost say, to preserve the interest of the piece, but my heart grew cold with morbid thoughts. In the morning I was like one hardly yet roused from a nightmare. Then I was told that the military officers had decided to abandon and throw down the western outwork—Sifat's enclosure—and to turn a certain erection called a flèche, in front of the main door, into a more complete work, named a tambour, loopholed to protect the walls ; and that the work of demolition had already begun. The military officers were unanimous, it seemed, about this retirement, holding that the risk of retaining the place was greater than the advantage of the convenient flanking fire it gave against any rush across the sand-spit.

Wafadár, my clerks, Sifat, and others, came with long faces to say that there was a feeling abroad that my being hit was a presage of further ill-luck ; they certainly looked melancholy enough themselves, and shook their heads in the saddest way. Lying in bed, aching and troubled in mind, was terribly tedious ; so, with help, I got up and paid visits to the hospital and round the fort as usual. The Sikhs were looking happy and cheerful, and we had some pleasant talk. Campbell's unfortunate orderly was in shocking pain. His efforts to restrain agonised groans were so evident, that it was necessary to cut short one's words of encouragement, and leave. The hospital was always a terrible place to visit. On this date,

Whitchurch had no less than eighty-five patients—including those who merely came for medicine, or to have slight wounds dressed.

I found that although Sifat's enclosure had been abandoned, only the shed-like portions were destroyed, the perpendicular walls still remaining. Everything, indeed, looked rosier than in my repulsive sleeping-room.

Here is an extract from the fort Commandant's diary:—"British Agent all right in spite of his wounds, and told me to tell Subadár Badri Nár Singh, 4th K.R., and Sepoy Awi Singh (wounded severely) that they would both be recommended for the order of merit for bravery. . . . Also, he wishes Boler Singh recommended for the order of merit." It was important that everyone in the fort should know that courageous deeds were recognised at once, and that brave men were certain to be recommended for that decoration, so highly prized by Indian soldiers, and described on page 223. Badri Nár Singh had already been recommended for the third class of the order, so now, if he had the luck not to be killed, he would, probably, at the end of the siege, find himself promoted into the second class as well.

During the afternoon I set about improving the loopholes in the Gun-tower, and making slanting apertures, for downward fire, in its lower storey. This last-mentioned work could only be done in the daytime; afterwards, a light would, by illuminating the interior, make the inmates easy marks, through the loopholes, for the skilful Chitráli and Pathán riflemen. But even in daylight the task was not easy. As already mentioned, the tower was solid up to the first floor; that is to say, it was filled compactly with stones and earth up to that level. To make a vertical, or rather (from within) a slanting loophole we first dug out a little well, some 18 inches square, and then sawed through the inner timber frame, to the required extent, and as low down as possible, in order to remove the stones embedded between it and the outer wood-work. It was after the saw had been thrust right through the wall and its point projected outside that the real danger began. The tool itself was of bad steel, and kept bending double. As soon as the masonry had been knocked away sufficiently for it to work easily, the enemy began shooting at the hole.

Harley's Sikh carpenter, naturally, did not much care for the job, but he was a capital fellow. I made him tie the saw-handle to a stick with the piece of a scarf, so as to keep his hands out of danger, and, as the firing came from across the river, seat himself in the square hole with his knees and ankles jammed against its sides. He worked in this awkward attitude with safety, but uncomfortably and slowly. The enemy's marksmen had keen sight even to see the small aperture in the outer wall; but no sooner was it the necessary four or five inches wide, than in came a bullet, plump, and stuck in the earth below where the Sikh was sitting, and between his legs. I had satisfied myself, anxiously, that while he remained in the same position he could not be hurt, so I enjoined him not to move, even an inch. He knew it also, I think, but every time a bullet came in he stopped working for an instant and glanced up at me with an aggrieved look. I would then give him a reassuring smile, with a few words of encouragement, and on he would go again. As the little saw worked away steadily all the same, the enemy, after a few admirable shots, stopped firing. They were always averse to burning cartridges uselessly. The point of this story is the child-like obedience these stalwart Punjáb soldiers have for an European superior, and the trust they put in his words. Such faith is, indeed, quite touching.

With the aid of Chitráli youths, I also set about making a long loophole, four feet long, to command the ground just short of the foot of the tower on the summer-house side. This required care, for fear the equilibrium of the whole structure might be disturbed. We worked as before, only on a larger scale. A big square well was dug against the wall, with a step left at the bottom. Upon this step the watching rifleman could lie and watch through the horizontal aperture, which was just below the level of his face. Any bullets —and many came in at first—lodged in the soft earth in the face of the step, while a man approaching close enough to try and shoot upwards must be so near the foot of the tower that half-a-dozen rifles would be trained upon him at once. The precaution was against a rapid dash at the wall with a lighted brand, followed by an equally quick retreat. It was terribly tedious and tiring work, for the old engineers had not only filled up the tower conscientiously, but had strengthened it by strong cross beams firmly fixed. The Chitrális, however, stripped of their upper garments, worked with extraordinary energy, and before night the long loophole was nearly finished.

The fort rumour of this date was that the activity of the enemy was due to desperation, because they knew that a relief was marching to us from Mastuj. Also, that the comparative quiet we had experienced all day was due to many of our besiegers having been hurried up the valley to occupy strong places on the road.

An uneventful night was followed by a quiet day— Tuesday the 9th. The enemy had now discovered a strange way of giving trouble. It has been explained that the officers' mess was in the verandah of a court in the southern half of the fort. This place had never been invaded by a bullet for three weeks; and, indeed, those which drove Harley out of his extemporised bedroom must have been chance shots fired from long ranges, for, much as the Sher Afzulites wished to cause us harassment, they never again succeeded in dropping bullets there. Nevertheless, full of resource, they now began slinging in stones, from behind the wall of the summer-house corner, which fell with remarkable accuracy into our court, or flew high over the dividing wall into the big yard. Such curious missiles, for employment in an Indian frontier war at the end of the nineteenth century, were effectual and galling. They rained thickly, and had to be carried away by the basketful; while everyone was compelled to seek shelter. It was irritating to keep dodging stones during the daytime, and exasperating at night to hear them rattle on the woodwork or thud into the ground at your feet. One or two of the garrison were severely hurt, and everyone felt that it would be inglorious to figure in a casualty list as "badly wounded by a stone."

My wooden shutters were banged against incessantly, and there was an endless bob-bob-bob down the stairs leading to my door. A Gilgit resident, a Pathán by birth, who had certain omissions, on the 3rd March, to atone for, like the man mentioned on page 304, declared that he was a good slinger, as was also one of his friends, and, with my permission, they two would show us how to pay back the enemy in his own coin. We collected to watch the exhibition. The Pathán carefully selected a pebble, preliminary to stretching and manipulating his sling with the parade of an expert. He then stepped back a yard or two, whirled it artistically, with much bustle of arms, head, and raiment, and delivered the projectile, which, to his gasping horror, instead of flying over the parapet, came off straight at a right angle into our midst, passing close between two startled heads. After that we made no further attempt to emulate the enemy; but the amusing discomfiture of our own man, in some odd way, proved so agreeable that it made the stone-throwing trouble ever afterwards easier to bear.

Our Chitrális all this day had a fit of sulks. They complained, and truthfully, it must be confessed, that I did not trust them, and, therefore, had taken away their arms. It was even reported to me that they had brought Shuja-ul-Mulk to their way of thinking, and that, with two or three exceptions, they would all, for national reasons, be miserable if in the end we were not defeated.

Towards the latter part of the afternoon I laboriously, and with much help, climbed to the top of the Gun-tower, and sat down to talk to a Sikh sentry whose village dialect was hard to comprehend. He was a heavy-featured man, but at that moment he was watching with an intentness which brought a half-startled look into his face, a gap in the upper part of the garden wall. Two people, one a Chitráli, the other a Pathán, had just gone by, he said, and must re-pass shortly. He modestly hoped to hit one of them, as he had formerly gained a rupee prize, he proudly observed, in a regimental competition, at a running-man target. After a look round I was helped down again, leaving the Sikh with his rifle all ready, and his eye still glued to the gap. Presently I heard him fire, and, shortly afterwards, on being relieved, he came down to tell me his story. The Chitráli, it seemed, had run along, doubled up, and so swiftly that it was impossible to draw a bead upon him; but the Pathán, scornful and swaggering, stalked past slowly with his nose in the air, probably by way of setting an example of courage to the other. But the poor chap got the bullet right through his lungs, falling down dead, and was finally dragged away by people creeping up under the wall and tying a rope to his legs. As one writes, it is odd to remember the plain matter-of-fact way in which such incidents as this are heard in war time; and then the contrast between a rough frontier life, with the law, order, and police of London, strikes one with curious force.

Later, a Pathán was heard lamenting close to the same gap. In accents of dramatic sorrow he proclaimed, that now his brother was dead, life meant nothing more to him; he only wanted to die also. Even we, fairly case hardened, were startled to learn that the moustached old subadár of the Sikhs, who happened to be on the tower at the time inspecting his men, had bawled out in reply, " All right, my father-in-law " (a term of opprobrium), " take two steps to the front and you shall go, without doubt, to your brother." Chivalry is not precisely the feeling that generations of war between Sikhs and Pathans has developed.

CHAPTER XXXI

A TIRED GARRISON

WEDNESDAY, the 10th April, passed away quietly, but there was much work to do, and more to plan for the night, in the way of additional defences. The tambour in front of the main gate was strong enough, but, as it was built hurriedly, it did not quite command the whole of the west fort wall, its side of the Flag-tower, in particular, being partially unprotected. It became more difficult now than earlier in the siege to get work properly finished. The labour gangs would sometimes run up a wall which fell down next day, or would make a big loophole by the simple process of knocking through an aperture large enough for a couple of men to enter abreast. Consequently, a good deal of work had to be done twice over. Everybody, in truth, was getting tired, and at two o'clock in the morning sleepiness and fatigue are harder to bear than at any other time.

We had a lively night. Just before one o'clock there was a terrible din, firing and shouting from all sides of the fort. We replied steadily. Then followed a sharp fusilade from the Gun-tower, and the Water-tower was also busy. On the west side the demonstration, or frustrated assault, was particularly noisy. After half-an-hour the enemy was supposed to retire in the direction of the bazaar; at any rate, we sent several volleys along that path. Upon this occasion, and

especially towards the end of the disturbance, our
shooting was particularly impressive. Out of a short
silence the shouted order would be heard, then following
an instant's pause came the flash and the thunder-clap.
Backwards and forwards rolled the mighty noise, echoing
and reverberating between towers and walls. A military
command given sonorously, in heavy darkness, when
one's nerves are highly strung, is solemn and thrilling.
We all thought at first that this was a real attack.
Scaling ladders, we had heard, were in the bazaar ready
for use, and Wafadár looked well to the long spears
with which my party were to thrust through the slit
loopholes of the south wall, the weak place in the fort.

The military officers had asked me to add, to my
scratch company, some Kashmír Gurkhas, on the supposition that my men were not altogether trustworthy.
I agreed, but the irregular regular soldiers were so
clumsy with their rifles, which they banged against
doors or fell down ladders with, and they were so hard
to talk to, seeing that they could not speak Hindustani,
and I knew nothing of Gurkháli, that after a short trial
I was obliged to send them away.

In one respect this was the most painful alarm I
ever experienced. When the outbreak of firing occurred
I was lying down, carefully bandaged. The noise was
so startling that I jumped up excitedly, dashed into my
coat, and ran out to discover the cause. As my arm
had never been into a sleeve since I was hit, and was
not again thrust into one till long afterwards, the pain
was great. Yet, for half-an-hour, so imminent seemed
an escalade that there was no time to relieve it. Whitchurch, of the multifarious occupations, the man who
worked hard for six hours daily, in the fetid atmosphere
of the hospital, and never seemed to have a moment's
leisure to indulge the high fever which racked him,

because of his exhaustion—yet who always had time to
help anybody else—came and eased me when, at length,
I got round to the inlying picket at the main gate. He
was a standing wonder to us all, a notable example of
how a man with a big heart can even triumph over the
high temperatures of an Indian ague.

Our untrustworthy Chitrális were unusually perturbed upon this occasion. They dressed themselves
hurriedly, being especially careful about their boots,
and waited with eager expectation as if for a promised
event. It is possible that they had been warned to
look out for something decisive. If so, they were
disappointed. Shuja - ul - Mulk was terrified at the
volleys, which, as I have said, were really awe-inspiring.
He broke down, poor little boy, and abandoned his
preternatural dignity for childish terror. It was only
by putting him to sleep with a stalwart Adamzáda
that his tremors could be soothed. We had very few
casualties, and in spite of the expenditure of many
cartridges we still had plenty remaining, for all men
hors de combat increased the number of rounds available
for those on duty.

Thursday, the 11th, was a glorious day, so beautiful,
that it increased our pangs at being imprisoned in a
small, evil-smelling fort. The great mountain to the
north, lovely and grim, once more showed its unruffled
brow against a wonderful sky, and yet again filled the
mind with thoughts of human insignificance. What
would it matter, it seemed to suggest, if all these
warring pigmies, assailants and defenders alike, were
swept off the face of the earth? Similar swarms of
tiny creatures had behaved with identical absurdity
through long generations, without even exciting the
notice of the great calm Spirit of the snow. At evening
time the Sher Afzulites began drumming away merrily

in the distance for polo or dancing, or because they merely desired to exult over us. Between nine and ten o'clock the stone-throwing all but stopped, and only one solitary voice continued the song of abuse, which was varied by an occasional trumpet-call. As the moon would not be up for several hours, we had to be vigilant; but the night was clear, and our machicoulis fires blazed bravely, sending floods of light fully thirty yards from the walls, making it impossible for a cat to escape undetected. This steady glare, on a windless night, must have looked pretty from the outside. I often caught myself wishing I could admire it from that standpoint. At one o'clock out came the moon, and some bright mind suggested we should have supper "after the theatre," so we sat down to pickled horse cheerily and with much make-believe. Afterwards, except the one officer on watch, all went to lie down with the possibility of having to turn out any instant. But there were hardly half-a-dozen shots fired before the dawn broke.

Wafadár, after supper, related to me a dream, wherein he had seen a British force victorious at the Nisa Gul, and the Chitrális flying in disorder. The interpretation was obvious; we were to be immediately relieved. Next day, it was reported that the other Chitrális were once more cheerful. They had also been dreaming dreams of good omen, and encouraged thereby they wreathed themselves in smiles, and were energetic in subservience to us, the lucky people. We had come into the fort with the earth sleeping and the trees bare. Now, outside, there was a wealth of fresh green foliage and the crops were well grown.

Many persons in groups, or singly, and several horsemen, were seen moving up the valley on the 12th April. Banners were displayed, and there were many

signs of a considerable movement of troops towards
Mastuj. Yet, we reflected that it was all a trifle
ostentatious. Why could not Sher Afzul have marched
his men by night, unless he wanted us to believe he
had unduly weakened his beleaguering force! So we
half made up our minds for a sharp fight during the
night. As an illustration of the nearness of the enemy's
works, we found, about five o'clock in the afternoon,
a Sikh lying dead on the west parapet over the main
gate; he was shot through the eye. He must have
crept up to the banquette, which could be reached by
a ladder, well screened by tent canvas, to peep through
one of the small loopholes, and, in that seemingly safe
position, was killed. No one missed him, and the body
had lain there for two or three hours, in Whitchurch's
opinion ; as a rule, no one ventured to show himself for
an instant on the parapets in daylight.

There was a lateral facet on the western edge of the
double-topped Tirich Mir, whose dead-white surface
used to glow with copper tints in the level rays of the
departing sun. It flashed upon us, like a promise of
peace, lingering after all else was in gloom. How
often have we not stood, regretfully, to watch it fade
slowly and die—the signal for Pandemonium to break
loose. So to-night; there burst forth a distressing
clamour from the summer-house corner, howls and yells,
accompanied by drum beating, and the strains of some
unusually lacerating musical instrument of the horn
species, while stones poured into the fort. The sentries
replied with occasional shots, and the night passed
away harmlessly, but with no lull of the noise.

Enclosed within four narrow walls, for a long time,
one gradually loses a just sense of proportion. Little
evils appear mountainous, while those of really large
size may, in the constricted space, be only partially

discerned. It may almost be said, that sometimes the
trifles of life are alone of importance.   One trouble
which caused us extreme irritation was a tiny monkey,
a rather pretty but hopelessly mischievous little creature. He was the delight of the garrison, and the
detestation of its officers. Official papers, diaries, and
small cherished articles were his game, which he pursued with unvarying success.   I suffered most from
his attacks. He was captured, and condemned to live
in a box, turned upside down, with holes in the bottom.
But sympathetic friends invariably released him after
each incarceration, and in the wildness of his glee he
perpetrated devilment seven times worse than before.
He finally made my sleeping-room a mere paper-strewn
rag shop, and emptied my box of " safety " razors, edge-
wise, on to the floor.   In desperation, this criminal had
to be arrested, and placed formally in charge of the
sentry over the Rághunáth ammunition, who was held
militarily responsible for his safe custody.   It was
strange that monkey was never shot, for he would walk
along the parapets, or climb the face of the walls from
one projecting wooden knob to another.   Our other
beasts were not so fortunate.   A large, good-tempered
dog had a couple of bullets through him, one of which
could be seen, and felt lying under the skin of his flank.
Another lay dead outside the waterway.   These animals
used to jump over the stable barricades and feed upon
the dead ponies and other carrion until they became
almost as offensive as the carcasses.

Probably noting the ease with which dogs could
get away from the fort, a Chitráli youth one morning
followed their example, leapt a barrier wall, and before
the guards had roused from their astonishment, was in
safety behind the trees.   It was never proved that his
countrymen in the fort were cognisant of his attempt,

but very likely he was the bearer of messages to Sher Afzul. However, his fate was tragic. Sher Afzul must have been in a vicious temper when the young man was brought into his presence, for he immediately ordered him to be put to death ; which was done there and then. After that no one tried to desert.

The 13th April was uneventful throughout its twenty-four hours. No less than seventy-six people still had to be attended to in hospital. Our food was holding out well, although I had decided that if we were not relieved before the 1st of May, the daily ration was to be still further reduced.

Groups of men were again observed at intervals, all day long, marching up the valley, a fact which might be speculated upon to the heart's content, without any definite result. As evening approached, the noise of drumming, singing, and abuse grew louder and louder from the summer-house side, and the enemy's slingers quitted themselves like men. One or two volleys were fired in the hope of moderating the clamour, but use-lessly. Did the enemy suppose that we should sur-render to the might of human outcry like a second Bastille? It was not only surprising but also ex-asperating. The morning light disclosed that the big sangar on the west had been connected with the older erection, immediately behind it, by a covered way. A shallow trench was dug between the two, and roofed over with sheaves leaning one against the other. This was quite as effectual against us as if it had been en-closed by solid masonry walls and a bomb-proof roof, for, as it concealed anyone moving through it, the enemy's object was gained, since we could no more afford to waste cartridges upon their screens than they could upon ours.

With the 14th, closed our sixth week of siege.

Y

All that day and the 15th our attention was still diverted by the constant going and coming of the enemy upon the Mastuj road, and there were incessant tom-toming, stone showers, and wild howlings both nights. Occasionally, when the shouting would suddenly swell into a deep roar, we would fire a volley, believing a rush was preparing, but nothing ever happened, and each morning we searched in vain to detect fresh approaches. What did it all mean? Someone suggested that the besiegers, having detached much of their strength Mastujwards, were trying by noise to conceal their scanty numbers. This seemed plausible, for it was hard to believe that the Sher Afzulites would exert themselves so much merely to keep our sentries awake.

Rab Nawáz Khán, the brave little cavalry man, terribly wounded on the 3rd March, made an almost magical recovery. One of his arms remained crippled, otherwise he was well. He kept warning us against a possible mine. It could only come from the summer-house, and the soldiers in the Gun-tower were urged to listen carefully, and always, for any sound of digging. But nothing occurred to justify Rab Nawáz Khán's suspicions, in spite of the numerous men with strained ears, who listened anxiously.

The 16th passed away also without incident, except that once a sentry thought he detected the sound of a pick. But it was never repeated, and the report caused no uneasiness; indeed, all fear of a mine was gradually passing away. Our Chitrális were happy because, they explained, our troops had not only reached Mastuj, but Sher Afzul must have set out in person to resist them. With the advent of soldiers from India, they averred that all the Khushwaktis would rise and declare in our favour.

CHAPTER XXXII

HARLEY SAVES US

ON the memorable morning of the 17th April, an hour or so after breakfast, there was another report sent down that the enemy were mining the Gun-tower. We thought it merely a scare, but, of course, an officer went promptly to inquire into the matter. It was Townshend, and shortly afterwards he called out begging me to come up. There was that in his voice which told something momentous had occurred. I hurried to the Gun-tower, where, from the long loophole I had constructed on the 8th, we distinctly heard, working underground, the muffled vibrating thud of a pick, with an occasional high-pitched ring as iron struck stone, and seemingly not more than ten or twelve feet from where we stood. We looked at one another in startled inquiry. He tentatively asked, "We must counter-mine?" Sifat, who had followed closely on my heels, knew what was passing between us as well as if he could understand English. He vehemently whispered over my shoulder, "Báhar Jána," which was his way of saying we must sortie. I acquiesced at once, and so did Townshend, for we perceived that there was nothing else to be done in time. Townshend went aside to listen once more to the dull strokes, so menacing, yet so full of fascination. "How many men, Sifat," I inquired ; "sixty?" "No, a hundred," was the reply ; and so it was finally settled.

The forlorn hope was to be made up of forty Sikhs, under their own jemadár (lieutenant), and sixty Kashmír Riflemen, the whole to be led by young Harley.

Gurdon begged almost pathetically to be sent also, but only one officer could be risked, and as Harley's Sikhs were to go, he, of course, must show them the way. He for some reason or other, thought the point was still in debate, and came to me with a terribly aggrieved face, to substantiate his claims to be the first man knocked on the head, in all probability. It is pleasant to reflect, that after forty-five days of close siege and bad food, with harassed nights as well as anxious days, these two young soldiers should vie with each other in generous rivalry to lead the desperate venture; for its desperate nature was evident. If, as was only too probable, the summer-house post were strongly fortified, our devoted men must be shot down long before they could tear away its barricades, as they would be assailed not only from the loopholes they were charging, but from those of the garden sangars, and from its end and river walls. Why Umra Khán's veterans did not make themselves impregnable against such a surprise as we gave them, cannot be fully explained. Their Chitráli allies still grow hot and cold when they think of it. Carelessness, fatalism, arrogance, all had a share, no doubt, but the chief influence at work was the contempt with which the Patháns had come to regard us, because of our persistently defensive attitude. For once it was not the Britisher who despised his wild enemy, but the wild mountaineer who underrated the Britisher. At heart, he believes, that man for man he is the superior of Indian troops, and that our numbers, armament, and organisation, alone enable us to conquer. These tribesmen have been known, it is said, to appeal to the sporting instincts of British generals to send away their artillery, and then see who would win in a fair open fight. I remember, too, that during the siege of Sherpur, in 1879, we were abused by the rascallions drumming and parading over Síah Sang as " Kila-bund badmáshes," which may be translated, rascals shut up in a fort or besieged (*i.e.* who dare not come out). However, it is certain that on this occasion, Umra Khán's trusted fighting - men at the summer-house post derided the possibility of our leaving the protection of the fort walls.

It was decided that Harley's perilous adventure, upon which so much depended, should be made at four o'clock in the afternoon. So Townshend set about writing out the necessary orders; and Harley started to select the explosives required to blow up the mine. He was our expert in such military engineering questions, and, moreover, possessed the only book on the subject—one written by General Brackenbury. During the early days of April he had occupied his leisure moments by filling canvas bags with gunpowder, which we found in considerable quantities in the fort. Into the midst of each of these bags, which weighed 50, 60, or 100 lbs., was thrust the end of a long, narrow canvas tube, many feet long, also filled with gunpowder—a substitute for a fuse. Each such explosive apparatus, when finished, was enclosed in a much larger bag, strong and made of waterproof sheeting, to guard against damp, and enable it to be carried about conveniently. When wanted for use, the long gunpowder hose was to be drawn out from the covering bag and used as the train to fire the charge, after the latter had been properly tamped. Harley, at the time he devised these appliances, had no particular object in view, but thought they might perhaps prove useful in demolitions

or similar work ; now they were invaluable. He selected
two bags, holding, respectively, 50 and 60 lbs. of gunpowder, a sufficient quantity, it was thought, to burst
open the mine ; and he also arranged to carry with
him a dozen pickaxes.

My business was, silently and cautiously, with Sifat's
men, to remove the heavy backing of big stones against
the garden door. The dropping or rolling down of one
such stone, so close was the enemy, might defeat our
plans, and uselessly sacrifice the soldiers ; for a surprise
was essential for the success of our scheme.

As the time drew near, nothing remained but to
speak a few words of advice ; and for an anxious re-
capitulation of all details, to see that nothing had
been forgotten. In a quiet talk, Townshend, Harley,
and I, carefully reviewed all the arrangements and
found them complete. Young Harley, whose customary
attitude partakes somewhat of gay Irish insouciance,
had now a quiet look of concentrated energy, in
which his limbs seemed also to participate. His unusual
manner inspired one with confidence, as also did his
alert self-possessed eagerness. At the close of our talk,
I personally begged him not to get on too far in front
of his men. I explained my meaning by instances from
my own experience, and strove to prove the theory that
an officer, heading a desperate attack, ought always to
have four or five trustworthy men close up alongside
of him. It was easy to show how a single isolated man,
a long way ahead, might be at once killed, and how
nearly certain it was that, if Harley were shot, the attack
would fail ; also, how ill the Chitráli garrison could
bear the loss of another British officer. I also explained
that I badly wanted prisoners, from whom to extract
information about outside affairs. Harley listened with
consummate coolness, and then went away to select

the men who were to be abreast of him in the first rush.

Finally, the parapets and towers were stealthily manned, and Harley's party collected in the passage leading to the garden exit, silent and crowded together, with their bayonets dimly gleaming, for there was to be no firing till the post was carried—nothing but white steel. All hearts stopped beating for an instant. Everyone knew, and at that moment felt more than ever, the awful significance of that incessant pick, pick, picking, at the foot of the Gun-tower, and approaching nearer and nearer; each stroke with suggestions of overwhelming catastrophe. It made one feel sick to reflect how everything depended upon the summer-house being merely occupied by riflemen, and not being invincible by reason of its defences. At four o'clock the gates were swung open, and Harley ran out, closely followed by his men. As they could only pass through two or three at a time, Harley took advantage of a built-up garden lounging place, a few yards away, to get about a dozen men together, when they made a collective tiger-spring for the summer-house, closely followed by the rest of the soldiers. The enemy, though completely surprised, had still that resourceful steadiness which comes from constant fighting. It enabled them to fire a volley into the faces of our men, killing two, and severely wounding a third, of those charging with Harley. One of them was a Gurkha, who had managed to squeeze himself into the front rank reserved for the Sikhs. But all the devoted little band were burning with fight, and responded to their leader as valiantly as he led them. There were no barricades—merely a wall of piled-up bundles of compressed green twigs to stop bullets. Short, sharp bayonet work soon cleared the building, and the enemy, except those imprisoned inside the mine, fled to the protection of the end corner of the garden wall, and at once began to pile out faggot bundles and construct a temporary sangar of fascines with all the method and rapidity of perfectly trained soldiers.

Our success had been paid for. Already from the parapet, over the sallying gate, melancholy uniformed figures could be seen dotted about amongst the trees in the massive limpness of death. Upon the copper bugle, at the back of a dead Gurkha, the sunlight flickered prettily.

Like a thunder cloud bursting over the fort was the violent outbreak of musketry, and from all sides fighting men were seen running up, bent double, to reinforce the sangars. In the firm belief that this was the despairing effort of famine - stricken wretches to cut their way out, the exulting enemy pressed forward to the fight.

Within the walls, the pent-up feelings of our men found vent in violent emotion, furious shooting, and deafening uproar. On every hand were flushed faces, glaring eyes, and features distorted with excitement. All shouted, and none listened. Rab Nawáz Khán, even, was flourishing a revolver at a loophole with wild gestures and a maniac laugh. Near him a Rág-hunáth soldier, his head whirling, was deliberately levelling his rifle at the summer-house. I took him by the shoulders and twisted him in the river direction, where he kept on firing automatically. The Sikhs in hospital came crawling out, seized rifles, and crept on to the parapets. Several of them had lost half their feet from frost-bite, and were obliged to hobble side-ways or even swarm up the notched poles which did duty for ladders. All alike were full of battle madness, and shouting with joy at the prospect of a fight in the broad day, and to support their "brothers" outside. It was long before there was a semblance of order.

In the midst of all this noise and turmoil, when everyone was literally standing on tiptoe, sweating with agitation, I understood a common remark of Harley's that Gurdon, in critical times, was even irritatingly cool. In the present instance he had experienced some trouble with the Sepoys on the west wall. Those men had not participated in the general thirst for a fight, and were dispirited still by their defeat prior to our investment. So much so, indeed, that Gurdon and their officers found a difficulty at first in keeping them on the parapets, but that once accomplished, Gurdon came to ask, "Is there anything you want me to do, sir?" with a quiet, kindly smile, astonishing to behold in such a scene. No wonder he succeeded in bringing his small detachment, the relics of poor Baird's party, safely through the very midst of Sher Afzul's men on the 3rd March.

The enemy, at the end of the garden and behind the wall on its river side, kept up a remarkably well sustained fire through their loopholes upon our waterway, stables, defences, and the garden face of the fort, which gave some people the strange impression that they intended to charge the solid walls in the full light of the sun. The open door had a natural attraction for the Pathán riflemen, and bullets streamed through. Small harm was done, however, as the guard formed a respectful lane for the missiles. Only one man was hit there. Wounded men soon began to stagger back, or were carried to hospital, where Whitchurch was busily plying his merciful work. One poor water-carrier came in with his jaw broken by a bullet. The wound was dressed and his face bound up. Regardless of the injury, and its accompanying "shock," he humped his great skin bag on to his loins, and was starting out again when I stopped him. He protested, and, finding me obdurate, sat down and wailed that his poor Sikhs were dying for the water he might not carry them.

All this time, Harley, in the captured summer-house, was galled by the tremendous fire of the enemy, and his men at first began to reply to it independently. He stopped that with his whistle, and then got in a volley or two, which had effect. While firing independently, no single Pathán had been hit. Next, he began to look about for the shaft of the mine, which was found immediately outside a wall of fascines, which had been broken down during the first headlong charge. Its mouth was also covered over with fascines—curiously enough. They probably had fallen into it during the surge of the *mêlée*. After clearing them away, volunteers were called for, and, as the Gurkha "kookri" (hacking knife) would be more useful than bayoneted rifles in the shaft, Harley asked the senior Kashmír officer for men; but none responded except one Dogra soldier, who threw down his rifle, dragged forth his "kookri," and jumped down into the pit. The Sikhs pressed forward with a single impulse, but only six could be selected, and of them no more than two could descend into the shaft at the same time. The remainder stood at the top, exposed to a heavy fire, and pulled out the Chitrális as they appeared; for the instant a man showed at the orifice of the mine, flaming forth sword in hand or unarmed, he was bayoneted, and hoisted out of the way.

Harley now brought up his powder-bags, and, having cleared the shaft of soldiers, descended into it with one companion. They did not know if there were any more workers in the tunnel. Suddenly a swordsman showed himself. With a flash, the Sikh with Harley grabbed at the sword with one hand, while he drove home his bayonet with the other. Several more continued to come out, some armed and some not, but all were slain at the top of the shaft, except two, that Harley somehow managed to save. In the noise, the reek, and the fury, sudden death alone would have restrained the blood lust of the furious Sikhs. The doomed mine-workers, if they emerged, must come singly, to meet their fate at the top of the shallow shaft, while if they remained inside they must be blown to pieces. About twenty had passed forth, when Harley, thinking the tunnel clear, placed his explosives a few feet inside its mouth and began to tamp them. Then a couple more Chitrális tried to struggle into the open. By their confused trampling, the long gunpowder hose got torn into pieces. Harley was almost in despair, for the men carrying the picks had cast them aside into the long grass, in order to use their rifles, and the tools could not be recovered. Luckily, he had a length of tubing still intact, some twenty feet of it, which he started to find. As he was about to jump down again with it into the shaft, a violent explosion occurred, knocking him down and burning the turbans of the Sepoys.

A minute previous I had run up to the machicoulis gallery in the Gun-tower to watch events. Thence I saw an enormous puff of smoke rise abruptly, like a beautiful white balloon, and Harley's men race back in two parties, their leader, last of all, bringing with him one of the prisoners. An extraordinary rifle-fire blazed about them as they dashed across the twenty yards of open space, but no one was touched ; the garden gate was banged to and quickly re-barricaded.

One glance showed me the never-to-be-forgotten horror of the summer-house shambles, then I ran down to congratulate Harley and praise his men.

The Sikhs, still raging with excitement, crowded forward to recite the numbers they had killed, and to exhibit their stained bayonets and splashed faces. Their eyes sparkled with measureless pride; they had the ecstatic look of religious fanatics. But Harley, with whom was Townshend, looked downcast and annoyed. They had indeed come to report to me that the powder bags had prematurely exploded, and that, with the exception of about three yards of its roof, the mine remained intact. While I live, shall I remember the bitter, the cold dismay this news caused me. But no time was to be lost; a second sortie was out of the question, for the enemy were already thronging the summer-house, and could not again be surprised. I ran to the spots which, in view of all possibilities, Wafadár and Sifat had indicated as the best starting-points for counter-mines, and we at once set to work digging. In the presence of Townshend and Gurdon, hastily summoned for the purpose, Sifat was promised a large sum of money if our mines penetrated beyond the walls in time to intercept that of the Patháns. With almost frenzied energy we were labouring, when Gurdon came down from the tower to observe, in a thoughtful tone, that the enemy seemed to have made a trench which reached nearly to our wall. Further examination o this last development proved that it was the mine, collapsed from end to end. We were reprieved. Harley's gunpowder had done its work after all. The frail roof of the tunnel, unsupported by beams—the mine was, in fact, a mere burrow—had slowly sunk down in great masses, leaving earth bridges here and there. Back swung the pendulum triumphantly. Now the stars in their courses were fighting for us, and our ultimate success was certain. With the conviction of a zealot, I declared to everyone that our troubles were over, for my seemingly lost luck had returned. Nevertheless, Townshend agreed with me that our countermines should not be stopped, so that if the baffled Pathárs attempted a fresh mine, they would find it anticipated.

The Chitrális plume themselves on knowing nothing about such methods of attack, which they look upon as a Pathán speciality. Consequently, the summer-house post and the loopholed garden walls had been handed over to Umra Khán's warriors, and completely they had failed in their trust. They under-estimated our spirit of enterprise, and let themselves be surprised. By asserting complete absence of personal responsibility, the Chitrális still find consolation for Harley's brilliant success, which not only saved us at the time, but made it impossible for Sher Afzul to induce his followers to directly assault the fort. One strange incident occurred during the thickest of the excitement. Some of our Chitrális began to weep for the fate of their fellow-countrymen inside the tunnel, and truly declared, as we found afterwards, that the diggers were not Pathárs, who merely acted as guards, but farmers from down the river, living upon the estate of one of the headmen with me. How they knew this fact can only be suspected, but our disconsolate allies formed a strong contrast to us in our over-brimming joyfulness.

What a cheery dinner we had that night! Even the famished smokers suffered less than usual. Our tobacco had long been exhausted, while cloves, chopped straw, and the bark of the plane tree proved wretched substitutes for the gentle narcotic. Whitchurch, I think, felt the privation most, and, next to him,

Campbell. Upon the rest of us it weighed less hardly. Wafadár, a few days before, had whispered, with the air of a conspirator, that the Mehtar possessed a few Egyptian cigarettes which he desired me to accept. There were about twenty altogether. I decided not to burden my conscience with the responsibility of so much treasure, and asked Wafadár to dole them out occasionally as I directed, seven at a time — one for each of us, and two for Campbell, on account of his bad luck in having been again ordered to bed by Whitchurch. Leaning on one elbow after dinner, and trying to smoke our single cigarette more slowly than was possible, we talked more and more of the Savoy and other tantalising thoughts. Whitchurch invariably finished his first, and then watched with wolfish eyes how we burnt our finger-tips and our moustaches in smoking ours to the very end. He would give a gasp of horror if anyone inadvertently raised an arm to cast away the last morsel, for such residues were priceless to him. No doubt, with his mouth watering, he would manipulate the fragrant particles, stuff them into the bottom of a pipe, and suck at it with simple faith, long after even the flavour of the encrusted bowl had passed away.

Our two prisoners were subjected to an exhaustive examination. They had plenty to tell, but hardly anything worth recording. The mildest of their beliefs was that the Amír of Kabul was backing Sher Afzul, and was already at Peshawer preparatory to an invasion of India! According to them, a great attack was planned for the previous day, when an attempt was to be made to fire the Water-tower, but it was deferred because the Patháns were confident that they could demolish the Gun-tower by their mine. Some vague statements were also made about pent houses already constructed and in the bazaar ready for use, under cover of which many fires were to be kindled against the walls simultaneously. We resolved that if such classic methods were employed, they must be met by modern bayonet charges.

Last of all was the bill for the day's proceedings; the reckoning when we laugh no more. Out of Harley's brave hundred there were twenty-one casualties—a large but not unreasonable proportion, considering the nature of the work. The Chitrális lost between forty and fifty killed outright, some five-and-thirty of whom were bayoneted in and about the shaft of the mine. Such was the rage of the Sepoys—Sikhs, Gurkhas, and Dogras alike—that they could not be restrained from slaughtering even unarmed men. Amidst frantic yells of "kill, kill," the poor wretches sank, one by one, in that tempestuous sea of hate. An hour later they would have been treated kindly, even tenderly; but at the climax of fury, when our men were intoxicated with their own and one another's excitement—the most catching of all mob influences—they could spare no one. It is astonishing that Harley contrived to save the two men, for, in a swaying throng of overwrought Eastern soldiers, bayonet thrusts cannot be identified. There is no doubt that this fierce ruthlessness startled the Sher Afzulites from the conviction that our troops were broken in spirit—what in India is expressively called "soft."

Of all duties, the most sorrowful is that of visiting the wounded after an engagement. One never knows how the poor fellows may be able to endure their pain. Usually, thank God, the shock of the injury, Nature's own anæsthetic, saves their manhood, for the power of endurance of wounds received in action depends, alas, less on the fortitude of the soldier

than upon the exact nature of the wound. The
North American Indians had devices which would
extort a scream from the most stoical victim at the
stake; so, to a certain extent, is it in battle.
One of the first hit of Harley's men was a grand Sikh.
He was carried to the hospital, where I afterwards
found him writhing on the ground, and shrieking from
the agony of his quivering nerves. Yet he was one
of the bravest of a brave race. Similarly, I remember
at the attack on Nilt Fort, in 1891, that one of the
Gurkha soldiers of the Maharajah's Bodyguard regiment, was conspicuous for a dashing impatience, which
he with difficulty restrained, to push forward against
the enemy. All at once this man, to the fury and
astonishment of his Kashmír leader, was seen to burst
into tears, throw down his rifle, and hide behind a tree.
Astounded, and burning with shame, his Gurkha officer
followed him; but an experienced Englishman, a
captain of a British India regiment, bade the subadár
be calm, as he was certain the man was badly wounded.
It happened that I also observed the incident, and ran
across a zone of fire to see what it meant. The man
was shot in the pit of the stomach and died soon afterwards. Another illustrative incident occurred at Chilás,
at the end of 1892. There, while Captain Wallace
was bravely trying to cover the retreat of five Gurkhas
rafting from the opposite bank of the Indus, where
they had been assailed by the treacherous enemy, one
of his Dogra Sepoys, to the Englishman's disgust,
suddenly cast away his rifle and ran behind a rock.
That man was marked by us for exemplary punishment,
afterwards, even when we learned that he was wounded;
and it was not until a skilful army surgeon inspected
the injury some days later, that we were able to forgive
the seeming cowardice. As a matter of fact, a bullet

had shattered the nerves in the palm of the right hand to such an extent, that no human fortitude could withstand the horrible pain the poor creature suffered. So it was heartbreaking to perceive that our splendid Sikh, stricken mortally, must, ere he died, go through the dreadful humiliation, worse than death itself, to such a man and his friends, of screaming out the remainder of his life. Truly, a soldier's prayer should be, that, when his end came, he might be killed swiftly, or, at least, be permitted to die with dignity and composure.

All the early part of the night the besiegers were known to be busily moving about, under cover, cautiously dragging away their killed. Our dead, though but a yard or two from the walls, had to be abandoned, and, with the carcasses of animals, the unburied of the friendless slain of the enemy, and more than one corpse in the mine, lay stark before Heaven, dumb protests against man's cruel anger. The actual fighting was one of the least evils of our long siege. Just before midnight the sound of great cheering twice came to our ears. Its meaning could not be conjectured, and dawn broke on the 18th April after a quietness inside the walls interrupted only by the customary odd shots of the sentries. But we still worked strenuously at the mines, and at our other protections, being resolved not to throw away a single point in the game. We particularly directed our attention to building screening walls to the hospital verandah, where bullets now began to drop at intervals.

Our prisoners informed us, with a reluctance that carried half conviction with it, that the beleaguerment of Mastuj had been raised by a mixed force of regular troops and levies from Gilgit, and that the Chitrális had fallen back ten miles nearer to us to defend the famous Nisa Gul cutting.

z

Soon after breakfast, we were temporarily paralysed by the Bengali Commissariat Agent bursting upon us with news of another mine. His dry lips could scarcely ejaculate the odd phrase, "Please, sir, I hear the voice of digging." Quietness was enjoined, in the usual way, by vociferous commands. Then we all went to the store-room, and even the most sceptical (myself and another) began to believe there was "something in it," when we heard the sickening echo of the thud—thud—thud we knew so well. After much wasted anxiety for a few moments, it was discovered that this exact reproduction of the stroke of a pick was simply caused by a Sepoy chopping firewood, for cooking purposes, in a distant apartment, the ground conveying the sound with horrible suggestiveness. Yet, once again during the day we had another less important scare of the same kind, which turned out to be the earth vibrations caused by our own mining tools.

However, nothing could for long destroy our optimism, for the whole garrison was eager and vigilant. No single face bore a trace of despondency now. The Rághunáths were bright and cheerful. They had done well, and suffered heavily in the sortie. Success, with its concomitant self-confidence, that prime essential of a soldier, which makes swaggering a military virtue now wiped away depression and warmed their hearts. As for the Sikhs, those off duty sat in' groups cleaning, nursing, or even fondling their rifles—their "fathers and mothers"—for "do they not protect their lives?" With happy smiles, they chatted gaily, and probably elaborated plans with one another for saving and gaining additional rupees; for it is difficult to say which god these magnificent soldiers most adore—steel (bayonets and cannon) or the silver of the Indian currency. Give them sufficient of both, with hard but just discipline, and bear in

mind that Sikhs of shortish stature have hardly yet
been tried—except against us in the Punjáb war—then
we shall get large numbers of recruits from the finest
martial folk within our own borders—a military sect
which probably only continues to exist for the sake of
our class battalions.

CHAPTER XXXIII

THE END OF A MINOR SIEGE

THURSDAY, April 18th, passed away with little commotion. Our men occasionally fired at parties of the enemy carrying off their dead, but there was no after-swell to the storm of yesterday. Night fell, and found us all watchful, for it was the eve of the Musalmán Sabbath, when Patháns, tortured with thoughts of vengeance, and with new blood feuds on hand, might be expected to "glut their ire." I spent much time devising little pent roofs, to enable men on the towers to fire downwards, and command the foot of the walls, while they themselves were protected; and everybody else was busy looking to walls and shelters.

About a couple of hours after dark, Townshend came to report that a man had actually crept up to the Sikhs on the west side, and, after shouting out something, had gone away again uninjured. Our indignation flared up and supplied its own fuel. What! were the Sikhs getting slack! So we rated, and the incident passed. Later, a man cried out again, and word flashed through the fort that all our besiegers had fled, and that Futteh Ali Sháh's brother was outside begging for admission, the first bringer of the good tidings. Directions were given for him to be admitted through the manhole in the main gate, and brought to me; but no precautions were to be relaxed. He confirmed the flying rumours, and supplemented them. Sher Afzul,

it seemed, with the two Bajour Kháns, had fled with
all their following. It appeared that Muhammed Isa,
after a severe beating at the Nisa Gul, had fallen back,
march by march, upon Chitrál, hoping for the reinforcements (2000 riflemen) promised by Umra Khán but
never sent ; that a final grand effort to capture the fort
was projected, but because of the losses inflicted by
Harley in his sortie, the enemy was so discouraged,
that all hope of getting men to attempt it had to be
given up. Finally, a Gilgit force, flushed with victory,
was but two marches away, and nothing remained but
general congratulations.

Nevertheless, we decided to wait for morning, when
Gurdon, with a company, was to move out and see
exactly how matters stood. We, however, sincerely
believed the news, and though still cautious against
possible treachery, gave ourselves up to pleasant
emotions. Wafadár produced the last seven cigarettes
—the only adequate incense and sacrifice combined
worthy of our feelings. Some shocking rum was also
brought out to make a grog. The decoction would
surely rack some of our heads, but there must be
something emblematic of festivity ; and so we sat over
the small fire, quietly happy, for we were all too played
out for boisterous joy, talking of our people at home,
and wondering, surmising, and guessing till daylight.
Nobody wanted to sleep. One or two made the
attempt, but soon gave it up and fell to talking again.
The reins of our tongues were loosed, so that we felt a
strange pleasure in easy speech, as though we had of
late only been allowed to converse in low tones.

Our Chitrális were exuberant in their loyalty ; no
more grumbling, but every man radiant for a short
time. Then, poor people, the truth was disclosed how
villainously Sher Afzul and his friends had behaved.

Hardly anyone was without terrible cause for sorrow. Sher Afzul had put to death the relatives of some, and had given away the wives and sisters of others. Their houses were mere ash-heaps, and all their property gone. Certain ingeniously shocking methods of vengeance— on Wafadár in particular—may not be written; there is a sickening horror about these vile retaliations which makes one glad to escape to other memories.

Gurdon marched out at nine o'clock, with a strong detachment, to find that every one had really fled. Bajouri traders came with presents of sugar, and small groceries—gifts of propitiation. It was astounding to find how much they had admired us all through, and what joy our release from the hateful fort prison gave them. No one could be more horrified, they declared, at the inexcusably bad behaviour of their fellow-country-men. They could give us little information, except vague rumours that Kelly was only two marches away; while another army, great and irresistible, was marching up from Peshawer and Hoti Mardán, accompanied by the old ruler of Dír, ousted by Umra Khán, and now restored to his own again. Ever since the 12th of the month it seemed that Sher Afzul and the Jandol Kháns began to show how uncomfortable their minds were, but they kept up their followers' spirits by asserting that the Amír's Commander-in-Chief was hurrying to help them.

Everybody was busy still. Sheep and goats, and decent clean food were requisitioned for the soldiers; it was pleasant work for Townshend and Harley to look after the brave fellows, while Gurdon and I had much writing to do, and many interviews. We had, of course, sent off a letter to Kelly as quickly as it could be composed.

Visitors trooped to Campbell, bidding him cheer up,

for the sky was blue, the breezes cool, and the valley waving with barley and wheat. He should be carried out to see for himself, as soon as any one had time to find a nice place under the beautiful trees, free from ill odours and the carcasses of dead animals. Poor Whitchurch, with his hospital, and his own fever, was, as usual, the heaviest and the quietest of workers. Letters were brought from the Chitrál Relief Force, giving us that information from outside for which we were greedy. Then, late at night, came a short note from Kelly, to say he would reach Chitrál on the following day (the 20th).

Next morning we were all up betimes. It was so sweet to move out from our sombre walls, although there was little inclination to wander far, for a strange inertness had to be contended against. For breakfast we had eggs and fresh milk and a skinny chicken, and could hardly eat for admiration of such delicacies. The men, too, were getting good rations; but none of those "extras" so dear to the Eastern soldier—tea, sugar, and butter. Perhaps Kelly might be bringing some. We little knew how lightly he was marching. At noon we began exchanging signals. Two hours more and they would be here.

Gurdon was in great trouble. We found out that a report of his death had been sent to his relatives in England. A groom, leading his pony, had been killed on the 3rd March, and the animal subsequently seized by Muhammed Isa, who set off for Reshun riding it. At that place it was seen and identified by Fowler. Somewhat naturally, as all Muhammed Isa's men knew an officer had been mortally wounded, and as that chief braggingly declared that he had done the deed, and captured the pony by his own prowess, it was accepted without hesitation that it was Gurdon who was dead.

It was painful to think of the sorrow such a mistake must have caused.

At two o'clock, Kelly's advanced guard was descried crossing the bridge, their bugles sounding an old familiar tune, which somehow made one melancholy as well as happy—in short, emotional. With the exception of Campbell, who could not be carried about safely until the fort was more clear, we all went outside to see them arrive. There were no extravagant greetings; I, for my part, welcomed them mechanically. All I could see were the dark-complexioned, sturdy Mazbis, looking admirably well, and much travel - stained. Officers passed me, but I only really saw two—Oldham, because he was wearing a turban, and Kelly, who waved a walking - stick from the Chitráli saddle on a sturdy little pony. My mind was weary, and my life seemed fatigued also. I felt, by anticipation, what it must be to attain a great age and feel a listlessness about all things. They declare, that we five standing stilly in front of the ruined outwork, were white - faced and strangely quiet. Perhaps nothing short of a Pathán battle-cry and the sharp clatter of rifle fire could have really roused us; for the long-sustained stimulus of danger and responsibility was gone; and only tiredness, a tiredness of brain and eyes and body, remained.

The women's durbar hall, occupied during the siege by Rab Nawáz Khán's wife and two other women, was turned into a banqueting-chamber for a dinner to Kelly and his officers, nine in number altogether, on Sunday the 21st. Campbell was carried to it at the cost of a bad jerk to his knee in the narrow doorway. So many British officers collected together in Chitrál was a strange sight to me, and all through the meal in lazy-brained reverie, I kept reverting to the circumstances which had brought it about. My mind kept going back to the visit

END OF A MINOR SIEGE

paid to Chitrál, in 1888, by Colonel Algernon Durand and myself, in the height of its picturesque remoteness, when we were conducted to dinner over strips of silk turban cloth, which we spoiled with our shooting boots, and were there entertained with wonderful hyperboles of conversation. Could old Amír-ul-Mulk have then foreseen that the most sacred apartment of the sacred part of his fort would ever witness a dinner-party of uniformed British officers, who sat at table with the matter-of-fact air one associates with a private dining-room or a mess chamber, how would the ancient man have gazed upon us?—the old autocrat beloved of God, and of the Prophet of God, whose royal brethren and chief nobles were proud to offer him their turban tails for kerchiefs, and the head-dresses themselves as basins when he desired to wash the snuff from his gums. The mere suggestion of the idea in a dream would have cost lives.

Kelly's officers were wonderfully nice fellows. Stewart, the gunner, with deep insight into the wants of men, sent us over two small tins of tobacco—every grain he possessed. Cobbe, similarly, made me ashamed of being powerless to resist his precious gifts of the same kind. All seemed to think, from Kelly downwards, that their march was a mere trifle, their hardships undeserving of reference. They were the most singularly generous and modest men I have ever met, and my admiration for them grew deeper and deeper, as the true facts of their story were brought to light. Campbell was languishing to see trees, and sky, and green fields, but no one had time to take him out till Monday, the 22nd, when he was put under a big tree and left to batten on the fresh air. To such a nature as his, with his love of outdoor pursuits, the dark, grimy room he tenanted so long must have been like a dungeon.

The following day we all moved into my old house—no longer "Sher Afzul's house"—and in the evening the thrice-blessed flag—our luck—was lazily flapping on its roof. We found it difficult to get Campbell in and out of the doorways, and finally decided to build him a makeshift hut in the garden at the back. Upon the 24th we learned, with a pleasure it is impossible to tell, that Edwardes and Fowler were both safe with Sir Robert Low's relieving force. Umra Khán, as we emphatically proclaimed, had behaved like a gentleman.

CONCLUSION

So the long, weary siege was ended, and already a thing of the past. Our total losses, including the reconnaissance of the 3rd of March were forty-one killed, and sixty-two wounded—one hundred and three casualties altogether. Of these, five killed and four wounded were followers, and not soldiers. My escort numbered three hundred and seventy combatants, all told. Colonel Kelly was now in military command of Chitrál, and had passed on his temporary "political" powers to me when he arrived. Consequently, Harley, Whitchurch, and all the Sikhs and Rághunáths were now under his orders. Townshend and Gurdon remained with me, the former as my Military, and the latter as my Political Assistant.

Congratulations and laudatory telegrams began to pour in. At a final parade of the garrison, the gracious message of Her Majesty, the Queen-Empress, was read out and translated to the Sepoys, and was subsequently repeated to those in hospital. Wonderful is the power of a great sovereign's words! An Eastern soldier's cheek takes a deeper hue, and his mien grows prouder at such august praises. Not even the British Tommy Atkins, with his capacity for sentiment and emotion, is more deeply moved. Many other messages came from the Viceroy, Sir Henry Fowler, the Commanders-in-Chief at home and in India, the Maharajah of Kashmír, and a great number more, both from official personages and from private friends, while it is unnecessary, perhaps, to say that Lord Roberts sent messages which filled the Sepoys, not to speak of others, with pride and gaiety. He never forgets ; and always says the exact thing to gladden the soldier's heart, which he knows so well.

All these messages were delightful to get, and helped to check the terrible reaction which followed our long insanitary imprisonment. But for me, Lord Elgin did an action which could only have originated in a very kind heart. He knew the strong attachment there was between myself and Colonel Algernon Durand, his military secretary, my long-time friend, fellow-traveller, and former chief, so he sent him to carry letters to me, and then conduct me to India and Simla.

INDEX